SOVEREIGNTY AT THE MILLENNIUM

Edited by Robert Jackson

Copyright © The Political Studies Association 1999

ISBN 0-631-215964

First published 1999

Blackwell Publishers Inc
350 Main Street, Malden, Massachusetts 02148, USA.

and

Blackwell Publishers Ltd
108 Cowley Road, Oxford, OX4 1JF, UK.

*Library of Congress Cataloguing in Publication Data has
been applied for.*

British Library Cataloguing in Publication Data.
A CIP catalogue record for this book is available from
the British Library

Printed in Great Britain by MPG Books, Bodmin,
Cornwall

This book is printed on acid-free paper

CONTENTS

Introduction: Sovereignty at the Millennium

ROBERT JACKSON

Sovereignty is a distinguishing feature of modern politics. It is one of those historical signposts, like experimental science or political individualism or industrialization or nationalism or mass public education, that points toward the modern era and away from the medieval era and all previous eras. Sovereignty frames and fixes the bounds of international relations. Without more or less contiguous independent states, each one having an outward aspect as well as an inward aspect, and without the consequent necessity of ordered contact and regulated interaction between them, the notion of international relations loses much of its intelligibility. Sovereign statehood anchors our concept of modern politics just as the notion of Christian empire anchored the concept of medieval politics. Presumably some new or renewed concept will have to anchor post-sovereign politics. That is the traditional or classical view of the subject.

Historically speaking, sovereignty has a birth (in the sixteenth and seventeenth century according to that view), a life (the past three or four centuries), and arguably just like any other basic political arrangement it will – sooner or later – undergo a transformation that will be so fundamental and consequential as to spell its death for all intents and purposes. Some scholars think that transformation is underway. Some are inclined to equate post-modernity with post-sovereignty. What will take the place of sovereignty, when the time comes, is not at all clear. Some scholars go so far as to envisage a global polity in which states, if they still exist, will be servants of the world community and no longer independent units and actors in their own right. Other visions and images of sovereignty transformed are briefly discussed below.

Whether we are reaching a historical turning point of consequence in the history of sovereignty, or not, is the subject of debate at the present time. With an eye on the turn of the millennium this special issue of *Political Studies* canvasses some of the most important arguments in the sovereignty debate among international relations scholars. The essays look into selected aspects of that institution seeking to assess its contemporary significance and the extent to which its framework and *modus operandi* may be changing. Where and when did sovereignty originate? Where has it been and where is it heading? What are its future prospects? Is it in stable health with a long life yet to come? Is it undergoing significant change, and if so what kind of change? Is it in terminal decline? Is world politics getting beyond sovereignty in its basic organization? Or should we speak, instead, of the evolution of sovereignty? Are we presently witnessing a reformation of sovereignty? These are some of the questions raised by the contributors.

Sovereignty is an academic or theoretical subject but it is also a profoundly practical arrangement of world politics. Sovereignty lays down the main conditions and standards of conduct of world politics. It calls for political activity of a distinctive kind by specifying certain bounds or limits. National leaders, diplomats, soldiers, international civil servants, and other such people must operate with some notion of, and attention to, sovereignty to carry out their foreign (and domestic) activities. But the practices and usages of sovereignty need only be as explicit as they have to be. The usual test of practice is workability and amenability. The sovereign state system has met that test for the past several centuries: on balance over time, it seems to facilitate unmistakable, stable, constant and predictable relations between states, and most statespeople involved seem content with it. The main thing is that international actors can understand sovereignty in terms that enable them to deal with each other. They need to know what the sovereign political role involves in order to perform it and respond to it. And that seems to be widely known and not at all obscure.

Perhaps the working notion of sovereignty is becoming unsettled in certain places and in certain respects at the present time. That may be the case in Europe where it is no longer as clear as it once was where the line of sovereignty should be drawn in politics involving EU states. Are those states still 'sovereign'. If not, how should we characterize the change that has occurred in that regard since they got involved in the EU project? Are they putting their sovereignty behind them as they build an integrated Europe on a novel foundation that they are organizing between themselves as they go along? Turning to a different example, it is not entirely clear what the French-Canadian politicians, who refer to themselves as 'sovereigntists', are asking from the rest of Canada when they demand sovereignty for Quebec. Does it involve political independence? Could it involve a new form of association looser than federalism but less than independence: perhaps 'sovereignty association' (another of their terms)? That question has not yet been answered. But there is a rough and ready idea of sovereignty and non-sovereignty on the part of political leaders and other people who get involved in such practical questions. That idea usually comes down to recognition as an independent state. When the Albanian leaders of Kosovo call for sovereignty everybody knows they want to separate from Serbia and either launch their own independent state or unite with neighbouring Albania. To date they have been refused international recognition.

Academics, on the other hand, operate with theoretical conceptions of sovereignty that are more elaborate and various. Sovereignty is a contested academic concept. Some concepts are categorically different than other concepts. Is sovereignty independence? Is it autonomy? The first is a notion of authority and right, but the second is a notion of power and capability. Historians, international lawyers and political theorists tend to operate with the first concept. Political economists and political sociologists tend to employ the second concept. The former scholars are content with the rule of thumb notions of practitioners. They see their research task as one of clarifying those practices and usages and rendering them intelligible in theoretical terms. That is, shall we say, a more traditional approach to the subject. The latter scholars are not satisfied with discerning, abstracting and understanding the practitioner's self-conceived ideas and self-styled activities. They are trying to answer explanatory questions, and they seek a concept that can be used to address those questions. They consequently are inclined to employ definitions of sovereignty that are 'scientific'. That is, shall we say, a more contemporary social science approach to the subject. Social science scholars are often tempted to stipulate their own concept for their own research. That leads to conceptual multiplication and can be a source of conceptual contestation and even confusion. There is evidence of these two categorically different approaches in political science definitions of sovereignty at the present time. And there are pitfalls waiting for anyone who is not fully aware of that. Readers of these essays should bear that in mind.

But regardless of their different conceptions of the subject I expect that most international relations scholars would agree that sovereignty is one of the fundamental subjects of political science. That view is taken by the contributors to this collection. These essays are, in their different ways, entering into current academic debates and controversies on the subject of sovereignty. It may therefore be useful to briefly outline some of the noteworthy issues involved in these academic disputes. Hopefully that can serve as a preface to the essays that are summarized below.

As indicated already, the traditional academic approach to sovereignty is usually driven by the aspiration to organize into more systematic and coherent terms the practices and usages of sovereignty that are evident from international political activity, past and present. That typically results in conceptions of sovereign statehood with two basic aspects: an internal aspect in which a government of a populated territory is supreme within its jurisdiction, and an external aspect in which that same government is legally separated from all other governments of the same sort and is recognized as such. Thus, in international relations, sovereignty is a mark of political independence of a state. It gives a state a right to engage in international activity and international organization in company with other sovereign states.

That classical view of sovereignty as political independence is sometimes dismissed as mere legality. Of course it is legality. But legality, i.e., legal authority and right, is not something that is trivial or of little interest or concern to practical politicians. On the contrary, in the case of sovereignty it is of profound interest and concern. Canada possesses sovereignty which enables its federal government to participate in international society, but Quebec – so far – lacks that status and the opportunities for international membership and activity that it brings with it. That is a big deprivation in the minds of Quebec separatists who seek to control and conduct Quebec's political affairs free of the Canadian government and constitution. Some states of the United States – California, New York, Texas, Florida – are far more substantial and powerful than all but very few sovereign states. They would be in the front rank if they were sovereign. But they are prevented by the American constitution from participating as independent actors in world politics. They must be content, and presumably they are content, to let Washington conduct a foreign policy that articulates their international interests and concerns.

In other words, sovereignty as classically understood is a qualification that makes certain political systems, about 190 at the present time, eligible to play a role on the stage of world politics. Eligibility is not based on any substantive political, social or economic merit or qualification. It is based on history and – one is tempted to say – the accidents of history: many if not most non-Western states have a sovereign existence largely owing to the particular course taken by Western colonial history. The role of a sovereign state is usually regarded as the most important of all roles that anyone could perform on the world stage. Sovereign states are the leading actors of world politics. The script of world politics is written mainly for them. Everybody else is a supporting actor. But there are other views nowadays that call into question the asserted pre-eminence of sovereign states in world affairs. Some scholars, often Marxists, see multi-national corporations as leading actors. Some see IGOs and NGOs as important actors too. Some see human beings, either as individuals or as bearers of various non-state identities, as performing significant roles that are being written into the script. They discern a new global polity that is coming into view, inexorably even if slowly and haltingly, as the sovereign state system decays. Some political economy or political sociology views of world politics are thus inclined to downplay or even debunk the paramount role of sovereign states.

Other academics argue that sovereignty is an instrument or resource that governments use to deal with each other. Governments calculate the advantages of holding on to some or all of their sovereignty or surrendering some or all of it. For example, the member states of the European Union are said to recognize that the instrumental value of sovereignty today is not as great as it used to be. EU states believe that they cannot effectively pursue their interests or concerns within the traditional framework of sovereignty. They are in the course of abandoning that old framework. They increasingly operate within a new frame-work that involves a 'pooling' of sovereignty by the member states. That concept of sovereignty is seen to apply more widely than Western Europe. The process of globalization, the economic integration of high income economies, the increasingly co-operative and consultative economic game played by OECD states, are seen to be changing the *persona* of sovereignty into something different from what it was.

Are we getting beyond sovereignty in world politics? Some scholars see the dawning of a new world of mobile individuals and organizations who have been liberated by modern technology to roam the planet, actually or virtually, and who are thus escaping from sovereignty. They point to the freedom and power of global financial markets in diminishing economic and specifically monetary sovereignty by shunting huge money trains back and forth around the world at the speed of light without consulting national governments or bothering about national borders. Here sovereignty is seen to be vulnerable to globalization which is displacing it. Others scholars detect a retreat from sovereignty in the moral practices of world politics and note an advancing 'humanitarian space', as exemplified by growing receptivity to humanitarian intervention and augmentation of human rights as a standard of international conduct. Still others see a system of global governance emerging in which the sovereign state, while still in existence, is subject to a universal civic ethic that reduces the independence of statesmen and stateswomen. On that view, norms of the community of humankind are beginning to have precedence in certain domains over norms of sovereignty.

Some scholars speculate whether sovereign states might disappear and be replaced by a new arrangement of some kind. The usual ways to think of that alternative political universe is in terms of a world federation or a world in which economic globalization undermines the autonomy of states or a world based on universal rights of the community of humankind. A less familiar image of a post-sovereign world is that of a secular equivalent of the political organization that existed in Western Christendom in the Middle Ages: the image of a 'new medievalism'. World politics in that image is an intermingling of the global, the local, and the transnational in which social forces penetrate and infiltrate and in some instances undermine, or even destroy, the bordered political space of the sovereign territorial state.

Sovereignty is also a contested value for international relations scholars. It is convenient to think of a value continuum. At the conservative extremity sovereignty is seen as upholding the value of freedom, i.e., political independence, and as fostering international order. At the progressive extremity it is seen as denying justice to countless individuals, organizations and identities that cannot fit into the territorial logic of sovereignty and are burdened by it. In between are value questions about the rationality of existing international borders and the worth of sovereign states in an interdependent world.

Sovereignty and its first cousin, self-determination, have been seen by most students of the subject as important values that are considered to require no further justification. Decolonization, for example, which involved the transfer of sovereignty from European imperialists to non-European nationalists was generally understood by most scholars to be a good thing. The nationalists thought it was a good thing. It was the imperialists, at least some of them, who thought it was a bad thing. But nowadays some scholars are raising the question whether sovereignty is equally good for every culture or society or people. What is the good of a world in which hundreds of millions, if not a billion, people are living on the edge of starvation and are enduring other forms of suffering that, it is argued, can be laid at the feet of the sovereign states system? For those scholars the end of sovereignty, which is often equated with post-modernity, would hopefully be a liberation from such chains and shackles.

Some scholars argue that a major reorganization of international life is underway that will lead to irrevocable changes to the world political system that has prevailed since the Peace of Westphalia (1648). Owing to rapid technological change and the consequent 'shrinking' of the planet, it is held that sovereign states individually and the states system as a whole can no longer insure basic values, such as peace, security, welfare, and conservation. The sovereign state is becoming obsolete. Alternative institutions and arrangements, of a more egalitarian and less elitist kind, are necessary and hopefully will be fashioned to provide such basic goods. According to that view, international theory based on the notion of sovereignty is increasingly irrelevant to the requirements of today and it therefore ought to be replaced by a new theory of a planetary political community in which the state is, at most, only one of several important institutions and is no longer paramount. They believe that would be a very welcome development.

Others argue, in a similar vein, that sovereignty is an institution which necessarily arranges and emphasizes some identities at the expense of other identities. Sovereignty denies and deprives the non-sovereign 'other' who is condemned to live a less than fully human existence as a result. It facilitates and reinforces the North/South divide by submerging millions inside of underdeveloped states or failed states. According to that critical way of thinking, the theory of the sovereign state impairs our capacity to envisage alternative and better arrangements of human life. The philosophical hegemony of the sovereign state is, if anything, even more of a barrier to the historical quest for human self-fulfilment than the political hegemony of the sovereign state. Our current theory of sovereignty is a mental prison. The international critical theorist is called upon to open the way in emancipatory thought to a more inclusive post-sovereign world which, because sovereignty and modernity are collaborators, would also be a post-modern world. That critical view of the subject is taken by those academics who believe it is their duty not only to make sense of the world of sovereign states but, following the example of Karl Marx's critique of capitalism, to expose the oppression and suffering that sovereignty is seen to involve and thus to open the door to liberation from it.

Turning now to the essays in this volume. They understandably reveal different although overlapping views and concepts of sovereignty. But it is clear that they consider the institution to be a fundamentally important subject of political science even as they differ in their assessment of its present condition and future prospects. The first three essays (by Robert Jackson, Alan James and James Mayall) see the institution not only as very significant but also as probably having a lot of life still left. The next four essays (by William Wallace, Christopher Clapham, Paul Taylor and Daniel Philpott) notice important ways in which the institution is changing into something different from what it has been. Maybe the age of sovereignty is nearing its end. The final essay (by Georg Sørensen) finds some merit in each view and maintains that although core elements of the institution of sovereignty remain firmly in place other elements have been transformed. What the future may bring is not the end of sovereignty but, rather, a new arrangement of sovereignty.

Robert Jackson presents an overview of the concept and history of sovereignty, as seen from a classical international society perspective, with the aim of understanding its character and *modus operandi*, and the extent to which that has changed over time. He views sovereignty as a legal institution that authenticates a political order based on independent states whose governments are the principal authorities in the world, both domestically and internationally. For him, sovereignty is a foundation institution and a basic frame of reference of modern political life. It is a premise or assumption, of a normative kind, that enters into and in some fundamental way defines political activity in the post-medieval world. He poses the following questions: What is sovereignty? What is its character and *modus operandi*? Who are the principals and agents of sovereignty? Who are the subjects of sovereignty? What would be involved in going beyond sovereignty in world politics? What are the values that sovereignty can be seen to uphold and defend? His essay is devoted to answering these questions.

Alan James explores the contemporary practice of sovereignty in a world of states. He argues that although states vary enormously in size and strength the one thing they have in common is their equal sovereign status which makes them eligible to participate in international activity. Since 1945 the number of states on the international stage has increased from about 75 to getting on for 200. All of them – new and old – say they are sovereign, and challenges to such statements are noticeable by their almost complete absence. This reflects the fact that all these states enjoy the condition which, according to the practice of the international society, makes them eligible for regular participation in international affairs. That is to say, they enjoy sovereignty, in the most basic and important usage of that term. The key features of sovereignty are threefold: it is a legal, absolute, and unitary condition. His essay examines the content of this concept and explains its significance. He also pays attention to the requirements which must be met if eligibility for participation in international affairs is to be translated into actual participation – as it is in respect of virtually all sovereign states.

James Mayall's essay carries on in the same international society tradition by investigating the evolving relationship between sovereignty and nationalism, with a focus on the changing theory and practice of self-determination. The impact of nationalism on international society was paradoxical. On the one hand, it challenged dynasticism as the traditional standard of international legitimacy within international society; on the other, it reinforced the dominant position of the state. The elevation of the principle of self-determination as the new standard of legitimacy after 1918 posed a problem that has never been satisfactorily resolved: which were the selves which could exercise this right? The post-1945 answer to this question, namely decolonization, avoided confronting it directly. The cold war also constrained the extent to which this answer was challenged. Conversely, the end of the cold war reopened the debate about the definition of the nation and the meaning of self-determination. It is not clear that a theoretically coherent solution to the problem is any more available now than after 1918 or 1945.

The next essay, by William Wallace, analyses the place of sovereignty in the European Union, with emphasis on the tension between sovereignty and integration. All West European states face crises of internal sovereignty, expressed partly in challenges to national identity and partly in a widening gap between the nationalistic rhetoric of domestic politics and the co-operative international practices of national governments. The logical way to reconcile the contradictions that are involved would be to move towards a more explicit federal European structure. The widening gap between the elites who run national governments or influence their policies and those who elect them, however, leaves room for populist challenges and popular resistance to further integration. Western European governments are now caught between an economic logic which drives them forward into each other's arms, and a political logic which holds them back; they have so far failed to develop a satisfactory framework of multi-level government which can reconcile these opposing inclinations and rationales.

Christopher Clapham's paper discusses the nature of sovereignty in the Third World, looking particularly at the weakest, poorest and most artificial states on the periphery, especially those of Africa. He argues that the newly independent governments took to Westphalian sovereignty 'like ducklings to water'. His essay demonstrates how international conventions designed to uphold sovereignty have often been appropriated, and in some cases subverted, by rulers to enhance their domestic control. Sovereignty in some Third World states has been implicated in the decline and disintegration of the territorial state. It has been turned into an expedient and lucrative political arrangement to serve essentially private ends of ruling elites. Thus, far from being a foundation of public life in the state, sovereignty in some Third World countries has produced the opposite effect. As the sovereign state comes under challenge the picture of the international system conveyed by multicoloured political maps is becoming inadequate and perhaps even misleading as a representation of political reality. Clapham concludes that the era of sovereignty as a universal organizing principle for the management of the global system has ended.

The following essay, by Paul Taylor, explores a shift in the interpretation of sovereignty at the United Nations. During the cold war sovereignty was narrowly defined as the inviolable right of independence of a sovereign state. After the end of the cold war more governments were prepared to demand that states whose internal policies were not up to international standards should mend their ways. The standards by which they were judged were increasingly those of the liberal democratic states. There were also developments in the concept of the international community which by the late 1990s had become more substantial and harder to ignore. There were, therefore, two contrasting notions of sovereignty: that it was a private world, based on the doctrine of non-intervention, with weak international authority; and that it was an international license to operate as an independent government, granted by the collectivity of states, which, it is argued, now constituted an international community. The essay examines the interplay between these two notions and argues that there was a discernible move to the latter after the end of the cold war.

Daniel Philpott recalls how during the sixteenth and seventeenth centuries in Europe, defenders of the medieval 'universal' international society of Christendom battled proponents of a new world of sovereign states, but the latter were victorious in 1648 at Westphalia. That victory involved a reconstitution of international society that displaced the old and 'thick' norms of Christian empire and established new and 'thin' norms of sovereignty. Today, several trends – the rise of humanitarian intervention, the expansion of the European Union, the increasing importance of non-state actors – suggest a change towards a thicker universal society once again. What insights does the early modern European transition provide for today? That question is addressed along three dimensions. First, the essay investigates how authority has shifted with respect to territorial sovereignty, transnational actors, and empire. Second, it shows the roots of both transitions in prior changes in ideas about legitimate authority, and not simply shifts in organizational structure, economics, or technology. Finally, it explores the ethical dilemmas and controversies that have come to the fore over questions of human rights, humanitarian intervention, and global obligations.

The collection is concluded with an essay by Georg Sørensen which raises the fundamental question of change in the sovereign state system. Is sovereignty a stable and unchanging institution or has it undergone dramatic change, both in present times and in earlier periods? If there is dramatic change, is the institution in the process of disappearing or at least losing much of its significance? Should we consequently talk about 'the end of sovereignty' or 'the illusion of sovereignty' as many scholars indeed propose to do? That debate about change and continuity is also apparent in the contributions to this collection with some (e.g. Alan James) arguing in favour of continuity and others (e.g. Paul Taylor) arguing in favour of change. This concluding essay makes an attempt at resolving the continuity versus change debate by arguing in favour of both positions; there are core aspects of the institution of sovereignty which remain unchanged and there are other aspects of the institution which have changed dramatically over time. In making that argument, Sørensen employs an important distinction between constitutive rules of sovereignty (which remain unchanged) and regulatory rules of sovereignty (which have changed in several ways), and he introduces the notion of different sovereignty 'games' played by different types of sovereign states.

Sovereignty in World Politics: a Glance at the Conceptual and Historical Landscape

ROBERT JACKSON

A Normative Premise of Modern Politics

Sovereignty is one of the foremost institutions of our world: it has given political life a distinctive constitutional shape that virtually defines the modern era and sets it apart from previous eras. As A. P. d'Entreves puts it: 'The importance of the doctrine of sovereignty can hardly be overrated. It was a formidable tool in the hands of lawyers and politicians, and a decisive factor in the making of modern Europe.'[1] And not only Europe: in the past century or two sovereignty has become a cornerstone of modern politics around the world. Sovereignty expresses some core ideas of political modernity including the fundamentally important notion of political independence. It was originally an institution of escape from rule by outsiders and to this day it remains a legal barrier to foreign interference in the jurisdiction of states. The basic norm of the UN Charter (Article 2) enshrines the principle of equal sovereignty and its corollary, the doctrine of non-intervention.

The institution is, shall we say, a basic element of the grammar of politics.[2] It exists as a normative postulate or premise or working hypothesis of modern political life. It may not always be explicitly acknowledged as such and may, like an iceberg, be mostly hidden from view. But it silently frames the conduct of much of modern politics nevertheless. Sovereignty is like Lego: it is a relatively simple idea but you can build almost anything with it, large or small, as long as you follow the rules. The British (English) used sovereignty to separate themselves from the medieval Catholic world (Latin Christendom). Then they used it to build an empire that encircled the globe. Then they used it to decolonize and thereby created a multitude of new states. It has other uses besides these.

My purpose is to investigate sovereignty in international relations in basic outline. Limitations of space dictate that this essay can only be an abridgement of a large historical subject. The main questions, although by no means the only ones, that can and I believe should be asked of sovereignty are the following: What is sovereignty? What is its character and *modus operandi*? Who are the principals and agents of sovereignty? Who are the subjects of sovereignty? What would be involved in going beyond sovereignty in world politics? What are the values that sovereignty can be seen to uphold and defend? The remainder of the essay is devoted to suggesting some responses to these questions, starting with the first and ending with the last.

---

[1] A. P. d'Entreves, *Natural Law* (London, Hutchinson, 1970), p. 67.
[2] The expression is Laski's. See H. Laski, *A Grammar of Politics* (London, Allen & Unwin, 1978).

Independence and Supremacy

What, then, is sovereignty? To begin, it is a constitutional arrangement of political life and is thus artificial and historical; there is nothing about it that is natural or inevitable or immutable. Sovereignty is a juridical idea and institution. A sovereign state is a territorial jurisdiction: i.e., the territorial limits within which state authority may be exercised on an exclusive basis. Sovereignty, strictly speaking, is a legal institution that authenticates a political order based on independent states whose governments are the principal authorities both domestically and internationally.

A caveat is necessary. Sovereignty is not an economic notion as it is sometimes made out to be. The expression 'economic sovereignty' is a conflation of two different concepts that are best kept in separate compartments if we wish to be clear. A better term might be economic autonomy. That is not to say that sovereignty and economics are unrelated. Obviously they are related. It is merely to point out that the relation is a contingent relation and not a conceptual relation. Economic autonomy is the notion that a country's economy is insulated from foreign economic influence or involvement or control. That may or may not be desirable in any particular case. But it is a matter of policy and not one of definition. Rather than speak of the decline or loss of 'economic sovereignty' it would be more to the point to speak of the difficulties that independent governments face in trying to pursue nationalistic economic policies, especially in our era of transnationalism and globalization.

Thus, like all independent states, Canada has the sovereign authority to issue and manage its own currency. The USA does not have the authority to do that in Canada. But for Canada and presumably for all states in similar circumstances of economic interdependence that right is a bit hollow. The Canadian government does not have much room for manoeuvre in that regard, because while monetary policy is set in Canada, the value of the Canadian dollar is heavily dependent on American monetary policy and on international currency markets. So, while Canada has the right to its own currency, it has limited power or capacity to determine the value of that currency. Canada is a sovereign state but it does not possess very much economic autonomy.

Sovereignty is the basic norm, *grundnorm*, upon which a society of states ultimately rests. If states were not sovereign political life would have to rest on a different normative foundation, such as suzerainty or empire or theocracy as was the case prior to the revolution of sovereignty e.g., the ancient Chinese suzerain-state system, the Roman Empire, medieval *respublica Christiana*, etc. A conceivable future world of non-sovereign states would have to be based on an alternative normative foundation of some kind e.g., global federation. But in a world of independent states certain norms are necessarily basic: norms of equal sovereignty, non-intervention, reciprocity, etc. That is the normative logic of the institution.

Brierly identifies the following basic norms of sovereignty: 'self-preservation, independence, equality, respect and intercourse'.[3] These norms are radically different than those which are basic in a world of Chinese suzerainty or Roman imperialism or medieval theocracy i.e., state inequality, dependence, intervention, paternalism, non-reciprocity, etc. In the absence of sovereignty the

---

[3] J. L. Brierly, *The Law of Nations* (London, Oxford University Press, 1938), p. 40.

normative shape of world politics would be significantly different and in all likelihood it would be fundamentally different. In a world federation, for example, states might resemble American 'states' which under the US constitution hold sovereignty jointly with the federal government but they do not hold it exclusively by themselves.

Hinsley captures the core meaning of sovereignty: it is 'the idea that there is a final and absolute political authority in the political community ... and no final and absolute authority exists elsewhere ...'.[4] In another place he notes that 'sovereignty ... is an assumption about authority'.[5] We might say that sovereignty is the basic assumption about authority of modern political life, domestically and internationally. By 'authority' I am of course referring to a right or title to rule. Sovereignty is the assumption that a government of a state is both supreme and independent. Regarding insiders, sovereignty is disclosed by the supremacy of a governing authority over everybody who lives in its territorial jurisdiction and is subject to its laws and policies. Internal sovereignty is a fundamental authority relation within states between rulers and ruled which is usually defined by a state's constitution. Regarding outsiders, sovereignty is disclosed by the independence of a governing authority from other governing authorities. External sovereignty is a fundamental authority relation between states which is defined by international law. Thus, as seen from inside a state, sovereignty is paramount authority, and as seen from outside it is self-governing authority.

Most of the time there is an established and recognized set of states in the world whose title to sovereignty is not contested to the point of serious uncertainty. There are of course occasions when things are not taken for granted and sovereignty is anything but habitual. Those are the moments when things get interesting from an academic point of view. There is a history of political controversies about sovereignty which this essay shall attempt to survey briefly. Sovereignty, in that respect, should be understood as an institution which is periodically renovated to respond to new historical circumstances. There are of course limits to the renovations that can be made to any institution, including sovereignty, beyond which it is changed out of all recognition and it can no longer be said to exist as such.

Because sovereignty is so fundamental, so much a fixture of modern political life, those occasions when questions are raised about sovereignty are likely to be highly contentious and sometimes even combative moments. In Canada the question of sovereignty in Quebec has been raised with increasing frequency and intensity. There is a deep division of public opinion on that issue which has been disruptive of Canadian political and economic life. A similar question, posed by certain Slovak politicians, led to the peaceful break-up of Czechoslovakia into two successor states after the Cold War: the Czech Republic and Slovakia. A comparable partition could yet happen in Canada. These are peaceful episodes whose international dislocations are local and minimal. However, that might not be the case if an existing sovereign is not only called into question peacefully but is also opposed by force. In recent years – to cite only a few well-known cases – armed secession movements have been mobilized by dissident Chechens

[4] F. H. Hinsley, *Sovereignty* (New York, Oxford, 1966), p. 26.
[5] F. H. Hinsley, 'The Concept of Sovereignty and the Relations between States', in W. J. Stankiewicz, ed., *In Defense of Sovereignty* (New York, Oxford University Press, 1969), 275.

in Russia, dissident Serbians in Croatia and Bosnia, and dissident Albanians in Kosovo in Serbia (Yugoslavia). These latter conflicts have disrupted international relations in the Balkans region.

We should probably regard periodical reshuffling of the title to sovereignty, even major redistribution, as something to be expected from time to time. That could dislocate the political life of certain states and regions for a period. But it would not challenge the institution itself. The extensive reshuffling of sovereignty after the Cold War in the former Soviet Union and the former Yugoslavia was disruptive. But it was also an affirmation of the popularity of the institution. Sovereignty clearly is something that many people want to keep and many other people want to have.

However, there are moments in world politics when the current *modus operandi* of sovereignty – i.e., the institution itself – is placed in some degree of doubt. The history of sovereignty has involved occasions of that sort e.g., when national self-determination became a basic norm of sovereignty or when colonialism became illegitimate and illegal. On both of those occasions the constitutional shape of sovereignty was altered significantly. There may someday even be another occasion, reminiscent of the 'Grotian moment' of the seventeenth century, that may come to be regarded as the end of sovereignty and the beginning of some fundamentally different post-sovereign arrangement of world politics. Some scholars believe that that revolutionary time has already arrived.[6]

One of the basic inclinations of the society of sovereign states, however, is to prevent international revolutions and to keep international reformations to a minimum. International society is fundamentally conservative. Sovereignty is a historical institution and change has therefore to be met, but the encounter does not have to be a capitulation on the part of sovereignty. Nor could it be without putting the state system at normative risk. That conservative bias is a striking feature of the arrangement. That is justified by reference to basic political values that the institution of sovereignty is intended to underwrite and indeed foster (see the final section). Among the most important of those values is international order and stability. As international circumstances change, however, requirements for order and stability also change, and the practices of sovereignty must change too. In the beginning sovereignty was dynastic and imperial. Then it became popular and nationalist. Today in many parts of the world it is locally-based and anti-imperial. The institutional arrangements have changed over time but the core notion of sovereignty as political independence has remained the same.

To sum up thus far: sovereignty in world politics is a distinctive way of arranging the contacts and relations of political communities, or states, such that their political independence is mutually recognized and they co-exist and interact on a foundation of formal equality and a corresponding right of non-intervention. The approach that I shall take in pursuing this argument is that of the classical international society tradition associated with the writings of Wight and Bull, among others.[7]

---

[6] See R. Falk, 'The Grotian moment', *International Insights*, 13 (Fall 1997), 3–34 and my reply to that claim in R. Jackson, 'The Grotian moment in world jurisprudence', *International Insights*, 13 (Fall 1997), 35–56.

[7] M. Wight, *Systems of States* (Leicester, Leicester University Press, 1977) and H. Bull, *The Anarchical Society* (London, Macmillan, 2nd ed., 1995).

Political Authority before Sovereignty

Because it is so easy to take sovereignty for granted it may be useful to recollect, if only in brief outline, the European political world before sovereignty became a standard of conduct in the relations of principalities, republics, monarchies, confederations, etc. – what we refer to as states and the states system. If we can understand, if only in brief outline, what that older historical world was like and what the political change from medieval to modern basically involved we should be in a better position to grasp the operational meaning and significance of sovereignty.

A striking impression that the middle ages convey to anyone looking back from our vantage point at the dawn of the third millennium is one of astonishing diversity concerning political authority. By comparison our international world has a remarkable degree of uniformity centred on the institution of sovereignty which is now global in extent. The only uniform institution that existed across western Europe and by far the most important institution of the middle ages was the medieval theocracy – Latin Christendom – which was at one and the same time a religious organization and a political organization. *Respublica Christiana* (defined below) holds the key to our understanding of that time.

In the middle ages political life was not sharply differentiated from religious life or family life or other departments of social life. Government authority was not clearly public; in most places a king's (public) realm was also his or her (private) estate.[8] Medieval commentators distinguished 'the king's two bodies': his or her personal body and the body politic.[9] Rulership was in many places largely the private affair of dynastic states. But in other places it was the corporate activities of religious foundations or commercial organizations and in yet other places it was the communal property of cities, towns, guilds or estates. There were many different kinds of 'political' authorities whose relations were ambiguous and whose responsibilities and activities could easily conflict. Sometimes and indeed quite often it was difficult to distinguish political and religious authority. Even to try to make such a distinction risks misconceiving the medieval world in which the political was entangled, inextricably, in the theological. Some of the leading political authorities were bishops or heads of religious orders who controlled extensive territories.

The medieval map was not a territorial patchwork of different colours which represent independent countries under sovereign governments whose populations had clearly conceived national identities. Instead, it was a complicated and confusing intermingling of lines and colours of varying shades and hues. 'Europe was not divided up into exclusive sovereignties, but was covered by overlapping and constantly shifting lordships.'[10] 'Lordship' involved 'a proprietary right to territory' but it did not imply sovereignty: a duke or a municipal government or the head of a religious order could exercise lordship which was not restricted to dynastic or even to noble families – although most lordships were the hereditary tenures of such families.[11] Kings and other rulers were the subjects of higher authorities and laws. They were

---

[8] Sir George Clark, *Early Modern Europe* (New York, Oxford, 1960), pp. 27–8.
[9] E. H. Kantorowicz, *The King's Two Bodies* (Princeton, Princeton University Press, 1957).
[10] Clark, *Early Modern Europe*, p. 28.
[11] M. Keen, *Medieval Europe* (Harmondsworth, Penguin, 1991), p. 262.

neither supreme nor completely independent. And much of the time local rulers were more or less free from the rule of kings: they were semi-autonomous but they were not fully independent either. 'The people' did not exist as such. Most people were vassals of superiors and some people were chattels of ruling families far more than they were subjects of independent states. Only rarely, if ever, were they citizens of states – and only the wealthy class enjoyed citizen status.

It was unusual for a king's realm to be concentrated and consolidated at one place. A ruler's territory would often resemble an archipelago: peripheral parts were scattered like islands among the territory of other rulers; core parts were perforated and interrupted by the intervening jurisdictions of other authorities. Some rulers held fiefdoms within the territorial domains of other rulers which gave them the status of semi-independent vassals. In short, many states were conglomerates whose rulers occupied different offices in their different territories which affected the way they had to rule those territories, such as the kings of Prussia, who were absolute monarchs in Konigsberg but were imperial vassals of the Holy Roman Emperor in Berlin, or the Habsburg's themselves, who later were autocrats in Vienna and Prague but were constitutional monarchs in Brussels.

If we can stretch a word and speak of 'sovereignty' in the Middle Ages in the first instance the sovereign was God whose commands were generally acknowledged by Christians as demanding obedience. In the second instance it was the pope, the bishop of Rome and vicar of Christ, God's representative on earth, who presided over Christendom.[12] The core political idea was that of the *respublica Christiana*: the notion that secular authorities no less than spiritual authorities were subjects of a higher authority, God, whose commandments were expressed by the precepts of Christianity. Both secular and religious authorities were Christ's subjects and servants. According to St. Paul: 'The state is there to serve God ... The authorities are there to serve God ... All government officials are God's officers'.[13] *Respublica Christiana* was based on a joint structure of religious authority (Sacerdotium) headed by the pope and political authority (Regnum) headed by a secular ruler designated as emperor (in the later middle-ages and early modern era that office was held by the head of the Habsburg dynasty). In short, if there was a 'sovereign state' in medieval Europe, it was the Christian empire: *respublica Christiana*. Before sovereign states could fully emerge the superior authority of the papacy and the imperial office had to be extinguished or at least rendered superfluous.

Respublica Christiana was thus a *universitas* rather than a *societas*. A *universitas* is a human association that has a commanding authority and an overriding purpose which is the standard against which all conduct is judged. *Respublica Christiana* was a unified authority in theory, however shaky in practice, that was devoted to the overarching purpose of Christian redemption and salvation.[14] Unlike a *universitas*, a *societas* accommodates different authorities and is thus governed not by any commanding agent or purpose

[12] J. Canning, *A History of Medieval Political Thought, 300–1450* (London, Routledge, 1996), p. 84.

[13] As quoted by Canning, *A History of Medieval Political Thought*, p. 19.

[14] This is a modification of the notion of *universitas* theorized by M. Oakeshott, 'The Rule of Law', in his *On History and Other Essays* (Oxford, Blackwell, 1983); also see M. Oakeshott, *On Human Conduct* (Oxford, Clarendon, 1975).

but, rather, by a general rule, or norm, which those authorities recognize, are subject to, and are expected to subscribe to. Following this reasoning, international *societas* consists of a variety of states each free to devote themselves to their own national interests providing that they observe international law, which is a set of general norms that vouches for the authenticity of sovereign states.

The Medieval *universitas* was a community of Christian believers which it was the duty of the pope and the emperor, of kings, barons, bishops, priests and indeed of every Christian to uphold. Christian rulers were defenders of the faith. Latin Christendom was a religious-political community that encompassed all social divisions, including those of political jurisdiction, and gave at least minimal unity and cohesion to Europeans whatever their language and wherever their homeland happened to be.[15] Even if the actuality of unity varied widely from one place to the next and was sometimes non-existent 'the belief in unity was deep-seated and died hard'.[16] Since it was based on the Christian religion there was no room in Latin Christendom for non-Christians, for Christian dissenters or reformers, or for pagans or non-believers. Medieval Christians thus drew a sharp line to separate their world of true faith from the non-Christian and the anti-Christian world. A similar border was later to separate the European and then Western world of sovereign states from the non-western world that was deemed to be incapable or unworthy of sovereignty and was thus a candidate for European colonialism.

Respublica Christiana presided loosely over European political-religious affairs not only by means of the papacy and the office of the emperor, but also by means of periodic councils of the church. One of the most important conferences in the emergence of sovereignty was the Council of Constance which put an end to the 'great schism' (1378–1417) in Latin Christendom when there were several popes each claiming to be the vicar of Christ and to represent the authority of the papal monarchy.[17] This conciliar intervention in papal authority was followed by the Council of Basle (1449) which finally gave up on the attempt to re-establish the unity of the western church by conciliar means. That opened a way for the emergence of states with greater authority than had existed previously.[18] Here, arguably, was the first clear intimation of a post-Medieval political world based on the *societas* of sovereign states as the defining and unifying institution.[19]

The Medieval ecclesiastical-political order began to fall apart during the sixteenth century under the dual shocks of the (initially Italian) Renaissance and the (initially German) Reformation which occurred at about the same time. The Renaissance involved the emergence of independent Italian city-states which formed a regional state system that soon spread north of the Alps. Other European rulers took their political cue from the Italians and the arts and sciences of the Renaissance, including the political art of independent statecraft, spread to all of Western Europe. *Raison d'etat* and more narrowly *realpolitik* or in other words the morality of the interest of the state, became the primary and

---

[15] Wight, *Systems of States*, p. 47.
[16] Keen, *Medieval Europe*, p. 12.
[17] Canning, *A History of Medieval Political Thought*, pp. 181–82.
[18] Canning, *A History of Medieval Political Thought*, p. 185. Also see Keen, *Medieval Europe*, p. 314.
[19] Wight, *Systems of States*, p. 151.

sometimes the only justification of statecraft.[20] By the sixteenth century the papacy itself had become a state and indeed a significant power: one among several rival Italian powers.[21] If the pope was now an Italian statesman could he still also be the presiding authority of *respublica Christiana*? The existence of increasingly self-regarding states was in turn furthered by the growing use of vernacular languages in political life, which prompted political theorists, such as Machiavelli, to articulate novel ideas of independent statecraft and statehood that were not readily available in medieval political theology which was expressed in Latin.[22]

The Reformation involved a struggle for religious freedom (by Protestants) against religious orthodoxy (by Catholics) and simultaneously for political authority (by secular rulers) over religious matters – which meant freedom from outside interference. The political theology of Martin Luther disengaged the authority of the state from the religious sanction of *respublica Christiana*.[23] One of the clearest instances of disengagement was King Henry VIII of England's divorce not only from Catherine of Aragon, which the pope refused to sanction, but also simultaneously from *respublica Christiana* – as registered in the Act of Supremacy (1534) which abolished papal authority and elevated the King to Supreme Head of the Church of England.[24] The notion of sovereignty is systematically explored at length and in depth for the first time in the French vernacular in Jean Bodin's sixteenth century political treatise *Les six livres de la Republique* (1576).[25] This was not a study of *respublica Christiana*. It was a study of the French monarchical state as a free-standing and self-regarding political entity. 'It is most expedient for the preservation of the state that the rights of sovereignty should never be granted out to a subject, still less to a foreigner, for to do so is to provide a stepping-stone where the grantee himself becomes the sovereign.'[26] That counsel was a rejection of the middle ages.

Westphalian Sovereignty

The great transformation from medieval to modern thus involved at its core the institution of the sovereign state and the corresponding *societas* of states. When, exactly, that happened is a subject of debate among scholars of world politics. Wight sees its tentative beginnings in the conciliar movement of the fifteenth century.[27] Hinsley sees its full historical manifestation only in the Concert of Europe in the 1820s.[28] Most scholars, however, see the seventeenth century and particularly the Peace of Westphalia which settled the bloody thirty years' war

[20] See J. Vincent, 'Realpolitik', in J. Mayall (ed.), *The Community of States* (London, George Allen & Unwin, 1982), pp. 73–85.

[21] J. Burckhardt, *The Civilization of the Renaissance in Italy*, vol. 1 (New York, Harper & Row, 1958), pp. 120–42.

[22] Keen, *Medieval Europe*, p. 318. Also see Wight, 'The origins of our states-system: chronological limits', in *Systems of States*, pp. 129–52; also the relevant discussion on pp. 110–14.

[23] S. Wolin, *Politics and Vision* (Boston, Little, Brown, 1960), p. 143.

[24] See Norman Davies, *Europe: A History* (London, Pimlico, 1997), p. 490.

[25] J Bodin, *Six Books of the Commonwealth* (M. J. Tooley, trans.), (Oxford, Blackwell, no date).

[26] Bodin, *Six Books of the Commonwealth*, book I, ch. 10, p. 49.

[27] Wight, *Systems of States*, p. 151. A similar view is taken by Keen, *Medieval Europe*, pp. 314–21.

[28] F. H. Hinsley, 'The Concept of Sovereignty and the Relations between States', in Stankiewicz, *In Defense of Sovereignty*, p. 285.

(1618–1648) as the best historical reference point for symbolizing that fundamental turn in European political life.

It is important to understand the Westphalian moment from the perspective of that time and not from the present time – insofar as that is possible. The conceptual and linguistic categories available to the statespeople at Westphalia were those of the late medieval era.[29] They understood themselves to be an assembly of Christian rulers and their representatives. They had a notion of being members of one community the basis of which was the Christian religion.[30] They still spoke of 'Christendom' and of their peace congress as the 'senate of the Christian world'. They expressed their agreements in Latin. The peace treaties do not specifically include much evidence for the claim that Westphalia is the crucial turning point in the emergence of sovereignty. There is no mention of the word 'sovereignty'. Westphalia was an important stage, perhaps the most important, in the long retreat that lasted over several centuries during which time *respublica Christiana* was obliged to surrender more and more authority to the emergent states of Europe. 'At Westphalia the states system does not come into existence: it comes of age.'[31] Westphalia is not a literal moment of political transformation but, rather, the symbol of that change.

After Westphalia the language of international justification gradually shifted, away from Christian unity and towards international diversity based on a secular society of sovereign states. By the time of the Peace of Utrecht (1712–1713) the rulers of Europe understood each other as 'essentially ... self-determining actors, none of which was entitled to dictate to others.'[32] The treaties of Westphalia and Utrecht still referred to Christendom but they were among the last to do that. For what had come into historical existence in the meantime was a secular European society of states in which overarching political and religious authority was no longer in existence in any substantive sense. The arch constituted by *respublica Christiana* had been broken. An anarchical society of sovereign states had taken its place. Europe displaced Christendom. Europe was now conceived as a plurality of territory-based political systems each with its own independent and supreme governing authority. What had been a political-theological *universitas* became an international *societas* of sovereign states. That is what Westphalia stands for.

The institution of sovereignty sorted out the uncertainty and indeed the confusion around the question of authority that existed in the middle ages. The new sovereign state escaped from the medieval system of dispersed authority and successfully established and enforced its own centralized authority. The state captured its territory and turned it into state property, and it captured the population of that territory and turned them into subjects and later citizens. Internally, there was no room for semi-independent territory or people or institutions. As indicated, in many cases the Christian churches fell under state

---

[29] 'Well into at least the seventeenth century, the juristic, theological and overtly political works of medieval scholastics continued to be prime sources for the discussion of political thought ... The writings of ... Hugo Grotius (1583–1645), amongst very many others, illustrated this trend.' Canning, *A History of Medieval Political Thought*, p. 186.

[30] See A. Osiander, *The States System of Europe, 1640–1990* (Oxford, Clarendon, 1994), pp. 27–8.

[31] Wight, *Systems of States*, p. 152.

[32] Osiander, *The States System of Europe*, p. 120.

control. Territory was consolidated, unified, and centralized under a sovereign government. The population of the territory now owed allegiance to the sovereign and they had a duty to obey the laws of the land. Externally, there was no room for any intervening overarching authority comparable to the pope or the emperor. *Rex est imperator in regno suo*: king is emperor in his own realm. There was no room for quasi-independent lordships either. The familiar territorial patchwork map of the world was brought into being in which each patch was under the exclusive jurisdiction of an independent state. All territory in Europe and, eventually, all territory around the world was partitioned by sovereign governments and placed under their independent authority.

Although the Christian empire survived until the early nineteenth century, it was reduced to a hollow shell. Westphalia confirmed the peace of Augsburg (1555) at which the principle of *cujus regio ejus religio* was formulated, according to which every ruler was permitted to enforce the religion of his or her choice, either Catholicism or Protestantism, within his or her territories. This was a principle of international co-existence.[33] As one historian puts it: 'This extraordinary compromise saved the theory of religious unity for each state while destroying it for the Empire'.[34] The religion of international society was still Christian but that was increasingly indistinguishable from the culture which was European.

Finally, there was intended to be a balance of power between member states to prevent any one state from making a successful bid for hegemony which would in effect re-establish an empire over the continent. Adam Watson captures the Westphalian moment very nicely: it 'was the charter of a Europe permanently organized on an anti-hegemonial principle'.[35] Kissinger has summarized this development:

> Europe was thrown into balance-of-power politics when its first choice, the medieval dream of universal empire, collapsed and a host of states of more or less equal strength arose from the ashes of that ancient aspiration. When a group of states so constituted are obliged to deal with one another, there are only two possible outcomes: either one state becomes so strong that it dominates all the others and creates an empire, or no state is ever quite powerful enough to achieve that goal.[36]

Europe no longer went to war in the uniform of *respublica Christiana*, as it had done in the Middle Ages. There was no overarching authority to sanction war, which was now the right of sovereign states, but there was deemed to be a common interest in peace the defence of which might require the collective action of such states. It was generally recognized, however, that all states had legitimate interests and statespeople were responsible for advancing and defending those national interests and could not ordinarily be expected to sacrifice them. The anti-hegemonial notion of a countervailing alliance of major powers aimed at preserving the freedom of all member states and maintaining the European society of states as a whole was only worked out by trial and error and fully theorized in the eighteenth and nineteenth centuries.

[33] Keen, *Medieval Europe*, p. 318.
[34] Wedgwood, *The Thirty Years War*, p. 42.
[35] A Watson, *The Evolution of International Society* (London, Routledge, 1992), ch. 17.
[36] H. Kissinger, *Diplomacy* (New York, Simon & Schuster, 1994), p. 20.

Ever since the seventeenth century the normative idea of Europe as a *universitas* under a unified hierarchical authority has been repudiated, notwithstanding major attempts to reinstate it by armed force: for example, in the later seventeenth century by French King Louis XIV in the form of universal monarchy. The greatest historical threat to the European *societas* of states before the twentieth century was posed by Napoleon's bid for continental hegemony (1795–1815). In the eighteenth and nineteenth centuries Britain often played the role of the defender of the balance of power by adding decisive military weight to the coalition which formed against the hegemon, most notably in the case of post-revolutionary Napoleonic France. The United States played a similar role in the Second World War against Nazi Germany and Imperial Japan, and in the Cold War against Communist Russia. Insofar as both Britain and the USA accepted and indeed defended the principles of the international *societas*, even when their power was at its greatest, they could not themselves be regarded as hegemons in the classical political meaning of the term.

The history of attempting to transform Europe into a *universitas* in which only one authority is 'sovereign' has mostly been a history of war and revolution. Recently, however, the old unity idea has been taken up in Western Europe in the peaceful form of the European Union which has some features of a quasi-*universitas*. But even if the EU became a fully fledged *universitas* – perhaps based on a federal constitution – the larger effect of that for world politics would be to create a new greater power where previously a collection of lesser powers existed.[37] In that event the balance of power might have a new balancer (see below).

To sum up to this point. The great transformation symbolized by the expression 'Westphalia' involved turning the medieval world inside out. During the middle ages Europe was a (loose) *universitas* based on the overarching (ramshackle and shaky) political-religious structure of Latin Christendom. At that time most 'states' were penetrated and compromised by external and internal authorities of one kind or another. In the modern era Europe was transformed into a *societas*, based on a multiplicity of states whose governments were intolerant of competing authorities or parallel jurisdictions in what they considered was their exclusive territory: they were supreme within their jurisdiction and independent of foreign authorities.

Imperial Sovereignty

When a government exercises supreme authority over a foreign territory that government can be said to possess imperial sovereignty. A foreign territory is somebody else's homeland. Imperial sovereignty is thus a denial of local sovereignty in foreign countries. Sovereignty gave imperial states independent status in their foreign territories while simultaneously imposing a dependent status on the populations of those same territories. That denial of equal status is often the seed of the demand for political independence on grounds of national self-determination.

---

[37] For a discussion of monism and pluralism in the legal systems of Europe see N. MacCormick, 'Liberalism, nationalism and the post-sovereign state', *Political Studies*, (1996), XLIV, 553–67.

After the Westphalian revolution imperialism within Europe carried a taint of medieval feudalism and was contrary to the political norms of a *societas* of independent states. There were of course empires and indeed many of them. But Europe was no longer an empire. The empires that remained within Europe were imperial states most of which occupied territory outside the core area of the West European *societas*: e.g., the peripheral lands in central, southern, and eastern Europe of the Habsburg (Austrian) Empire which was the remnant of the Holy Roman Empire. As indicated, attempts to reinstate an overarching empire across the heartland of *societas* Europe – e.g., by France on several occasions – were resisted and prevented.

But empire-building by European states outside Europe was the fashion until the twentieth century. European rulers saw the commercial and military advantages of holding non-European territory in the Americas, Asia, Africa, etc. Many European states projected their military power and commercial enterprises into non-European oceans and continents, where they inevitably made contact and frequently came into conflict with non-European political systems. The historical outcome was most often victory for the Europeans. Conquest, colonization, and other actions to extinguish the independence of non-European political systems were lawful in the eyes of Europeans. In their acquisition of non-European territory the European states were guided by Roman principles and practices: i.e., occupation of *terra nullius*, cession, prescription, inheritance, accretion, and conquest.[38]

When European states began to penetrate non-European continents and oceans, usually in competition with each other, sovereignty was conveniently available as an institution for annexing new territories. The imperialists understandably preferred a recognized title to foreign territory, rather than the uncertainty of holding it by force in competition with each other. European states consequently recognized each other's empires while agreeing not to recognize non-European political authorities. European imperialism was initially sanctioned by the *respublica Christiana*: e.g., the pope's jurisdictional division of the Americas between Portugal and Spain in the early sixteenth century. But the notion that territorial occupations could be authorized by anyone other than European sovereigns themselves disappeared. When the East India Company and the Hudson's Bay Company asserted claims to territories in South Asia and North America they did so by reference to royal charters that they had obtained from the British Crown. Sovereignty was a means of instituting the European states' claims to imperial authority over the rest of the world. In that way sovereignty initially became a global institution.

Sovereignty was then understood to be a distinctly European institution. European states did not extend a right of membership in their *societas* to political authorities outside Europe; their international association was closed to outsiders. Non-European political systems were regarded as lacking legitimate or credible claims to sovereignty and were consequently subjected to unequal treaties and other discriminatory measures. The justification for that discrimination had a medieval ring: it was the right and indeed the responsibility of Europeans to rule non-Europeans and other peoples of different and by implication lesser civilization than their own. There was believed to be a 'standard of civilization' which non-western societies had to measure up to

---

[38] M. N. Shaw, *Title to Territory in Africa* (Oxford, Clarendon, 1986), p. 17.

before they could make a legitimate and credible claim to sovereignty. The high point of European imperial sovereignty, in this regard, was reached in the second half of the nineteenth century. It is captured in the rationalization of a prominent British international lawyer published in 1880:

> It is scarcely necessary to point out that as international law is a product of the special civilization of modern Europe, and forms a highly artificial system of which the principles cannot be supposed to be understood or recognized by countries differently civilized, such states can only be presumed to be subject to it.[39]

Thus, in the relations of European states to each other Westphalia inverted the practices of medieval Europe. But in the relations of European states to political authorities outside the European heartland and in the rest of the world Westphalia reiterated Medieval practices which asserted the superiority of Latin Christendom or Western civilization, the moral inequality of peoples, the right of intervention, the right of conquest, and ultimately the right of colonization. The old medieval boundary between Christendom and the non-Christian world was redefined as a line between the civilized Western world and the not yet fully or properly civilized rest of the world.

European states that acquired imperial possessions governed them in the manner of a *universitas* with each one managing its own empire with a view to enhancing its own military or commercial interests. Some European empires, most dramatically the British Empire, held numerous dependent territories that were dispersed in a fashion reminiscent of the empires of medieval Europe. The British Empire is an excellent example of such a conglomerate state which consisted of its homeland, Great Britain, the British Dominions (Canada, Australia, New Zealand, South Africa), British India, and an assortment of crown colonies, colonial protectorates, protected states, and – in the twentieth century – mandated and trust territories scattered around the world.

In the late nineteenth and early twentieth centuries European imperial states adopted a posture of paternalism in which they assumed the responsibility for educating their non-European subjects in the arts and sciences of Western civilization. That is evident in the General Act of the Berlin Conference (1884–1885) which sanctioned the partition of Africa and called upon 'all the Powers exercising sovereign rights [in the continent] ... to watch over the preservation of the native tribes, and to care for the improvement of the conditions of their moral and material well-being ... bringing home to them the blessings of civilization.' (Art. VI) It is evident in the League of Nations Mandates System which spoke of non-western 'peoples not yet able to stand by themselves under the strenuous conditions of the modern world' whose 'tutelage' 'should be entrusted to advanced nations'. (Art. 22) And it is evident in the UN Trusteeship System which aimed 'to promote the political, economic, social, and educational advancement of the inhabitants of trust territories, and their progressive development towards self-government or independence as may be appropriate in the particular circumstances of each territory and its peoples ...' (Art. 76) The aim clearly was to eventually erase the normative distinction between the West and the rest of the world thereby making a global *societas* of states not only equitable but also possible. But that was expected to take time and probably a long time in some cases.

---

[39] W. E. Hall, as quoted by Wight, *Systems of States*, p. 115.

What proved fatal to the institution of imperial sovereignty, however, was the liberal political idea that there was something inherently wrong about a government that laid claim to foreign territories and populations – even if its intentions were benevolent. Increasingly it was felt that there was no longer any room in international society for governments that asserted a right to govern foreign territories and their populations. The *societas* of states was now understood as an institution in which membership could not be denied on grounds of religion, civilization, geography, etc. That postulated an intrinsic right to sovereignty which is usually portrayed as a right of national self-determination. In spite of the thorny problem of determining who ought to exercise that right or in other words what is the nation for purposes of political independence in particular cases – which is anything but straightforward (see below and also the essay by James Mayall) – that came to be virtually the only valid ground for asserting and claiming title to sovereignty. After centuries of legality imperial sovereignty become unlawful. That is explicitly registered in various UN General Assembly resolutions: e.g., Resolution 3103 (1973) which portrayed colonialism as nothing less than 'a crime'. It now takes an effort to remember that little more than half a century ago Western imperialism was a global political arrangement that seemed destined to continue indefinitely.

Popular Sovereignty

By 'popular sovereignty' I shall refer to the notion that sovereignty resides in the political will or consent of the population of a territory, rather than its ruler or government: i.e., the independence of a people considered as a political community. Sovereignty begins its career as dynastic sovereignty. Political authority is autocratic or absolutist: 'I am the sovereign, and I shall exercise authority over my subjects, wherever they live, at home or abroad'. Sovereignty logically would seem to end its career as popular sovereignty. Political authority is democratic or at least representative: 'We are sovereign over ourselves. Nobody else has any right to intervene in our country and exercise sovereignty over us without our consent.'

The doctrine of popular sovereignty is anything but new. The idea was registered in the French and American revolutions of the late 18th century. It was evident in the American Declaration of Independence (1776) and the United States Constitution (1787). The American Federalists spoke of the virtues and advantages of 'popular government' even while recognizing the vices and dangers.[40] The French constitution of 1791 declared that 'Sovereignty is one, indivisible, unalienable and imprescriptible; it belongs to the Nation; no group can attribute sovereignty to itself nor can an individual arrogate it to himself.' The ghost of Rousseau's 'general will' is not difficult to make out. Martin Wight sees the seed of popular sovereignty in the challenge to dynastic and absolute monarchy in the English 'glorious revolution' of 1688–1689.[41] One could argue, however, that the seed was already planted by the revolt against *respublica Christiana* and the creation of independent territorial realms – even if it took about three centuries for the flowering of the idea that state authority is rooted in the people who make their home in the territory.

---

[40] James Madison in *The Federalist* No. 10, reprinted in R. M. Hutchins (ed.), *Great Books of the Western World* (Chicago, Encyclopaedia Britannica, 1952), vol. 43, pp. 49–53.
[41] Wight, *Systems of States*, p. 159.

The explicit principle of national self-determination came late in the history of sovereignty. President Woodrow Wilson's efforts to establish a League of Nations based on consent made national self-determination a primary consideration in the formation of new states in Central and Eastern Europe in the areas of the defeated Habsburg and Ottoman empires. In the Atlantic Charter (1941), with Nazi occupied Europe in mind, the USA and Britain called upon sovereign states to 'respect the right of all peoples to choose the form of government under which they will live'. The UN Charter committed its members to 'friendly relations among nations based on respect for the principle of equal rights and self-determination of peoples' (Art. 1). In 1950 the UN General Assembly 'recognized the right of peoples and nations to self-determination as a fundamental human right'.

If the people or nation were easy to recognize in practice the story might end there. But that is not the case. That can come as no surprise after a moment's reflection on the relationship between peoples and territory which is usually an awkward fit even at the best of times. The practical problem of determining who shall count as comprising the people is anything but easy to solve. Even if it is clear who are the people the problem still remains that territory and people are not usually neatly aligned. Furthermore, it is always problematical, both politically and morally, either to redraw territorial borders or to relocate people in an effort to achieve alignment. That is one of the big lessons not only of the attempt to create new national states in central and eastern Europe at the end of the First World War, but also of various territorial partitions (e.g., Ireland, India, Palestine, Yugoslavia, etc.) and population transfers (e.g., at the end of the Second World War in Europe).[42]

That is perhaps most evident from the issue of national minorities. When the people or the nation, rather than the ruler or the government, become the referent for sovereignty, the issue of national minorities arises at the same time. Point 12 in President Woodrow Wilson's famous 'Fourteen Points' speech (1918) acknowledged that post-war Turkey should be 'assured a secure sovereignty', but he immediately added that 'the other nationalities which are now under Turkish rule should be assured an undoubted security of life and an absolutely unmolested opportunity of autonomous development.' That came to be read as political independence. New nation states were subsequently recognized in those areas outside the Anatolian heartland of the Turkish nation. As it turned out, however, it proved impossible to draw sociologically rational borders that perfectly divided nationalities into separate territorial compartments of their own: e.g., Greece and Bulgaria had Turkish minorities. The same problem arose in the partition of the Habsburg Empire into new states. Redefined Hungary ended up with Slovak minorities, Romania and Czechoslovakia had Hungarian minorities, etc. In short, the attempt to draw international boundaries to create new nation-states out of the debris of empires inevitably created new national minorities.[43]

The issue of national minorities alerts us to the problems that surround the principle of national self-determination in a society of sovereign states

[42] Jennifer Jackson Preece, 'Ethnic cleansing as an instrument of nation-state creation', *Human Rights Quarterly*, 20 (1998), 817–42.
[43] See Jennifer Jackson Preece, *National Minorities and the European Nation-States System* (Oxford, Clarendon, 1998).

organized, fundamentally, on a territorial basis. National self-determination, strictly speaking, is realized in practice only in a comparatively small number of cases of sovereign statehood. Most sovereign jurisdictions include several nations and peoples, and some jurisdictions contain many of them.

Uti Possidetis Juris

Do a people determine the sovereignty of a territory, or does a territory define and delimit the sovereign jurisdiction of people? The latter situation is nearer to historical reality. The current practice is to vest sovereignty in a bordered territorial homeland rather than a distinctive people or nation. That should not be surprising insofar as sovereignty is an institution that expresses a territorial definition of political authority.

In the twentieth century the political map of the world was frozen in a territorial pattern shaped by the outcome of the Second World War and also by the colonial borders established in the non-western world by the European imperialists. Those jurisdictions defined the post-war and post-colonial territorial *status quo*. Existing borders became sacrosanct and lawful border change correspondingly difficult. The right of territorial conquest was extinguished in the twentieth century. No longer could states acquire territory or lose territory by means of armed force. Nor, for all intents and purposes, could territory any longer be purchased or exchanged or rearranged or altered in any way without the agreement of all affected states parties. In short, the current territorial jurisdictions of states acquired entrenched legality.

The League of Nations Covenant undertook 'to protect and preserve ... the territorial integrity and existing political independence of all Members' (Art. 10). The League failed but the UN Charter upheld the same juridical value using identical language (Art. 2). The 1960 UN Declaration on Granting Independence to Colonial Territories and Countries stated that 'any attempt aimed at the partial or total disruption of the national unity or territorial integrity of a country is incompatible with the purposes and principles of the Charter of the United Nations'. Respect for borders is a sacred norm of the 1963 Organization of African Unity. The 1975 Helsinki Final Act expressed the principle that 'frontiers can [only] be changed, in accordance with international law, by peaceful means and by agreement'. The 1990 Charter of Paris for a New Europe reiterated the same principle. It was the basis of the Dayton Agreement signed between Bosnia-Herzegovina, Croatia and Serbia. The two key articles read as follows:

> The parties ... shall fully respect the sovereign equality of one another ... and shall refrain from any action, by threat or use of force or otherwise, against the territorial integrity or political independence of Bosnia and Herzegovina or any other state. (Article I)
> The Federal Republic of Yugoslavia and the Republic of Bosnia and Herzegovina recognize each other as sovereign independent States within their international borders. (Article X)

The territorial *status quo* has been preserved almost without exception even in the face of armed challenges. In Europe the major apparent exception is the unification of East and West Germany. It should be noted, however, that the external post-1945 borders of former East and West Germany were not altered in the slightest degree by reunification. It might be thought that the new states that emerged after the Cold War in the territory of former Soviet Union and former Yugoslavia contradict the juridical practice. But the internal borders of each federation were used to define the territorial jurisdiction of the successor sovereign states. The new borders have subsequently been upheld even in the face of armed efforts to change them e.g., in Croatia, Bosnia, Russia (Chechnya), and Serbia (Kosovo). It seems nowadays that boundaries cannot be modified even to punish an aggressor state: Iraq retained its borders despite having committed the crime of aggression and having suffered an overwhelming military defeat in the Gulf War.

Virtually all of the new states of the Third World previously were colonies or other territorial jurisdictions created by Western imperialism. Not only in Africa but also in Asia and the Middle-East existing borders are virtually identical to those of the colonial era. The exceptions are minor and few. In Africa that is all the more surprising in light of the profound weakness of the existing states most of which are seriously deficient in political stability and country-wide unity.[44] Even in the Middle-East the old colonial frontiers which divided the Arab 'nation' into many territorial jurisdictions have been declared as lawful by the vast majority of Arab states: a juridical ethic which in Arab eyes not only condemned the borders of Israel, which ignored colonial divisions, but also Iraq's invasion of Kuwait.

We are living at a time when existing state territorial jurisdictions are vested with exceptional value. The principle involved is that of *uti possidetis juris* according to which existing boundaries are the pre-emptive basis for determining territorial jurisdictions in the absence of mutual agreement to do otherwise. The principle seeks to uphold the territorial integrity of states by demanding respect for existing borders unless all of the states who share them consent to change them. If consent is not forthcoming and change must occur, as in the disintegration of Yugoslavia, then the external border of the former state shall remain in place and internal borders shall be used to determine the jurisdictions of the successor sovereign states. That is the accepted norm for determining international boundaries in ex-colonial situations and in the break-up of states.

That principle originated in nineteenth century Latin America.[45] Colonial administrative boundaries were largely followed in drawing international frontiers in the absence of any alternative territorial norm that could secure general acceptance. Thus the Spanish colonial territories of Peru, Chile, Ecuador (Quito), Columbia (Caracas), etc. became independent states.[46] The same norm was recognized in Africa at the time of decolonization in the 1960s: colonial borders were the only generally acceptable basis for determining the

---

[44] Robert H. Jackson and Carl G. Rosberg, 'Why Africa's weak states persist', *World Politics*, 35 (1982), 1–24.

[45] For the origins and development of this practice in the emergence of independent states in the new world see Fred Parkinson, 'Latin America', in Robert H. Jackson and Alan James (eds), *States in a Changing World* (Oxford, Clarendon, 1993), pp. 240–61. Also see A. Kacowicz, 'The Impact of Norms in the International Society: The Latin American Experience' (delivered at the Leonard Davis Institute Conference on International Norms, Hebrew University, Jerusalem, Israel, 26–27 May 1997).

[46] As Fred Parkinson remarks, 'The principle of *uti possidetis juris* was a great help in enabling the region to weather the storm of state succession'. Parkinson, 'Latin America', p. 241.

new international frontiers of the continent. When colonial territories proved unworkable for self-determination and self-government, as in the cases of French West Africa and French Equatorial Africa, internal administrative borders that had also been defined by the occupying colonial powers were raised to the status of international boundaries. The Organization of African Unity is based on that principle which is expressed in Article 3 of its Charter. In both Latin America and Africa *uti possidetis juris* was closely connected to the search for a viable normative foundation for regional peace after colonialism.

In 1991 the EU created an Arbitral Commission chaired by Robert Badinter, President of the French Constitutional Council, to rule on the validity of various claims for political independence in former Yugoslavia. The Commission underlined the crucial importance of *uti possidetis juris*: 'The territorial integrity of States, this great principle of peace, indispensable to international stability ... has today acquired the character of a universal and pre-emptory norm. The people of former colonial countries were wise to apply it; Europeans must not commit the folly of dispensing with it.'[47]

In twentieth century world politics the 'self' in self-determination is juridical and not sociological. Ernest Gellner has pointed out that in the fewer than 200 states of the contemporary world, 8,000 languages are spoken.[48] Virtually all the new states that were created or resurrected (Poland) by the League of Nations in Central and Eastern Europe in the aftermath of the First World War were multi-national in social composition. Many nationalities that could not secure independent statehood for themselves were internationally recognized as national minorities.[49] The new state jurisdictions of ex-colonial Asia and Africa were also multi-ethnic and usually contained significant minority communities but they were not recognized internationally either by the UN or by regional international organizations. Most of the world's numerous ethnonational communities have no international status either as independent states or recognized national minorities. They remain submerged within or between existing state jurisdictions. One important consequence of that is a world of multi-ethnic states. In short, neither ethnonationality nor any other exclusively sociological definition of the collective self is, by itself, a valid basis for a claim to sovereignty.

To sum up. The twentieth century normative practice of upholding a universal right of national self-determination has effected a revolutionary expansion of international society which multiplied the number of independent countries in the second half of the century. But the previously outsider groups who have become sovereign insiders have in almost every case had an immediate prior existence as a juridical entity. Acquisition of sovereignty has almost always involved an elevation of the legal status of a territory. Most of these elevated territories formerly were either colonies of empires or internal administrative units of federal states. The principle of national self-determination has thus became subordinated to the practice of *uti possidetis juris*. In international

---

[47] A. Pellet, 'The opinions of the Badinter Arbitration Committee', *European Journal of International Law*, 3 (1992), 178–85.

[48] E. Gellner, *Nations and Nationalism* (Oxford, Blackwell, 1993), p. 74.

[49] Jennifer Jackson Preece, 'Minority rights in Europe: from Westphalia to Helsinki', *Review of International Studies*, 23 (January 1997), 75–92.

politics during the twentieth century the juridical-territorial clearly and decisively trumped the sociological-national.

Beyond Sovereignty?

Sovereignty, as that idea has been employed in this essay, is a distinctive status that opens the door for a government to engage lawfully in certain political activities, domestic and international. Sovereign status qualifies a government to participate in the *societas* of states. Canada can participate but – so far – Quebec cannot. That is not because Canada is more worthy or more capable: there is little difference between the two entities in that regard. It is because that is the way it was decided historically. In that traditional way of thinking, sovereignty is a right of membership, historically determined, in what amounts to a very exclusive political club.

The *societas* of states is the most exclusive political club in the world and has been so for several centuries. There are always more polities that seek membership than have it, and states who presently enjoy membership are almost always unwilling to part with it. Given that universal appetite for sovereign statehood and the premium conservative value placed on the existing distribution of territorial sovereignty it would seem rather surprising if any states were prepared to surrender their sovereignty either in whole or in part. It has happened in the past. The political unification of Italy and Germany in the mid-nineteenth century are instances of smaller states and statelets transferring their sovereignty, either voluntarily or under military duress, to a government of one larger resultant national state. Nationalism was a powerful impetus in each case.

Another example is the American colonies who, after liberating themselves from the British Empire, elected to form a larger sovereign state, the United States of America, and thus to constitute and exercise their newly acquired independence jointly instead of each colony becoming independent on its own territory – as usually happened in twentieth century decolonization. Americans were determined to avoid what they understood were the lessons of European history, namely that state systems foster incessant conflict and warfare. According to Alexander Hamilton, 'to look for a continuation of harmony between a number of independent, unconnected sovereignties in the same neighbourhood, would be to disregard the uniform course of human events, and to set at defiance the accumulated experience of ages'.[50] So to avoid the errors of Europe the American ex-colonies formed a federation, a *universitas* rather than a *societas* of states, among themselves.[51]

That constitutional arrangement has had a few predecessors and imitators: e.g., Switzerland, Canada, Australia. North America is noteworthy for its two transcontinental federations, its paucity of sovereign states, and its consequently limited international political life. But most of the world's states have been determined to hold sovereignty exclusively rather than divide it and hold it

---

[50] Alexander Hamilton, *The Federalist*, No. 6.

[51] That is not to suggest that the Americans turned away from war in their continent. They obviously did not. They fought the British Empire in the north and the Mexican republic in the south. But the most important wars for them were their wars of territorial conquest as they moved the frontier westward and, of course, the American civil war.

jointly with somebody else. Africa stands in sharp contrast to North America in that regard. Most post-colonial federations in Asia, Africa and the Caribbean collapsed into their constituent ex-colonial parts not long after independence. *Societas* Europe and not federalist America has been the wave of the future in most parts of the world.

Sovereignty clearly is not a status that is lightly surrendered or easily foregone. The most noteworthy instances of the widespread transfer of sovereignty (discussed above) are those in which imperial states gave up sovereign title over what had been their colonial territories. But those same states retained sovereignty over their homelands. They relinquished some of their territorial sovereignty when they could no longer decently or effectively hold on to it – usually the former. It is all the more interesting, therefore, that in Western Europe since the 1950s steps have been taken by a growing number of sovereign states, including several former imperial states, to establish a European Union in which the question 'Who is sovereign here?' has increasingly come to be asked.

There is a continuing debate on this question which cannot be investigated in any detail. But the main arguments can perhaps be reduced to the following two opposing views: (1) There is something that is fundamentally new in the EU: its member states have come together to form a European political and legal authority which is constitutionally distinct from those states and with regard to which the states have limited their sovereign rights and prerogatives in certain important respects. That is a fundamental political change that moves Europe some distance beyond a *societas* of states and toward an emergent *universitas*. (2) There is nothing new in the EU: the member states of the European Union remain sovereign. They have merely formed an international organization devoted to improving their socio-economic conditions which does not involve any permanent and irrevocable transfer of sovereignty. The EU is a 'union of sovereign states' and nothing more. (In his contribution, Georg Sørensen argues that the EU is neither an emergent *universitas* nor a continuing *societas* but, rather, it is an unusual intermediate entity.)

The EU, according to the first argument, is not merely an international organization but, rather, it is a polity of novel kind whose member states have relinquished some of their independent jurisdiction with the effect that EU Europe is in certain important respects moving beyond the *societas* of states in its political life. The European Court of Justice can rule on the validity of national legislation in certain areas of common policy, such as social and economic policy, some aspects of which have been placed under the jurisdiction of the Treaty of Rome and subsequent EU treaties.[52] The Court has ruled that the various EU treaties as well as the norms set up under their authority have established 'a legal order of a new and unique kind to which the member states have freely transferred certain of their sovereign rights'.[53]

The EU is a new kind of polity in the following ways. On the one hand, the member states are no longer fully independent; they have endowed the EU with some of their sovereign authority, especially as regards the making and

[52] K. J. Alter, 'Who are the "masters of the treaty"?: European governments and the European Court of Justice', *International Organization*, 52 (Winter 1998), 121–47.

[53] N. MacCormick, 'Liberalism, nationalism and the post-sovereign state', *Political Studies*, XLIV (1996), p. 555.

conducting of social and economic policy. Common obligations under EU law remove from member states some of their previous freedom of action in these policy areas. On the other hand, the EU does not constitute a fully sovereign entity either, at least not yet. The relations between the EU and its member states have been characterized as 'co-ordinately valid legal systems' in that each side of the relationship 'for certain purposes presupposes the validity of the other'. There is not so much a sharing of sovereignty as a mutual acknowledgement of co-ordinate jurisdiction between the EU and its member states in certain policy areas in which the states used to enjoy exclusive jurisdiction.[54] In that regard, it is argued, the EU is an important instance of Europe going 'beyond the sovereign state'.[55]

In the same vein, the EU is seen to be fostering a 'supra-national citizenship'. That argument has been made in connection with a celebrated case of the European Court of Justice (the Van Gend en Loos case) which found that the EU 'constitutes a new legal order' with regard to which member states 'have limited their sovereign rights'. According to that judgement, EU law imposes direct obligations and confers direct rights on individual Europeans regardless of the member states of which they are citizens. Here again the EU is seen to constitute a new legal and political order in which member states have 'limited their sovereign rights' within certain areas. And the subjects of that new constitutional arrangement are not only the member states but also their nationals who are becoming, in a somewhat awkward arrangement, citizens of Europe while still remaining citizens of their own country.[56] Some legal scholars argue that the EU should therefore be understood as not merely 'an agreement among States' but also as 'a "social contract" among the nationals of those States'.[57]

One such analysis concludes: 'It is not inevitable, but it is possible, that what we are now embarked on in Western Europe is a thoroughgoing transcendence of the sovereign state as the essential model for legal security and political order'.[58] This image of the EU as an emerging polity that is more than the sum of its partner states is reminiscent, somewhat, of the old European *universitas* with the Christian religion replaced by a secular European civic identity and with EU citizens, like their medieval Christian ancestors, retaining a significant attachment to their individual homelands. Here, too, is an intimation that Europe has seen the light and is now belatedly following in the footsteps of Alexander Hamilton's federalist America.

The EU, according to the second answer, is still basically an international organization: we might call it the European 'union of sovereign states' view. According to that way of thinking, the member states have authorized all its basic rules, institutions, and organizations. Its authority rests on international treaties rather than a domestic constitution. If we probe the constitutional basis

---

[54] For an argument that sovereignty is a bargaining resource that is being shared among EU states see Robert O. Keohane, 'Hobbes's Dilemma and Institutional Change in World Politics: Sovereignty in International Society', in H.-H. Holm and G. Sorensen (eds), *Whose World Order: Uneven Globalization and the End of the Cold War* (Boulder CO, Westview, 1995), pp. 165–86.

[55] MacCormick, 'Liberalism, nationalism and the post-sovereign state', pp. 561–7.

[56] Quoted by J. H. H. Weiler, 'European neo-constitutionalism: in search of foundations for the European constitutional order', *Political Studies*, XLIV (1996), 520–1.

[57] Weiler, 'European neo-constitutionalism: in search of foundations for the European constitutional order', pp. 526–8.

[58] MacCormick, 'Liberalism, nationalism and the post-sovereign state', p. 555.

of the EU, in an effort to discern the justification for the authority of EU law, what we find is a familiar and traditional norm of a society of states, namely *pacta sunt servanda* or in modern terms the principle of reciprocity between equally sovereign EU member states who remain fully in charge of the EU. On that view, the international agreements upon which the EU is built are entirely consistent with international law which rests squarely on the institution of sovereignty.[59] The EU is the child and not the parent or even the sibling of its member states.

That subordinate status of the EU as an international organization rather than a supranational organization is particularly evident in those areas of international activity that traditionally indicate the presence of sovereign statehood, namely foreign policy and military policy. Far from the EU taking over responsibility for security and order in Europe, some of its member states as well as some other states continue to bear that responsibility on an individual basis or in free alliance with each other. The Western European Union, the defence component of the EU, plays a minor role. The security of Europe remains firmly in the hands of the USA supported by Britain, Germany, and France. NATO is still the most important security organization in Europe. According to this view, then, the EU is the joint property of the states who created it: i.e., it is a typical international organization. In short, there is nothing new about the EU.[60] Europe continues to be a *societas* of states rather than an embryonic *universitas*.

Let us suppose, for the sake of analysis, that the first argument is more accurate. An important element of that argument is the claim that territory in Europe is being redefined and reconstituted, away from the states and towards the EU.[61] At the same time that internal borders within the EU come down to foster easier movement of people and goods the external EU border goes up to prevent illegal migrants, smugglers, etc. from coming into the EU and taking advantage of the situation. That is a line of security to protect the citizens of the EU not so much from attack as from infiltration and exploitation of the civic liberties and socio-economic opportunities they now enjoy on a wider European scale.

In whatever ways it might make sense to conceive of the European Union as 'going beyond sovereignty' it still remains the case that there is a sharply defined external border around the EU which is increasing in height at the same moment that the internal EU borders between member states are coming down. That there is a border that separates Europe from the rest of the world is nothing new, as we have seen. What is new is that the rest of the world today is a world of sovereign states, whereas the rest of the world in the past was a world of European empires and, before that, a world of separate civilizations based on different religions. If the EU were to become an independent polity there would then be about fifteen fewer states in the world and, possibly, one new superpower. Europe would look more like North America. That would be a revolutionary change for Europe. It would realign the balance of power. But it would not alter the *societas* of states on a global scale in any other fundamental way.

---

[59] This argument is presented and rejected by Weiler.

[60] Weiler, 'European neo-constitutionalism: in search of foundations for the European constitutional order', p. 518.

[61] U. Preuss, 'Two challenges to European citizenship', *Political Studies*, XLIV (1996), 543–4.

In that regard it would not be a revolution or even a reformation of the sovereign state system. It would recollect comparable changes in the past which significantly reduced the number of sovereign states or potential sovereign states. A politically united Europe would still be part of a world of sovereign states.

The first argument is sometimes supplemented by a globalization thesis concerning the withering away of sovereignty in the face of rapidly increasing economic transactions and traffic around the world. The thesis basically turns on a notion of sovereignty that is economic in character. In that vein, Robert Keohane views sovereignty as a 'bargaining resource'.[62] Sovereignty is considered to be the same as autonomy i.e., the capacity to insulate oneself or protect oneself from outside influences and forces. The EU e.g., its common market regulations or common policies on economic competition or common currency, is seen to entail a loss of economic sovereignty for its member states. The states who have entered the common market or adopted the common currency no longer have their own national market or currency. Keohane speaks of states 'bargaining away' their sovereignty to the EU as if it is something that is instrumental rather than constitutional.[63] If we think about sovereignty in that way there is no question but that the EU involves a voluntary loss of sovereignty on the part of its member states.

But that is a misleading way to think of sovereignty. The EU states that are opting to join the 'euro' currency zone are deciding to exercise their sovereignty in that way. That is a matter of policy and not of sovereignty. Their sovereignty is being used to authorize certain common rules and activities in co-operation with other EU member states. Their sovereignty has not been transferred in the permanent, non-refundable way that British sovereignty over its colonies was transferred. The EU does not involve a transfer of sovereignty. There is nothing to prevent Britain from legally withdrawing from the EU. There are of course policy considerations that might make that unwise. By comparison, Quebec cannot legally withdraw from Canada without first obtaining the consent of Ottawa.[64] Sovereignty is not a resource to exchange. It is a status, i.e., a legal standing, and thus a right to participate and to engage in relations and to make agreements with other sovereign states. As indicated earlier, the expression 'economic sovereignty' is a conflation of two different concepts that are best kept in their separate compartments if we wish to be clear. Rather than speak of the decline or loss of economic sovereignty it would be more to the point to speak of the difficulties that independent governments face nowadays in trying to pursue nationalist economic policies in a rapidly integrating global economy.

In whatever way we decide to understand the EU, either in the first way or in the second way, there is no doubting that it is a very significant development in European politics. Even if the first argument is more accurate, the EU as an embryonic *universitas* should be understood against the background of earlier periods of European history. That Europeans would give up on their *societas* might come as a surprise when we recall that it was they who conceived of

---

[62] Keohane, 'Hobbes's Dilemma and Institutional Change in World Politics: Sovereignty in International Society', p. 177.

[63] Keohane, 'Hobbes's Dilemma and Institutional Change in World Politics: Sovereignty in International Society', p. 177.

[64] I am indebted to Will Bain for this important point.

sovereignty in the first place, ran with it for centuries, and in the course of doing so expanded the *societas* to the rest of the world. But it is less surprising if it is understood against the background of European medieval and Roman history. Maybe Europeans are again leading the way, either backwards or forwards depending on how we view the endeavour, to a more politically and legally integrated world, perhaps along institutional lines of confederation or federation. But that too has happened before.

The Values of Sovereignty

The final question to be addressed, the most fundamental, is a value question. Why is sovereignty pursued so constantly and possessed so jealously? Why do the people of the world, or at least their political leaders, want to have it, to hold on to it if they have it, to obtain it if they do not have it? And where governments are prepared to submerge some of their sovereignty in a larger community, as perhaps in the EU, why do they immediately turn around and safeguard their newly united jurisdiction against external encroachments? In short, why is sovereignty and the *societas* of sovereign states so deeply ingrained in world affairs? That surely is because, like any basic human institution, it is an arrangement that is particularly conducive to upholding certain values that are considered to be of fundamental importance.

Whenever a human institution survives for a long time and is adopted on a wide scale some basic values are likely to be involved. The core values of sovereignty are the following: international order among states, membership and participation in the society of states, co-existence of political systems, legal equality of states, political freedom of states, and pluralism or respect for diversity of ways of life of different groups of people around the world. There may be other values involved, but these do seem to be the most fundamental.

International order is one of the basic values of the anarchical society, and for some scholars it arguably is the most basic.[65] How does sovereignty fit into that value? A clue is given by James Madison in *The Federalist* number 51 where he justifies a constitutional separation of powers for a republican government: 'In order to lay a due foundation for that separate and distinct exercise of the different powers of government ... it is evident that each department should have a will of its own; and consequently should be so constituted that the members of each should have as little agency as possible in the appointment of the members of the others ... The interests of the man must be connected with the constitutional rights of the place.'[66] A parallel argument can be made about sovereignty and international law: the interests of the rulers, or government, must be connected with the constitutional rights of the country. Sovereignty and the *societas* of states provides that connecting juridical framework. It is a norm that prohibits one state from acting authoritatively within another state.

It is important to add that this legal arrangement is not based on fairness: as indicated, many political communities are arbitrarily denied recognition as sovereign states. That is particularly evident in Africa: why should Nigeria be recognized as having interests and rights internationally, but Biafra (Eastern

---

[65] H. Bull, *The Anarchical Society* (London, Macmillan, 2nd ed., 1995).

[66] James Madison in *The Federalist*, No. 51, reprinted in Hutchins, *Great Books of the Western World*, 43, 162–5.

Nigeria) not be? Madison would probably say: it is not about fairness; it is about convenience and prudence. Nigeria was the British colony that conveniently emerged at decolonization. It would have been risky if not dangerous to partition Nigeria in order for Biafra to be recognized as a sovereign state. That might set off a chain reaction of partition conflicts across the continent. That was evidently a widely held concern at the time. In the Nigerian civil war (1967–1970) almost all states, African and non-African, rallied to the side of Nigeria, and only a very few states recognized and sided with separatist Biafra.

The *societas* of sovereign states has been referred to above as a political 'club', the most exclusive political club in the world. Politicians and polities of diverse interests, concerns, beliefs, ideologies, etc. want to participate in world politics, they want their voices to be heard in the places where the activity of world politics is carried on, which means they want to be inside the room and around the table. They want that opportunity even if their political voice is not as weighty as some other political voices. It is their presence in those places where their voices have a right to be heard that sovereignty makes possible. It is an issue of inclusion versus exclusion. Sovereignty based on state equality is inclusive: it underwrites the value of representation and participation in world politics. Of course it does not guarantee any separate international hearing for non-sovereign voices. But in accommodating the voices of sovereign states on a global scale at least it creates the possibility that other voices within those states can be heard if the statespeople are prepared to register their concerns internationally which they have every right to do.

Sovereignty discloses the value of co-existence. That was a commonly-used expression during the Cold War when it referred to the reluctant mutual toleration of Soviet Communism and Western Democracy: ideological co-existence. That is not quite what I mean by the expression. What is meant here is mutual regard of separate states as, *prima facie*, worthy of recognition and respect. A *societas* of sovereign states is based on the value of co-existence in this latter meaning of the term. Sovereignty thus gives expression to the value of international legal equality, i.e., equal status between independent states. That intimates a classical liberal view: the best international law is the one that makes provision for the greatest freedom. The *societas* of sovereign states underwrites the value of political freedom on an international scale. Sovereignty is an institutional expression of the freedom of groups politically organized as states.

That has to be qualified. Sovereign states are free political systems in the negative meaning of freedom: freedom from.[67] They enjoy a right of non-intervention. They are not necessarily free in the positive meaning of freedom: freedom to. Moreover, the state jurisdiction and its government may be free while the citizens or subjects may not be free. Often they are not free. That is the situation of 'failed states' and 'quasi-states' which are not uncommon in contemporary international society.[68] The global expansion of sovereignty is of course implicated in the existence of such states. That may be one of the prices of international freedom based on sovereign states that not everyone is prepared to pay.

---

[67] I. Berlin, 'Two Concepts of Liberty', in *Four Essays on Liberty* (London, Oxford University Press, 1969), pp. 118–72.

[68] R. Jackson, *Quasi-States: Sovereignty, International Relations and the Third World* (Cambridge, Cambridge University Press, 1990).

The alternative, however, is some kind of substantive qualification for sovereignty upon which recognition and non-intervention would be based. States might be judged by the quality of their domestic political institutions and practices which might be defined by those of liberal democratic states. Sovereignty might be conceived as an international license granted by the international community. (That argument is explored by Paul Taylor's essay.) Presumably the UN would issue the license. The UN would become at least in that one important respect a *universitas* recollecting the role of the medieval papacy in authorizing and indeed licensing the religious institutions and practices of European monarchies. If that were the case at the present time presumably not all states would be recognized. Presumably not all states would enjoy an equal right of non-intervention. Conceivably some states would be subject to international supervision or trusteeship until their rulers and peoples mended their domestic ways. World politics would once again contain two sorts of states: those which are sovereign and those which at least for the time being are not. That is reminiscent of the semi-sovereign world that was abandoned half a century ago. That would be a shift away from political diversity and toward political uniformity in world politics based, once again, on the Western model. That could be seen as a step backward rather than forward.

The *societas* of sovereign states accommodates the phenomenal diversity of human social organization around the world that must be taken into account if the world political system is to have some general basis of validity. Montaigne famously put the point as follows: 'Let every foot have its own shoe'.[69] That could mean a different law for different states.[70] But it could also mean a law sufficiently general to embrace human diversity. That is what Montaigne was driving at: 'the most desirable laws are those that are rarest, simplest, and most general'.[71] That is what sovereignty is. Notwithstanding its very real limitations and imperfections, to date the *societas* of sovereign states has proved to be the only generally acceptable and practical normative basis of world politics. At present there is no other world-wide political institution that can perform that service for humankind. Another way of putting that is to say that the above-noted values are among those very few values around which the world can unite politically even if that union is a minimalist one.

[69] Montaigne, *The Complete Essays of Montaigne*, D. M. Frame (trans.) (Standford, Stanford University Press, 1958), book 3, ch. 13, p. 816. This translation is from P. Burke, *Montaigne* (Oxford, Oxford University Press, 1981), p. 33.

[70] See Oakeshott, *On History and Other Essays*, p. 145n.

[71] Montaigne, *The Complete Essays of Montaigne*, book 3, ch. 13, p. 816.

The Practice of Sovereign Statehood in Contemporary International Society

ALAN JAMES

The absence of legislative control over semantic practice is, in one's more authoritarian moments, a matter for regret. In respect of discourse about international relations, no better ground for this reaction can be found than the use of the term sovereignty. On every hand, it seems, the term is freely introduced; and on inspection (for writers are in this regard rarely self-conscious) it emerges that an almost equivalent profusion of concepts is being paraded. However, this situation at least provides grist for the familiar academic tasks of drawing distinctions and – International Relations falling within the province of social science – the establishment of categories.

Concepts of Sovereignty

It may therefore be noted that, speaking very broadly, the subsequent contributions to this special number of the journal fall into three broad groups. In this they reflect the contemporary concerns of the discipline and the associated literature. In the first place, sovereignty is used to refer to the extent to which a state is free to behave as it wishes (see the articles by Philpott, Taylor, and Wallace). This has two aspects: jurisdictional and political. Jurisdictional sovereignty has to do with the extent to which a state is under no specific or general international obligations regarding its internal behaviour and decision making. To that extent it is legally free to conduct itself as it sees fit, or sovereign.[1] As these comments imply, this concept of sovereignty is not an absolute. It is not something which a state either has immutably or not at all. Rather, it is relative in nature. It is like a bundle of separable rights. Thus the bundle remains in existence notwithstanding the renunciation or involuntary loss of some of the individual items of which it is, collectively, composed. It also remains in existence even if the state is in some political disarray. The state continues to be sovereign, in the sense of having jurisdictional rights, over those areas of its affairs which are not subject to the direct requirements of international law.

The other aspect of this first concept of sovereignty focuses on political rather than jurisdictional freedom.[2] Like the latter, its nature is necessarily relative.

---

[1] This approach can be traced back to Bodin's well-known assertion, made in 1577, that 'sovereignty consists of absolute and perpetual power within a state': quoted in F. H. Hinsley, *Sovereignty* (London, Watts, 1966), p. 22.

[2] One well-known approach to sovereignty which is rooted in the idea of political independence is that of J. H. Herz, who argues that impermeability is the essence of the traditional sovereign state: see, generally, J. H. Herz, *International Politics in the Atomic Age* (New York, Columbia University Press, 1959).

Even a state with huge political assets finds that there are many circumstances in which, as a practical matter, it cannot do what it would like to do. Lesser states are likely to find themselves more circumscribed although there are also occasions on which, paradoxically, their smaller size may give them a greater immediate freedom. Nonetheless, constraint is the general factor of which participants in the international political game are perhaps most aware. Only up to a varying point (which varies with the hour and by the issue) are states sovereign in the sense of being politically free.

As colleagues will later make clear, there have been large developments in the second half of the twentieth century which have notably diminished the freedom of the state, and hence (in this sense) its sovereignty. In some cases the emphasis has been on legal restrictions; in others, on political. Either way, the outcome is that states tend, at the millennium, to be less free than they generally were 50 years ago; and there is no compelling reason to believe that this process has now reached its end. But it must be remembered, especially insofar as legal restrictions are concerned, that an obligation is often accompanied by a corresponding right or advantage.

The second broad approach to sovereignty which finds expression in these pages focuses not on the activity of sovereign states but on the identity of those who control its decision-making processes (see Clapham's article). Instead of analysing the position or predicament of the state in relation to its individual fellows or to the collectivity of states as a whole, it probes into the distribution of power within the state. It asks, who rules – or, who is sovereign? In so doing, it echoes a famous definition of politics as the business of deciding 'who gets what, when, how'.[3] This issue is, of course, always of supreme importance to those who are engaged in the domestic political conflict. But where there is an agreed or accepted constitutional structure within which the battle takes place, the appearance of a new set of rulers is rarely described as a switch of sovereignty. Such governmental changes as occur are, in keeping with the democratic ethos of the age, seen as normal and fair – and hence not requiring the emotive depiction which tends to be associated with the use of the term sovereignty. Where, however, a group has succeeded in riding roughshod over the indigenous democratic procedures, it is likely that there will be references to it having 'seized' sovereignty, to the sovereignty of the state having been 'captured' by a minority. State sovereignty, in other words, will be widely deemed to have fallen into tainted hands. At the turn of the millennium, such situations are not uncommon, albeit less so than has often been the case since 1945.

In contrast to the first two concepts of sovereignty, which concern the state's international freedom and the use made of its internal procedures, the third concept approaches the state only indirectly. It rests on the premise that sovereignty is an immediate attribute not of the state but of the nation (see Mayall's contribution). It then asserts that a legitimate state is one which can plausibly claim to be acceptable to its national constituents, which is their genuine representative.[4] In other words, the legitimacy of the state depends on

---

[3] This was the title of a famous book by H. D. Lasswell, *Politics: Who Gets What, When, How*, (New York, Whittlesey House, 1936).

[4] For two recent expressions of this approach, see: J. S. Barkin and B. Cronin, 'The state and the nation: changing norms and the rules of sovereignty in international relations', *International Organization*, 48 (1994), 107–30; and G. Starovoitova, *Sovereignty after Empire. Self-Determination Movements in the Former Soviet Union* (Washington, DC, United States Institute of Peace, 1997).

its embodiment of national sovereignty. And, as a practical if not a theoretical requirement, in most cases such a state will probably need to embody just one nation. During the twentieth century this normative position has become orthodox, and thus carries with it large possibilities of change. Huge change there certainly has been. On the whole, imperial states which faced diminution in the cause of national sovereignty offered relatively little resistance. But similarly-challenged metropolitan states have naturally been less compliant, and it may be expected that they will continue to express vigorous opposition to their dismemberment. Used in this third sense, therefore, sovereignty is a likely associate of conflict and disruption.

In the writer's view, these three usages are not aspects of a single institution known as state sovereignty. They are not each of them facets of the same concept or phenomenon. Rather, they represent different uses of the term sovereignty, and hence distinct (albeit loosely-linked) concepts of sovereignty. A linkage exists because each usage refers to the state – the type of territorial unit which has been dominant in global politics for the last half millennium. But of the state each of them has a different and important thing to say.

Constituents of Statehood

This draws attention to a further and no less important issue regarding the state: what is it which an entity has to possess to be so designated? Generally this question receives a threefold answer. First, territory. This is, as it were, where a state starts, territory being the element on which its other elements exist. Each of the world's states represents a demarcated physical sector of the land mass of the globe, and at the international level nowadays represents it exclusively (the difficult governmental device of a condominium having gone out of fashion). Thus, apart from Antarctica (where various competing claims have in effect been put on one side), the world's land mass may be imagined as wholly divided into states by frontiers rather as a farm is divided into fields by hedges, fences, and walls.

Secondly, a state must have people. Their number may and does vary hugely from one state to another, from a few thousand here to hundreds of millions there. But every state supports human life. This points to the third characteristic of a state: government. By one process or another, some of the people of a state are designated as its official representatives, constituting its government. A state, like a university, a church, a company, or a club, is not a human person. It does not walk, think, and talk as an individual human being does. No one has ever seen a state (as distinct from the territory of a state). But, like universities, churches, and so on, a state is deemed to act like a person – to take decisions, to communicate, to undertake responsibilities, to act.

In other words, a state is a notional person. It must therefore have a way of determining who is entitled to speak and act in its name, and this applies as much to its internal affairs as to the conduct of its foreign relations. Such people are those who compose its government, and those who are employed by the government. Through these human agencies, the state lives, moves, and has its being. Thus when it is said that 'Britain decided to do such and such', what has happened is that the person (e.g. the Foreign Minister) or the group of persons (the Cabinet) with the relevant responsibility has decided on behalf of Britain, to do it. Or, when I say that 'the state has treated me very badly', what may have happened is that an official in, say, the Inland Revenue, has reached what I conceive to be a bad decision.

A state is therefore made up of territory, people, and a government. This is often as far as the matter is taken, and for some purposes it is sufficient. But it is insufficient if one wishes to discover what it is which enables some states to play a full and active role in international relations. For there are many states (i.e. governed territorial entities) which do not participate in international relations, not just because they do not wish to do so but – more importantly because they lack the relevant capacity.

For example, the territory of Gibraltar, while only a couple of square miles in extent, has a population which is somewhat greater than one or two states which participate in international relations, and is more prosperous than a number of others. It undoubtedly satisfies the characteristics of statehood which have been mentioned above, yet it has no international part. True, it is not usually called a state. But that is inconsequential, there being several terms which are used to refer to governed territorial entities – 'province', for example, is another. The best known instance of territorial units called states but which lack international statehood is, very probably, the constituent units of the USA. Each of the 50 of them has a defined territory, people, and a government (each government being sub-divided into an executive, a legislature, and a judiciary). Moreover, a number of them have bigger populations and most of them are a lot wealthier than many of the states which appear, as a matter of course, on the international stage. Yet (like Gibraltar) none of the states making up the USA are regular participants in international relations.

The reason for this is to be found in one of the most important distinctions – arguably the most important – which can be drawn between states. It is the distinction between states which have an international capacity, and those which do not. Gibraltar and similar territories, and the constituent members of federations, fall into the latter category. They lack what is required for part-icipation in international relations. On the other hand, getting on for 200 states do enjoy this capacity – and hence are the ones which make up the still-Westphalian international society. They possess, in relation to Gibraltar and the states of the USA, an extra characteristic, an extra qualification. For better or ill, the states themselves call it sovereignty.[5]

Sovereignty – in the Sense of Constitutional Independence

It happens that individual states seem never to have spell out, in so many words, what they mean by this usage. And as the international society is simply the collectivity of states, with absolutely nothing by way of organizational structure or written procedures, no guidance is to be derived from that quarter. Of course, the society of states has its own legal norms and arrangements; but they apply to

---

[5] What follows draws on the writer's more detailed work on sovereignty and diplomatic relations, notably: *Sovereign Statehood, the Basis of International Society* (London, Allen and Unwin, 1986); 'Diplomatic Relations and Contacts', *The British Year Book of International Law, 1991*, (Oxford, Clarendon, 1992), pp. 347–87; and 'States and Sovereignty', in T. Salmon (ed.), *Issues in International Relations* (Edinburgh University Press, forthcoming). See also, R. H. Jackson and A. James, 'The Character of Independent Statehood', in R. H. Jackson and A. James (eds), *States in a Changing World: a Contemporary Analysis*, (Oxford, Clarendon, 1993), pp. 3–25.

territories which already, as it were, possess an international capacity, and do not stipulate what the essence of that capacity is. Similarly, the international society is nowadays awash with international organizations; but they are organizations of and for territories whose eligibility to join flows from an existing international capacity. Again, there is no indication – beyond, perhaps (as, allusively, in article 2.1 of the United Nations Charter) the use of the word sovereignty – of what it is which makes states eligible for admittance. In other words, the international society is without a written constitution. However, there is no problem in determining what sovereignty, meaning an international capacity, entails. For there is a very real sense in which the international society can be said to have an unwritten constitution, one which is enshrined in practice. And the relevant international practice is crystal clear. It can therefore confidently be stated that sovereignty, in this most fundamental sense, amounts to constitutional independence.

A sovereign state may have all sorts of links with other such states and with international bodies. But the one sort of link which it cannot have (for thereby it would lose its international status) is a constitutional one. For sovereignty in the sense now being discussed consists of being constitutionally apart, of not being contained, however loosely, within a wider constitutional scheme. A territorial entity which is so contained is not sovereign and hence is not eligible to participate on a regular basis in international relations. Once any such connection is severed, the territory concerned has become sovereign and thus ready, if it and others wish it, to join in the usual kind of international activity.

The constitution of a state, like that of any human enterprise, consists of the body of principles and basic rules in the light of which it is to be governed. Such principles and rules can, in principle, be minimal. If authority is highly centralized, the state's constitution may amount to no more than that the word of the ruling individual or group is law: *l'état, c'est moi*.[6] In the twentieth century, however, democracy has become highly orthodox, and despotism correspondingly unorthodox. In consequence, virtually all states are equipped with constitutions which fulsomely embody democratic principles. They indicate how, in general terms, the state is to be organized and administered, saying what institutions are to be set up, how they are to be manned, the way in which they are to proceed, what they may and may not do, and how they are to relate to each other.

Such a constitution does not need to be written, but except in the case of a country with a long and relatively untroubled internal history (Britain is in fact the only clear extant case, New Zealand being the sole ambiguous one), it is difficult to imagine how a modern democratic state could work effectively without a written constitution. It may well be that, in common with all normative as distinct from scientific rules, the constitution will not always be observed. But in that event the state concerned will need either to get back to its constitution, or to amend it, or to equip itself with a new one. Such a change may occur in a merely *de facto* way, with the shiny democratic constitution being ignored by an individual or group who wield power on an entirely personal basis. In such circumstances the formal constitution has become a sham, and a form of

---

[6] For a highly abstract but pellucid representation of the transition from despotic kings to democratic kingdoms, see, C. A. W. Manning, *The Nature of International Society* (London, Bell, 1962), pp. 101–2.

personal rule exists.[7] But nonetheless, to the extent to which such rule is accepted, and therefore effective, it can realistically be said to be constitutionally based. The *de facto* constitution indicates how, at least *ad interim*, the state is governed.

This point perhaps requires a little emphasis. A constitution is not a synonym for democracy. The word 'constitutionalism' is sometimes used to refer to democratic rule, but it must be distinguished from rule on the basis of a constitution. That phenomenon is not necessarily indicative of democracy. A constitution can provide the entity to which it is attached with any kind of political complexion, establishing authoritarian as well as democratic government, and also everything in between. Nor need a constitution provide for government on a rigidly centralized basis. In fact, some powers are likely to be delegated to regional bodies. And if a state is particularly large, socially complex, or geographically extensive, it is very probable that the degree of delegation will be such that the subordinate entities will be equipped with their own constitutions. But they exist within the state's overall constitutional umbrella.

Government, at any level, requires a constitution, whether *de jure* or *de facto*. For the attempt to govern without any kind of constitutional basis will assuredly entail disorder and perhaps chaos – out of which a new kind of *de facto* constitutional arrangement is likely soon to arise. Thus a constitution indicates that government is under way. In the case of subordinate entities equipped with their own constitutions, it will undoubtedly be made clear, both in those constitutions and in the practice of their relationships with the central government, that they are not constitutionally independent. They have powers of government, but as they look outwards the essential point about their situation is their subordination. At least some competencies, perhaps just the conduct of the territories' defence and foreign relations, will be reserved to the central, or metropolitan, government. In consequence such territories are not sovereign, in the sense which is required to participate in international relations on a regular basis. For the international society admits only those governed entities which are sovereign in the sense of being constitutionally independent.

Key Features

The key features of sovereignty are threefold. (From now on the qualifying phrase 'in the sense of constitutional independence' will usually be dropped when reference is being made to this concept of sovereignty.) It is a legal, an absolute, and a unitary condition. To say that sovereignty has legal characteristics is not meant to imply that to be sovereign is lawful, whereas a different condition might be unlawful. Instead, what is meant is that sovereignty is founded on law, inasmuch as a constitution is a set of arrangements which has the force of law. Thus, the observation that a state is sovereign is an observation about the standing of the state in the eyes of its own constitutional law. It indicates possession by the state of a set of legal arrangements of a certain kind – ones which equip it with a constitution.

---

[7] See, generally, R. H. Jackson and C. Rosberg, *Personal Rule in Black Africa* (Berkeley, CA, University of California Press, 1982).

This point is worth the sentences which have just been expended on it. For although it is quite widely assumed that sovereignty has something to do with law, it is almost as widely assumed that the relevant law is international. This is a mistake. It is indeed the case that international law applies to sovereign states and regulates their mutual relations. But it is not a provision of international law which has to be satisfied for a state to be ascribed sovereign status. It is a certain kind of constitutional law which is requisite. So far as international law is concerned, the position is that it applies to entities which have already become sovereign. In other words, international law presupposes sovereignty. It makes sense only on the assumption that there are sovereign states to which it can be applied. And those sovereign states are sovereign because they are independent in terms of their own constitutions.

The second main feature of sovereignty is that it is an absolute condition. Absolute, not in the sense of possessing unlimited power, but in the sense of not being relative, of an attribute being either present or absent, with no intermediate possibilities. This, too, is a particularly important point to make because, as shown earlier in the article, there are other conceptions of sovereignty which are relative, such as jurisdictional independence and political independence. They refer to situations which exist in degree, in terms of more or less. Thus when one is talking about either of those usages of the term sovereignty, it would be natural to say that X was more sovereign than Y, or (if one was feeling bold) that Z's sovereignty was in the order of 70%.

But when sovereignty is used to mean constitutional independence, one is referring to a different type of phenomenon. It is not one which can exist in degree, in terms or more or less. In political terms, a sovereign state may be weak; it may barely be able to support itself by its own efforts. This is the sort of entity which has been graphically described as a quasi-state.[8] But such a condition does not detract from the state's constitutional status – nor, consequentially, from its ability to play at least a diplomatic role in international relations. For constitutional independence is either possessed, or not. The relevant entity is sovereign (and therefore 100% sovereign) or lacks sovereignty – lacks it totally.

A statement of this sort is entirely appropriate – indeed, it is called for – when one is speaking of the formal standing, position, or status which a person (real or notional) has attained. When someone is, for example, appointed as a vice-chancellor of a university, that person holds the office absolutely. There is no question of being a 70% vice-chancellor. The individual in question is a vice-chancellor, and the man or woman who lives next door is not. It may be that critical comments are made about the vice-chancellor's efficiency or industry, so that he or she may be adjudged deserving of a grade of, say, no more than 50%. But that in no way detracts from the fact that the appointee is fully a vice-chancellor. And he or she will be no less or more so than someone else holding a similar position, whatever the relative sizes, levels, or reputations of their universities.

The same line of argument is exactly applicable to states when one is talking about whether or not they enjoy constitutional independence – and hence sovereignty. Whether or not a governed territorial entity is constitutionally

---

[8] See, generally, R. H. Jackson, *Quasi-States: Sovereignty, International Relations and the Third World* (Cambridge, Cambridge University Press, 1990).

independent is a matter of fact which in principle can only be answered negatively or positively. No matter how close a territory approaches constitutional independence, if it does not reach it the territory has to be adjudged as without it, completely without it. This means that it cannot be sovereign, in the sense which is requisite for normal participation in international relations. Thus (tiny) Monaco, (developing) Mexico, and (much-troubled) Mozambique are all sovereign, and hence absolutely so; whereas New South Wales, Nova Scotia, and Nebraska (all being constituent parts of federal states) are not. Sovereignty, in this usage, is an absolute condition.

The third, and final, main feature of sovereignty is that it is unitary. It may, and does, have different implications in different contexts, leading some to speak of internal sovereignty and external sovereignty. But that is a dangerous terminology, for it can all too easily be taken to mean that sovereignty can, as it were, be split down the middle, enabling one of its halves to exist without the other. In fact, a sovereign state is all of a piece. Constitutional independence means that no other entity is customarily in the position of being formally able to take decisions regarding either the internal or the external affairs of the territory in question.

Of course, it is always open to a sovereign state to pass over to another state or an international body the legal right to take decisions which are binding on the state concerned in respect of certain specific internal matters. Equally, a sovereign state may wish to listen very carefully to what a powerful and important state has to say on certain aspects of its foreign policy. But the point is that the decision to grant such rights or adjust its policy is the decision of the sovereign state. Were it not sovereign, there would be another entity which, because of its own constitutional dispositions, would be regularly entitled to have a controlling or an overriding voice with regard to both the internal and external affairs of the territory concerned.

In sum, the control of both internal and external policy flows from the same source, so that each is inextricably bound up with the other. Just as a vice-chancellor will have certain powers within his or her institution and also, by virtue of the same office, represent the university externally, so also will a sovereign state have both an internal and an external role. Both are a consequence of its condition as a constitutionally independent, or sovereign, entity.

The Acquisition of Sovereignty

In 1945 the number of constitutionally-independent states was about 75. In 1999 it is in the region of 190. In international terms, this is veritably an explosion. The relatively sudden emergence of so many states was an entirely new and totally unexpected phenomenon. (And there is hardly a case during this period of a state disappearing from the political map.) Sovereignty, in the constitutional sense, has clearly been much sought after, and secured.[9]

No less than almost 100 of the 115 or so new entrants were former colonies – territories lying overseas from the metropolitan centre of the colonial state

---

[9] For a view of the acquisition of sovereignty which takes a much longer historical perspective than this paragraph, see, P. Lyon, 'New States and International Order', in A. James (ed.), *The Bases of International Order, Essays in Honour of C. A. W. Manning* (London, Oxford University Press, 1973), pp. 24–59.

concerned. At one moment a colony would have been part of the imperial constitutional set up. It may well have had a measure of self-government, perhaps a considerable measure. But ultimate authority over the colony lay with the metropolitan state – in the case of British colonies being exercised by the Crown on the advice of the British government of the day. In this way it was open to the colonial power to make herself felt – to a degree and in a manner which would have been specified in the colony's constitution – in the colony's internal affairs. And certainly it was imperial power who spoke for the colony in international relations. Thus the final governing authority lay outside the colony's physical limits.

Then, however, as the outcome of a political process which may or may not have been stressful (or even violent), the colonial power decided that she would cut her constitutional links with the colony. In respect of Britain's colonies, formal decisions to that effect would have been taken by the British Government and Parliament, respectively expressed through Orders in [the Privy] Council and Acts of Parliament. Thus, for example, in what became the standard British formula, the Nigerian Independence Act of 1960, in section 1(2), decreed that:

> No Act of the Parliament of the United Kingdom passed on or after [independence day] shall extend, or be deemed to extend, to Nigeria or any part thereof as part of the law thereof, and as from that day(a) Her Majesty's Government in the United Kingdom shall have no responsibility for the government of Nigeria or any part thereof, ...[10]

In this manner Britain's legislative and executive power in respect of Nigeria (including her responsibility for defence and foreign policy) was relinquished, and the government-in-waiting in Nigeria stepped into, the thereby-created vacancy. It may be noted that such arrangements made no reference to the amendment of the British constitution, for the reason that Britain's constitution is unwritten.

Nigeria had, typically, already been supplied by Britain with its own independent constitution (by way of an Order in Council), which took effect on independence day. That constitution naturally included provision for its amendment, and in fact Nigeria (as has often happened) had before long enacted for itself a completely new constitution.

In consequence of this type of development, the constitutional position of hitherto colonial territories underwent a massive change. At a specified time on a specified day their constitutional links with the colonial power were ended, and henceforth ultimate governmental authority lay within what now became new states. Symbolizing the change, the imperial flag flying at the centre of the colony's capital would very probably have been run down the flag pole at the exact moment of the transfer of power, with the flag of the new sovereign state being run up in its place.

From now on, it was up to the new state to reach its own decisions about all of its internal affairs. It could take advice and assistance from abroad, and could make promises to other states or international organizations about how, in certain respects, it will proceed. But there would be no question of another state

---

[10] This quotation, and other material in this paragraph, is taken from W. Dale, *The Modern Commonwealth* (London, Butterworths, 1983), pp. 61–2.

taking decisions for the territory, and certainly no possibility of an external power disallowing an internal decision on the basis of that power's superior constitutional position. Likewise in international relations, it was now up to the new state to decide for itself what to do. That is not to say that it had complete legal freedom to do what it liked. It had obligations under customary international law, and rights too, and could add to both by treaty. But decisions regarding its international situation were now its alone.

This is the sort of thing which happened in respect of getting on for 100 of the states which have gained admittance to the international society since 1945. In some, such as Algeria, Angola, and Indonesia, it took insurrection or even fierce fighting before the colonial power formally accepted that its authority had come to an end. But the constitutional essence of the process was the same as elsewhere. The remaining new states – about 20 – represent territories which were once part of the metropolitan territory of a larger state: chiefly the former Soviet Union, but also the former Yugoslavia and Czechoslovakia. So far as these territories were concerned, the legal processes involved in the acquisition of sovereignty were often rather messy, mainly because of administrative disorder in the metropolitan state. But at bottom, as elsewhere, the procedure involved the replacement of one constitutional set-up by another. Prior to their emergence as sovereign states these territories were constitutionally subordinate to the state of which they formed a part. Their breakaway was marked by the adoption of independent constitutions, which thereby fitted them for entry into the usual run of international life.

Eligibility and Participation

On a number of occasions in this article, when referring to the difference which sovereignty makes to a territorial entity, such words as 'capacity', 'fitted', and 'eligibility' have been used. This is because sovereign status does not in itself confer on a state the right to participate in day-to-day international affairs.

When a territorial entity becomes constitutionally independent, and so becomes sovereign, it does not thereby acquire an entitlement to force its diplomatic company on any of its sovereign fellows. What is has acquired, rather, is the capacity to do the sorts of things which are commonly done, internationally, by sovereign states: to 'talk' to other states (through diplomatic representatives), to make agreements with them, to apply to join international organizations, to campaign for certain goals, to press other states to do, or not to do, something, and so on. To do any and all of these things sovereignty is necessary. But it is not sufficient. Additionally, and preconditionally, other states must first, and individually, agree to have dealings with the emergent state.

This process is something like securing membership in an exclusive club. One has to have the relevant credentials, such as the appropriate expertise, affiliation, or whatever, and the money to pay the fees. But they are not enough, as membership also depends on the existing members being willing to grant admittance. Internationally, the equivalent procedure involves two preliminary steps: recognition and the establishment of diplomatic relations; and a third step of establishing diplomatic missions. This last step will be taken if it is anticipated or hoped that relations between the two states concerned will be relatively close or important.

Recognition is a formal device which is unilaterally exercised by the state bestowing recognition. It is in the nature of notice to the other that, in the view of the recognizing state, the other state has met the requirements for normal international activity, that it possesses the characteristics of sovereign statehood. The recognizing state is announcing that it judges the other state to have, as it were, 'arrived' on the international scene.[11] That clears the way for the two states to have normal dealings with each other. But there is no necessity for them to do so. In principle, nothing at all need follow recognition. In practice, however, it is probably unusual for a state to recognize a new state without also going on to establish diplomatic relations with it. Indeed, it seems that the two steps are now often combined – to the extent of recognition being bestowed by implication through the establishment of diplomatic relations. In turn, this could suggest that recognition is becoming anomalous. But as against that it should be noted that recognition can still have important consequences for legal disputes in the courts of the recognizing state.

Logically, the establishment of diplomatic relations follows recognition and, unlike that device, is a bilateral act. The two states concerned must agree on the establishment of diplomatic relations, which is usually done by way of a specific agreement to that effect. Once a pair of states are in diplomatic relations, they may engage directly in any kind of official contact, relating to each other freely. It is the normal bilateral relationship between sovereign states. It is also peculiar to them.

Procedural difficulties may ensue if a pair of states are not in diplomatic relations (and unlike recognition, diplomatic relations may be broken, either party having the unilateral right to take such a step). In those circumstances, when their diplomats encounter each other in third states or at international organizations, they are entitled (and may be expected) to cold shoulder each other. If one such state wishes to communicate with the other it may first need to make a special check (perhaps through a third party) about the acceptability of such a contact, and make a special arrangement for its execution. In practice, things are not usually as difficult as this in the absence of diplomatic relations, devices being employed to get over some of the problems which would otherwise arise. But there is no requirement to use such devices. States not in diplomatic relations are entitled to ignore each other totally. And even if they do make arrangements to get in touch with each other as and when they need to, it is very likely that they will find the situation at least somewhat less convenient than being in diplomatic relations.

The establishment of diplomatic relations simply clears the way for whatever sorts of contacts two states may wish to have. Contrary to what is sometimes thought, being in diplomatic relations is certainly not synonymous with the setting up of residential diplomatic missions in the capitals of the two states. In fact, two states in diplomatic relations may have very little to do with each other. But if one or both think that their interests justify it, embassies (or, as between members of the former British Commonwealth, high commissions) will be established in the foreign capital(s) concerned. This greatly facilitates contact between the two states, and so makes it more likely that the sending state will be able to influence the receiving state in the direction it would like. A residential

---

[11] See, generally, I. Brownlie, *Principles of Public International Law* (Oxford, Clarendon, 4th ed., 1990), pp. 87–106.

diplomatic mission also has a number of other advantages, such as giving the sending state a good listening post in the receiving state, and enabling the former to assist such of its nationals who are anxious to do business in the receiving state.

The diplomatic system thus enables states to have contacts with other states, and so to advance and protect their interests at the international level. It is an arrangement which is exclusive to sovereign states. Accordingly, the fact that a state is active in this way is an irrefutable sign that it enjoys sovereignty. But it must be remembered that sovereignty is not bestowed through getting involved in the diplomatic system. Rather, it is a precondition of involvement that one is sovereign.

Getting Beyond Westphalia?

Sovereignty, in the sense here elucidated, is the constitutive principle of inter-state relations. This remains as true when those relations are generally warm as it does when they are generally hostile. Nor is the assertion in any way weakened by an increased degree of cooperation within international organizations. Such bodies are created by states and remain their creatures. Organizations, do not have independent lives of their own; they do not have independent sources of finance; they do not have independent armed forces. All they have comes from or is loaned to them by states. Consequentially, organizations are unable to, as it were, devour their creators, and therefore present no threat at all to states' constitutional independence, and hence their sovereignty. Indeed, international organizations presuppose sovereign states.

However, one theoretical qualification must be made to the argument of the last paragraph. There is no reason in principle why a group of states should not set up an organization and, either initially or subsequently, transfer to it such far-reaching powers that it is, or becomes, not a treaty-based international organization but a constitution-based sovereign state. In that case the states setting it up would lose their sovereignty and in consequence would have to withdraw from international activity. They would have become subordinate entities within a wider constitutional and governing structure, and it would be that single structure which would now speak and act internationally for all the territory which it contained. The number of sovereign states in the world would have gone down, for a number of sovereign entities would be renouncing their individual sovereignties to create a bigger sovereign state.

This, of course, is what may happen in respect of the European Union, and which some hope will happen. But although, over the last 40 years, this grouping has grown in strength and resources, and is not the usual type of international organization, it is also not anywhere near becoming a single state. Most of its members presently display a keen desire to maintain their sovereign individuality, as do its aspirant members. They do not wish to become units within a federal state. For as long as those desires are maintained, the European Union will continue be represented on the political maps and in most international activity, by fifteen (or more) states rather than one.[12]

Some, however, envisage that sovereign states will disappear, and are even now disappearing by a different route. It is suggested that their sovereignty is

[12] See, D. J. Puchala, 'Western Europe', in *States in a Changing World*, pp. 69–92.

becoming, or will become, eroded and indistinct through its increasing irrelevance. This is seen as due in part to the heightened profile of non-state actors throwing, as it were, sovereign states into the shadows. Additionally, or alternatively, the suggestion is that states are becoming so involved with others, so entwined by both cooperative ventures and technology, that their frontiers are losing significance and their individual features are becoming blurred. Either way, sovereignty in the sense of constitutional independence is seen as a concept which soon will be, if it is not already, of interest to historians only.

Non-state actors are a heterogeneous group, including such varied bodies as terrorist groups, multi-national corporations, and non-governmental international organizations. Without doubt, such bodies occasionally have some impact on the behaviour of states. But things also work the other way. Non-governmental bodies often wish to secure the support of states. Multinational corporations are very well aware that even in a very poor state the government controls economic and legislative levers which can do them much harm. Terrorists can be routed by states, and are unlikely to receive much personal consideration in the process. Moreover, states generally find much more on their plates than the need to deal with non-state entities. It follows that there is virtually no reason to think that sovereign states are, as it were, being put out of business by such bodies.

So far as references to the growing involvement of states with each other are concerned, there can be no doubt about their material accuracy. States have more dealings with each other in regard to more issues of mutual concern than ever before. Almost everything, it seems, comes nowadays on to the international agenda: the traffic in drugs, the status of women, the environment, bacteriological weapons, outer space, population issues, economic development, cultural interchange, and so on. Elaborate and extensive cooperation occurs in a multitude of fields. This is the background to the powerful impression that the world has shrunk dramatically in the last half century. The headlong speed and mind-boggling complexity of developments in the technological field does nothing, of course, to undermine this impression.

But it by no means follows from this that sovereign states have become outmoded. Indeed, as in the consideration of non-state actors the evidence can be interpreted to the opposite effect. Up-to-the-minute technologies are being used by states to bolster their strength and extend their control over their domains. International cooperation is the cooperation of states, and to the extent to which it finds expression in agreed programmes of action, that action has to be coordinated or conducted by states. Cooperative activity, in short, does not necessarily imply that the cooperating actors somehow fade into the background; in practice it does not have this effect, and it is hard to see how it could possibly do so. The world remains politically organized, as it has done for 500 years, on the basis of the sovereign state. The idea that this type of arrangement is somehow becoming insignificant seems, to this observer, totally unreal. International behaviour patterns have changed, and are changing, certainly. But the basis on which the world is politically structured – a basis which finds expression in the idea of sovereignty – remains unchanged.

It is indeed an oddity that so many observers have asserted that the day of the sovereign state is coming to an end. It could (almost) be argued that the day of the sovereign state has only just begun! National groups have during the last half century been tumbling over themselves in their zeal to claim and grasp the constitutional condition which is expressed by the term sovereignty. The outcome, as was noted, has been a huge increase in the number of sovereign states. Many other groups are still trying to achieve the same goal. Basques, Kurds, Quebeckers, Sikhs, Tamils, East Timoreans and a host more assert that it is only sovereignty which will enable them to escape oppression and, or, enable them fully to express their national culture. Meanwhile, those long in possession of sovereignty show no disposition at all to give it up, not even in what are at first sight such favourable contexts as Scandinavia or western Europe.

The reason for this attachment to the idea of sovereignty is not hard to find. It seems that when people have come to feel affinities of the kind which are summed up in the word 'national', they also feel that the only proper form of government for them is one which is in the hands of their fellow nationals. Of course, this response is likely to be particularly keen if the group concerned has suffered sharp persecution or discrimination at the hands of the governing, and different, nationality. But it does not seem to be dependent on such treatment. Even those who have been governed relatively well by another national group are not slow to claim the presumed benefits of 'national self-determination' – one of the most potent ideas ever experienced in political affairs. Accordingly, while there is nothing inherently sacrosanct about the concept of sovereignty, it seems likely that the world will remain politically organized on its basis for a long time to come.

Wider Considerations

Is this a bad thing? Manifestly, the answer to that depends partly on one's analysis of the influence of sovereignty, and partly on one's values. Certainly, there has been no shortage of observers who believe that the world would be better organized on a different basis. In general, this belief seems to rest on the assumption that the sovereign state is prone to abuse its power, both internally and externally. That is to say, those who wield power in the name of the state tend so to behave. As has recently been observed, 'state sovereignty ... is inherently dangerous'.[13]

There would probably be little argument over the proposition that innumerable crimes have been committed in the name of the state, against both the citizens of the state in question and against foreigners. What is less clear is whether the abuse of authority would diminish were the world to be politically organized on some basis other than that of state sovereignty. Necessarily, any response to that query must emanate from speculation rather than evidence. And a not insubstantial part of the speculation would need to relate to the sort of governmental and administrative structures which could replace the contemporary arrangement.

Were the world still to be based on the idea of the state, the only alternative to a system of states is one alone. As to differently-based schemes, it is possible just to imagine a worldwide system of overlapping functional authorities. But whatever emerged, two observations refuse to leave the mind of the present writer. The first is that significant power would still rest in the hands of

---

[13] Robert H. Jackson, as reported in the *Annual Report of the Leonard Davis Institute for International Relations, 1996–1997* (Jerusalem, Hebrew University of Jerusalem, no date), p. 38.

particular individuals and groups; and the second that such human beings would still be likely, from time to time, to act with appalling heartlessness and depravity. It is also thought that no realistic scenario offers itself whereby there could be a change from the existing set up of sovereign states to one of an entirely different kind.

It may, therefore, be more fruitful to consider whether the scheme now in place has more advantages than is sometimes supposed. Two will be touched upon. In the first place, the territorial division of the world into sovereign states contributes notably to international order. It does so by identifying the entities which have the capacity to act internationally – and hence, also, those which do not. This is of great formal importance, in that the existence of an accepted concept of sovereignty establishes which territorial units are subjects of inter-national law, which are eligible to establish diplomatic relations with other such bodies, to negotiate and sign treaties, to apply for admission to international organizations, and engage in all the day-to-day activity which constitutes the on-going business of the international society – which, collectively, these sovereign states comprise.

To say that such matters are of a formal nature all too often elicits the response that they are thereby of little substantive importance, the actual relations of states being what really matters. This is a grave misunderstanding. What the formalities provide is a framework for relations, without which it is impossible to envisage how such relations could be well ordered. Of course, such a framework does not guarantee good relations. But the absence of an accepted framework would – as in all walks of life – guarantee bad ones, as no-one would know what behaviour was acceptable and what unacceptable. The hazards of such a normless context would certainly give rise to much fierce contention and huge disorder.

An instance may help to clarify this point. As it is sovereignty which bestows international capacity, it is well understood that, unless some modification of the principle has been specifically agreed, a sovereign state does not deal directly with subordinate elements within another state. Sovereign states speak to each other, and only to each other, i.e., the relevant officials of one state commun-icate with their counterparts elsewhere. Breaches of this principle are rare, as states know that such behaviour can cause much offence even between otherwise friendly states. But in the mid-1960s there occurred a notable breach of this established international practice.

It concerned Franco-Canadian relations. France, under President de Gaulle, chose time and again to by-pass the Canadian Government and deal directly with the Provincial Government of Quebec on matters which were clearly within the federal domain. It was a concerted effort to advance Quebec's claims to sovereignty. The campaign had very serious consequences for Franco-Canadian relations.[14] On one occasion, and it was by no means an isolated instance, the Prime Minister was 'fuming', and the Minister for External Affairs 'beside [him]self with rage'. So aggravating were the activities of the members of the French Embassy in Ottawa that 'the entire diplomatic corps' was instructed to notify the Department of External Affairs of any plans they might have for travelling and speaking outside Ottawa'. Subsequently, some Canadian ministers wanted to break off diplomatic relations with France. The Canadian

---

[14] P. Martin, *A Very Public Life. Vol. II: So Many Worlds* (Toronto, Deneau, 1985), pp. 572–605.

government held back from that, on the ground that it would 'play into de Gaulle's hands'. But relations between these two closely-connected states reached their nadir. Only with the fall of de Gaulle did the turbulence abate. If the behaviour of France were to be replicated on all sides, the consequences for ordered international relations can hardly be imagined – that is to say, they can be imagined only too well!

In this direct manner, therefore, the concept of state sovereignty – in the sense of constitutional independence – is of fundamental importance for the maintenance of international order. It has enormous functional value, permitting the assertion that sovereignty is at the very basis of international society. The second advantage which sovereignty offers also has functional value, and also relates to order, but order within rather than between states. Here the contribution of sovereignty is indirect, in that the link with order occurs via the principle of national self-determination (on which Mayall writes separately in this issue of the journal). The influence of this principle has already been alluded to, when mention was made of the number of territorial entities which have acquired sovereignty during the past half-century. They did so on the basis of national self-determination – more particularly, of the idea that the nation and the independent (or sovereign) state should coincide. Nor was this the first time during the twentieth century that this principle had been hugely influential in altering the political map of the world.

What happened was that in the concept of sovereignty nations found an admirable pre-existing envelope into which they could, as it were, insert themselves to achieve their goal of independent self-government. And to the extent to which this process satisfies the people of the now self-governing territories, the cause of internal order is thereby served. Politics can proceed within such states in the absence of the often disastrously debilitating issue of whether a particular group within the state should be allowed to secede. It happens that the principle of national self-determination has not always been operationalized in such a felicitous way. On the one hand, the national-demographical complexity of particular territories has here and there obstructed the best intentioned plans to implement the principle to the satisfaction of all concerned. On another, insistence on historical or strategic considerations or just the influence of political bias has sometimes interfered with the application of the principle.[15] On a third, many states have in the last forty years been created allegedly in the service of nationhood but in reality just on the basis of the administrative boundaries of the colonial era, which often encompassed hardly anything by way of national consciousness.[16]

Nonetheless, sovereignty has contributed significantly to the maintenance of internal order, both in states without secessionist problems and in ones where time and the conscious process of nation building have filled out the sovereign envelope with a more content domestic society. This is not to say that such states are havens of internal bliss. What is being said is that where a clearly-identifiable nation is more or less coextensive with a single sovereign state, it is unlikely that the state concerned will be subject to one of the most serious possible of threats

[15] For both of these matters see, generally, H. Nicolson, *Peacemaking 1919* (London, Constable, 1933).

[16] See, generally, R. H. Jackson, *Quasi-States*. The writer may perhaps be permitted to add the comment that a 'quasi-state' is no less sovereign, i.e. constitutionally independent, than a non-quasi one.

to its internal harmony. One has only to glance around the world to be aware of the huge disruption which can be caused by highly dissatisfied and powerful minorities. A slightly closer look will reveal that states not so cursed are benefiting from the fact that the nations they envelop enjoy sovereign status.

This draws attention to the fact that this second sovereign dividend is not just functional in nature. It also serves the idea of democracy, in that it provides a means whereby a people can secure a value which is generally espoused with great fervour: that of independent self-government. There is no reason at all, as a matter of principle, why a people should wish to govern every aspect of its life, as distinct from just having its culture protected, or enjoying autonomy within a multi-national state. But such alternatives are, as a matter of fact, rarely welcomed. Accordingly, for at least a century the route to democratic fulfilment has been intimately associated with the demand for sovereignty, representing yet another benefit of this maligned and much-misunderstood concept. As yet there is no sign at all that this approach is falling out of favour.

Sovereignty, Nationalism, and Self-determination

JAMES MAYALL

The desires of the heart are as crooked as corkscrews,
  not to be born is the best for man:
The second-best is a formal order,
  the dance's pattern; dance while you can

From W. H. Auden, *The Dead Echo*

Sovereignty, we are repeatedly told, is not what it used to be. Indeed, according to Professor Falk, the concept is in such deep trouble that its use should be left to politicians but discarded in serious academic analysis.[1] I shall consider this view insofar as it affects the principle of national self-determination in the final section of this paper. For the moment, we can safely ignore it. The formal order of international society continues to be provided, in the main, by the collectivity of sovereign states. Nationalist, and other, movements that challenge this order seldom attack the principle itself, since, in the last analysis, they mostly wish to acquire sovereignty for themselves. Their challenge is directed, instead, at the claims to legitimacy of those who exercise state authority. It is not states that nationalists wish to abolish, if necessary by force; it is existing, allegedly illegitimate, non-national states.

One of the consequences of the Cold War was to close down debate about the nature of international legitimacy. This observation may seem paradoxical, since the Cold War was, at one level, an ideological confrontation, each side claiming to represent the only just world order. Yet so long as it persisted, a principle of strategic denial to the other side more often than not prevented any close examination of the democratic or popular credentials of existing governments. The Cold War notoriously made for strange ideological bed-fellows.

The Cold War also cut down virtually all challenges to the state order that were mounted by state-less groups claiming their right of self-determination. Only Bangladesh fought its way to independence and international recognition; and even then only after the decisive intervention of India. We should be clear about what is and is not being said here. The Cold War did not prevent nationalist insurgencies, far from it, but from the vantage point of the major players in world politics, it rendered them largely invisible. Conversely its end, and the collapse of communism, led not only to the creation of more than twenty new states, but simultaneously reopened the debate about the meaning of the principle of self-determination, the nature and role of national identity in international politics, and the limits of sovereignty.

---

[1] R. Falk, 'Sovereignty,' in J. Krieger (ed.), *The Oxford Companion to Politics of the World* (Oxford, Oxford University Press, 1993). pp. 851–3.

The debate opened in a spirit of high optimism which hid more than it revealed. The then United Nations Secretary General, Boutros Boutros-Ghali, caught both the optimism and the confusion of the post Cold War public mood in his *Agenda For Peace*, the document that was commissioned following the first ever Security Council Summit in January 1992. In his discussion of the new international context he made three statements that seemed to hint at a process of managed constitutional reform for international society. First, he insisted that the state must remain as the foundation stone, but that its authority was not absolute. 'Respect for its fundamental sovereignty and integrity are crucial to any common international progress. The time of absolute and exclusive sovereignty, however, has passed; its theory was never matched by reality'. Secondly, he argued, that the United Nations had not closed its doors to new members, but that 'if every ethnic, religious or linguistic group claimed state-hood, there would be no limit to fragmentation, and peace, security and economic well-being for all would become ever more difficult to achieve'. Finally, he suggested that the way to resolve the rival claims of sovereignty and self-determination, was through respect for human rights, particularly the rights of minorities, on the one hand, and democratization on the other. 'Respect for democratic principles at all levels of social existence is crucial: in communities, within states and within the community of states'.[2]

What, beyond these high-minded but somewhat bland pronouncements can be said about the relationship between nationalism and the principles of sovereignty and self-determination? In answer to this question, this paper advances two arguments. The first is that, paradoxically, there is not, and indeed cannot be, any final or determinant answer. This is because the meaning of the concepts themselves is contested, so that the relationship between them will shift over time, as political actors confront new opportunities and constraints and adjust their ideas accordingly. The second argument is that, despite this indeterminacy, a conventional understanding of the relationship between sovereignty, nationalism and self-determination emerged after 1945. Further, this understanding seems likely to prove more stable than some revisionists assume.

The core of this conventional interpretation was the belief that international society consisted of sovereign, i.e., independent states; that they formed a society because they recognized each others sovereignty and what this entailed, namely their territorial integrity and right to manage their domestic affairs without outside interference; and that consequently the right of self-determination referred only to colonies. This consequence, it should be noted, was historical and circumstantial: it was not a logical deduction from the principle of sovereignty.

At the end of the twentieth century, this conventional interpretation remains largely intact, except that it is no longer plausible to argue that strategic necessity rules out territorial change, as it was during the Cold War. This may seem a small change, but it opens the floodgates. An illusion of stability has given way to an equally illusory sense of flux. Because the Cold War had so effectively frozen the political map, there was a tendency, to assume that it had

---

[2] Boutros Boutros-Ghali, *Agenda for Peace*, paragraphs 17 and 18. For text see A. Roberts and B. Kinsbury, (eds), *United Nations, Divided World: The UN's Roles in International Relations* (Oxford, Clarendon, 2nd ed., 1993) Appendix A, pp. 468–98.

also interrupted the process of democratizing the international order according to the principle of national self-determination. The validity of this assumption is not self-evident – while self-determination can reasonably be held to imply self government, the establishment of democracy cannot itself create a political identity which does not already exist. Nonetheless, the revival of the assumption that an international order which respected the right of self-determination would also entrench democracy certainly undermined the view that the national question had been finally resolved by the post-World War II settlement.

Sovereignty and Self-determination

Sovereignty is a much older principle in international politics than self-determination. The first aspect of the problem to consider, therefore, is what happened when the latter principle was injected into a world of pre-existing sovereign states. Traditional international society was largely composed of dynastic sovereign states. The patrimony of the rulers – and with it the borders of their states – could be changed as a result of the fortunes of war or the construction of dynastic alliances through marriage, and consequently also by the acquisition of title through inheritance. The members of international society were thus the sovereign states, not their populations. This conception was challenged by the American and French Revolutions, but the United States was only peripherally involved in international relations during its early years and, after the defeat of Napoleon in 1815, the old real-estate system was restored in Europe. It survived, dented but more or less intact, until the First World War.

Since 1919, international society has ostensibly been based on a principle of popular sovereignty, namely national self-determination. The collapse of the Hapsburg, Hohenzollern, Romanov and Ottoman empires dealt a mortal blow to the dynastic principle. It was no longer possible to defend the state as a private possession of particular individuals or families. But if prescription was out, consent had to be in; ownership of the state, in other words, had to be transferred to the people. The difficulty in effecting this transfer arose because, in the last analysis, individuals alone can give or withhold consent. Yet individuals do not, and cannot, live alone. Which, therefore, are the appropriate collective selves, whose right to self-determination must be recognized as the basis of the new political order?

This question arose in the immediate aftermath of the First World War. It seemed to imply that statehood – and hence membership of international society – should be based on a democratic test of opinion. In practice, new states were created out of the debris of European dynastic empires, theoretically along national lines but with little attention to their democratic credentials. Similarly, after 1945 the European overseas empires and after 1989 the Soviet Union broke up into their constituent parts. Since the implied principle of consent has not featured prominently in the three twentieth-century waves of state-creation, it is worth asking whether the questions, what is a nation, or who are a people, are theoretically answerable at all; or, on the contrary, can only be resolved pragmatically?

The rise to political prominence of the theory of self-determination was, in a sense, an accident. Empires had, after all, risen and fallen many times before in all parts of the world. At any other time in world history the revolt against the

West would not have required theoretical support. At the time when the spectacular worldwide advance of European imperial power was halted, however, the arguments that were used to sound its retreat were those of Western political philosophy, all of which rested on their claims to universal validity.

Self-determination was a central concept in this tradition, independent of, and prior to, the rise of nationalism. From the late eighteenth century both contractarians and idealists had conceived of human freedom in terms of the political obligations of self-determining individuals. Rousseau made the crucial move by identifying the rational individual will with the General Will, so that obligations owed to the State were, in the final analysis, owed by the citizen to him or herself. From whichever direction the argument was started, it finished up advancing the claims of nations to the allegiance of individuals. Thus, at one end of the spectrum, Mill held that for the concept of freedom to have any meaning at all, human beings had to be able to choose 'with which of the various collective bodies of human beings they choose to associate themselves',[3] while at the other, Hegel insisted that only the nation 'possessing in its own eyes and in the eyes of others, a universal and universally valid embodiment in laws' could form the basis of true, i.e., ethical, as opposed to formal sovereignty.

From the point of view of international relations, the problem with all these reconciliations of political obligation with self-determination, is that they take the identity of the nations themselves for granted. To be sure Hegel has criteria for distinguishing between true historical nations and groups which are, so to speak, suffering from arrested development, such as hunters and gatherers or pastoralists.[4] Mill did not explicitly rely on such evolutionary arguments, but his use of the distinction between civilized and barbarian peoples suggests that he too believed that a people's right to free institutions was evolved rather than natural in any *a priori* sense. But for neither writer was the identity of the group itself, as distinct from the issue of its rights, viewed as being problematic and therefore a suitable subject for theoretical analysis.

The theoretical problem emerges whenever it becomes necessary to decide which national claims to statehood should be recognized. The original Wilsonian solution to this problem was the plebiscite. It failed, not merely because of the irreconcilable territorial claims in Central and Eastern Europe after World War One, nor because the great powers had no intention of testing their legitimate title in their own possessions by this method, but also because it too regarded the identity question as self-evident. As Jennings famously put it in 1956, 'On the surface it seemed reasonable: let the people decide. It was in practice ridiculous because the people cannot decide until someone decides who are the people.'[5]

[3] J. S. Mill, *Representative Government*, ch. XVI, numerous editions.

[4] G. W. F. Hegel, *Philosophy of Right* (T. M. Knox, trans) (Oxford, Oxford University Press, 1979), Part 3: Ethical Life, (iii) The State (c) World History. 'Civilized Nations [are justified] in regarding and treating as barbarians those who lag behind them in institutions which are the essential moments of the state. Thus a pastoral people may treat hunters as barbarians and both of these are barbarians from the point of view of agriculturists etc. The civilised nation is conscious that the rights of barbarians are unequal to its own and treats their autonomy as only a formality. When wars and disputes arise in such circumstances, the trait which gives them significance for world history *is the fact that they are struggles for recognition in connection with something of specific intrinsic worth.*'

[5] W. I. Jennings, *The Approach to Self Government* (Cambridge, Cambridge University Press, 1956), p. 56.

The absence of an uncontentious definition of the nation forced international society into settling the issue pragmatically, a step which was rendered doubly necessary once the right of all peoples to self-determination had been listed amongst the fundamental human rights in both the United Nations Charter and the Universal Declaration of Human Rights. It did not lead, however, to the obvious, and in my view correct, conclusion that no generally applicable and objective definition is available,[6] but to a prolonged, if inconclusive, debate about the identity and origin of nations. The fact that the Cold War had virtually ruled out territorial change seems merely to have convinced the rival protagonists that it was the strategic stalemate that had removed the issue from the realm of practical politics, rather than its inherent insolubility.

Nationalism and Self-determination

Safely removed from any danger of influencing governments on such vital questions as the international recognition of insurgent or liberation movements, or intervention in support of, or opposition to, such movements, the quest for the true identity of the nation was transferred from the negotiating table to the classroom. Nationalists, who were involved in liberation movements, of course, had their own views on the identity question, and some of them indeed probably drew inspiration from the ideas of particular social theorists, just as nationalist governments used the school curriculum to perpetuate national myths and construct national cultures which both justified and ran congruently with state boundaries. But, in neither case, could they appeal to an agreed definition which would put their claims beyond dispute.

Two broad theoretical answers have been advanced to the question of national identity, although within each of them there are a number of variations, some of which overlap. Primordalists maintain that the national map of the world was laid down a very long time ago, even if very few these days cling to the belief that it accurately reflects the natural world, which can therefore be assumed to have remained essentially unaltered since the beginning of human history. By contrast, modernists see the nation as a recent invention, dating, except for a few somewhat anomalous, or at least unexplained, cases, only from the American and French revolutions.

For primordialist writers, assigning the right to self-determination is, in principle, a soluble problem, however difficult it may be in practice. Perhaps, just because it is so difficult, they do not often address the matter directly. The recipe is deceptively simple. First find your ethnie. This is done by identifying a group of people who share one or more of a list of 'objective' characteristics (the 'one or more' is normally added to accommodate Switzerland) – a name, a common language, a homeland, in which they generally although not invariably reside, common symbols, a common myth of origin or ancestry and a sense of themselves as a people with a shared history of triumphs and disasters and, on the basis of these, shared hopes and aspirations.[7]

---

[6] For a similar conclusion from an author who nonetheless argues for a moral right to self-determination 'in the civic nationalist mode', see J. Charvet, 'What is Nationality, and is there a Moral Right to National Self-determination?,' in S. Caney, D. George and P. Jones (eds), *National Rights, International Obligations* (Boulder CO, Westview, 1996), pp. 53–68.

[7] See A. D. Smith, 'Ethnie and nation in the modern world', *Millenium*, 14 (1985), 127–42.

Next extract your ethnic group from wherever it has been washed up by the tide of history, be it within an empire or a multicultural state. Endow its members with a state, under a government of their own kind, and of which they are citizens rather than subjects. This last step will effect the transformation of the ethnic group into a nation and will equip the new state for entry into international society. Opinions seem to differ on cooking times: for some, providing the ethno-genesis has occurred at a distant point in the past, a nation-state can be expected to arise naturally on defrosting after the Cold War. Others, like Connor, are more cautious, pointing out that the emergence of national self-consciousness from its ethnic base is a slow and uncertain process, about which it is difficult to generalize.[8] Much, it seems, depends on the oven.

Modernists hold that, far from nations rising up naturally from the ethnic subsoil in which they are rooted, they are created by nationalists, that is by those who subscribe to the political doctrine that nation and state should be congruent. Some nationalists may be able to adapt pre-existing ethnic myths and symbols for their own purposes, but they are also capable of inventing nations – Estonia is often used as an example – where prior to the age of nationalism, none existed.

The original modernist account of the nation was provided by those who attacked the *ancien regime* at the end of the eighteenth century. Their conception was broadly consistent with the liberal idea of self-determination as democratic self-government. The nation, in other words, was a civic association, not an ethnic one. Although the French insisted on the importance of French culture and language as defining elements of the French nation, it is worth recalling that, for much of the nineteenth century, France was a host country for immigrants not, of course, on the scale of the USA, but in significant numbers nonetheless. Official policy was certainly assimilationist, but it did not pay much attention to social or ethnic origins.

Academic modernists have paid almost as little attention to the international implications of their theories as the primordialists. For the most part, their interest is in the historical and sociological conditions that ushered in the nationalist era, rather than the justification offered for a state's entry into international society. Thus, for example, Gellner argued that a national culture was a necessary accompaniment of the transition from agricultural to modern society, largely because the division of labour on which industrialism depends, and the competition to which it leads, requires occupational mobility and therefore a literate and trainable labour force. Peasants, who mostly stay in one place, do not need to read and write in order to function and tend to regard whoever governs them with deep suspicion. Modern states, on the other hand, require educated citizens whose loyalty they can command. In attempting to explain why citizens, for their part, identify with the state, another modernist author Benedict Anderson has traced the rise of the nation to the development of print capitalism; the profit motive requiring a market of readers, which in turn puts a premium on the production of literary works in the vernacular and allows for an *imagined community* of people who do not know one another directly.

---

[8] W. Connor, 'When is a nation', *Ethnic and Racial Studies*, 13 (1990), 82–100. See also E. Weber, *Peasant into Frenchman: the Modernisation of Rural France, 1870–1914* (Stanford University Press, 1976).

In neither of these two accounts does the demand for self-determination feature prominently. Yet it is the modernists who point the way to the practical resolution of the self-determination problem. For Gellner, the crucial factor in determining a state's borders along national lines is the existence of a high culture, which is already widely diffused amongst the population at large, rather than being confined to the landed aristocracy and the clerisy, as it mostly was in traditional agrarian society. In explaining the political mapping of Europe during the nationalist era, Gellner divides the continent into times zones. Only along the Atlantic coast was there no great need to redraw political boundaries.

> The point about the zone is that from the late Middle Ages, if not earlier, it was occupied by strong dynastic states, which roughly, even if only very roughly, correlated with cultural areas ... This meant that when, with the coming of Nationalism, political units had to adjust themselves to cultural boundaries, no very great changes other than a kind of *ex post* ratification were required.

Consequently, with the exception of Ireland, 'the map of this part of Europe in the age of nationalism does not look so very different from what it had been in the age when dynasty, religion and local community had been the determinants of boundaries'.[9]

Elsewhere it was different. In the lands of the former Holy Roman Empire, two high cultures – Italian and German – had been codified since the Renaissance and Reformation respectively, although politically the area had long been fragmented. Political rather than cultural engineering was therefore required in the Italian and German speaking lands. It was carried out fairly successfully, from on top, by Piedmont and Prussia respectively. It was the area to the east that posed the greatest problem. In the Hapsburg Empire and those parts of Europe under Ottoman rule which confronted it, there were many peasant communities which lacked both a high culture and a distinct polity.

> Here both cultures and polities had to be created, an arduous task indeed. Nationalism began with ethnography, half descriptive half normative, a kind of salvage operation and cultural engineering combined. If the eventual units were to be compact and reasonably homogenous, more had to be done: many, many people had to be assimilated, or expelled or killed. All these methods were eventually employed in the course of implementing the nationalist political principle, and they continue to be in use.

The same story might well have been repeated in the lands ruled by the Romanovs, had the Tsarist Empire not, in effect, been taken over by the Bolsheviks.[10] Apart from a hint of structural determinism, what is striking about this account is that, wherever possible, an existing state was used as the basis for the creation of a nation-state.

A similar conclusion emerges from Anderson's analysis of non-European nationalisms.[11] Specifically, he confronts the failure of Bolivar's attempt to create a United States of Latin America. Why, given their access to a common

---

[9] E. Gellner, *Conditions of Liberty: Civil Society and its Rivals* (London, Hamish Hamilton, 1994), p. 133.

[10] Gellner, *Conditions of Liberty*, p. 116.

[11] B. Anderson, *Imagined Communities, Reflections on the Origins and Spread of Nationalism* (London, Verso, 1983), pp. 50–65.

literate high culture, did the South Americans not follow where the USA had led? Essentially his answer is that the formative experience of South American nationalists took place within the provinces of the Spanish Empire: for the Creoles – the Spanish speaking but locally born elites who aspired to independence – their 'career-pilgrimages' not only defined the imagined community but were constrained by the administrative boundaries established by Spain. Only those born in Spain could serve anywhere in the Empire; the locally born were confined to their home province. The territorial units existed before nationalism and exercised a real rather than a visionary prize for those who aspired to exercise power.

With minor adjustments, Anderson's argument can be applied to most non-European nationalisms. Certainly, it seems to fit quite well in Africa where the appeal of Pan-Africanism was quickly subordinated to the territorial principle after independence; and in India following the partition of 1947 any concessions that were made in response to demands for regional and linguistic autonomy – and many were – were never allowed to challenge the territorial borders of the state inherited from the British Raj.

Most modernist writers on nationalism adopt a broadly realist approach to international relations, to the extent that they consider them, which is not often. They seldom address legal or normative questions at all. At the same time, implicit in their arguments is the recognition that political identity – like political boundaries – are contingent matters. This is the crucial point. What is contingent cannot be settled by rational argument or a democratic vote. For political argument to take place, boundaries must be in place, but they lie behind or beyond such argument all the same. It was the reluctant recognition, born of bitter experience between the wars, that this is indeed the case, that led the international community to impose an official interpretation on the principle of self-determination after 1945. Note again, that while the Cold War delayed any serious challenge to this interpretation, it was *not* responsible for its initial adoption.

The Conventional Interpretation

When the drafters of the United Nations Charter, and the Universal Declaration of Human Rights, turned their attention to the right of self-determination, they referred to peoples rather than nations, presumably in an attempt to avoid the destructive confusion that had accompanied the reconstruction of Europe after 1918. The result was not a huge improvement. Finding objective criteria to define 'a people' is no easier, indeed, no different, to defining a nation, unless that is, the right is assigned to pre-existing states or territorial units and the people, whoever they may be, are simply assumed to be identified with and represented by state governments.

Whether or not those who drew up these documents were already clear about what they were doing, the principle was in practice interpreted as applying – *ex post facto* to all existing states and to the overseas colonies of the European imperial powers. Despite a rear-guard action by defenders of the imperial idea,[12]

[12] See for example, A. Burns, *In Defence of Colonies* (London, Allen & Unwin, 1957) and H. Seton-Watson, *Neither War nor Peace: The Struggle for Power in the Post-War World* (London, Methuen, 1960).

it was not seriously advanced in relation to the Soviet Union's imperial legacy, on the eastern fringes of Europe, around the Baltic, in Central Asia and beyond.

Nor were most governments willing to insist on a democratic test of opinion before extending international recognition to states which underwent a revolution. It is true that the United States attempted – for more than 20 years successfully – to blackball the People's Republic of China from the United Nations, but even Washington's closest allies were unimpressed by this attempt to force ideological conformity across international borders and in obvious defiance of Article 2 (7) of the Charter. Irredentism got equally short shrift. Around the edges of their inheritance, some colonial successor states consolidated their territory without suffering serious international consequences: thus India swallowed Goa, Indonesia, first West Irian and then in 1974 East Timor, and China, Tibet, a decidedly pre-modern form of conquest which the outside world accepted because the country had never enjoyed formal sovereignty or international recognition. But in general during the Cold War there was widespread antipathy to opening up the domestic political arrangements of sovereign states to outside scrutiny, and no indication that the forceful pursuit of irredentist claims – outside the immediate context of European imperial withdrawal – would be tolerated.

Irredentist claims are seldom abandoned altogether, but the ambitions of governments which harboured them, such as Spain to Gibraltar, the Philippines to Sabah, Morocco to Mauritania, the Republic of Ireland to Ulster, the Argentine to the Falklands, and Taiwan to the Chinese mainland, faced formidable practical constraints. They were prohibited under international law from using force as an instrument of foreign policy; with the partial exception of the Spanish claim to Gibraltar, which was sympathetically viewed by African states on anti-colonial grounds, it was impossible to generate diplomatic support within the General Assembly or other international organizations; and, above all, they were unable to obtain support for territorial change from either superpower.

The main challenge to the conventional interpretation of self-determination, as de-colonialization, came from secessionists: these were, after all, precisely those who took the principle seriously, and who understandably drew the conclusion, that if self-determination was a fundamental human right, it should apply to them. Of the three Cold War secessionist crises, which spilled onto the world stage – Katanga, Biafra and Bangladesh – only the Biafran case was debated seriously in terms of the substantive meaning of self-determination. The reintegration of Katanga into the Congo was the price the USA was prepared to pay to marginalize Soviet influence within the United Nations peace-keeping operation. The rebellion in East Bengal was often explained by academic analysts in terms of a theory of internal colonialism, but, as we have already noted, it was the Indian army which expelled Pakistan, not the Bangladeshis themselves.

Biafra's bid for independence collapsed because, unlike Bangladesh, the Biafrans failed to secure a powerful external patron who was prepared to defy the international consensus in favour of the territorial *status quo*. France came close, but in the end de Gaulle indicated that he would be guided by African opinion. By 1969, four African states – Ivory Coast, Gabon, Tanzania and Zambia had broken ranks and recognized the Biafran government. A number of others were rumoured to be sympathetic to its cause. At the annual OAU Summit in 1969,

President Nyerere of Tanzania, who had himself proposed the 1964 OAU resolution which committed African countries to accept the boundaries inherited at independence, circulated a memorandum to his fellow African Heads of State arguing that, in this case, they should abandon the commitment. His argument was straightforward and compelling. Colonial borders, Nyerere suggested, had been accepted for practical reasons – to facilitate inter-state co-operation, minimize opportunities for conflict and to release energies that could be better devoted to development and improving the lot of Africa's peoples. Nonetheless, the right of governments to rule rested on their ability to serve the population as a whole. When a government could no longer protect the lives of all of its citizens, and when a particular group believed itself to be threatened by genocide, it forfeited its legitimacy. In these circumstances, the same political considerations that had earlier led him to accept existing territorial arrangements could now (and in his view, should) be advanced in support of partition.[13]

This attempt, to establish internal standards of accountability and good government as relevant criteria for international recognition, failed. No surprise in that perhaps. By 1969, there was some truth in the jibe that the OAU was little more than a trade union of rulers; few governments were genuinely answerable to their populations, and the life presidents and military dictators who attended its meetings, had no interest in lowering their sovereign guard to accommodate international criticism. In most cases, internal opposition had been broken, or driven into exile. Also, in general, secessionists could neither appeal to international law nor dent the government's monopoly of the symbols of nationalism at the United Nations.

The lasting significance of Nyerere's failure, however, is that, unlike the failure of the USA to excommunicate communist China from international society, it had virtually nothing to do with the Cold War. The episode should give pause for thought to all those who may wish to argue that the end of the Cold War has created an opportunity to redraw the international map on the basis of 'genuine' self-determination.

The Search for a New Convention

The amazing sight of the communist regimes of Eastern Europe falling one after the other like a pack of cards in 1989, followed by the disintegration of the Soviet Union itself, may have temporarily led would-be revisionists to fantasize that an open season had been declared for secessionist self-determination. If so, the major players quickly disabused them. Even when, in March 1990, the Lithuanian parliament voted democratically to seek independence from the Soviet Union, western governments withheld recognition and urged the nationalists to reach an accommodation with Moscow. Indeed, there is much truth in Misha Glenny's observation that, initially, the west 'understood self-determination to mean the right of east European countries to leave the Soviet bloc',[14] not the right of the Soviet republics to secede from the Union itself.

---

[13] 'Tanzania's memorandum on Biafra's case'. For text, see A. H. M. Kirk-Greene (ed.), *Crisis and Conflict in Nigeria: A Documentary Sourcebook*, Vol. 2, July 1967–January 1970 (Oxford, Oxford University Press, 1971), pp. 429–39.

[14] M. Glenny, *The Fall of Yugoslavia* (Harmondsworth, Penguin, 1992)

When eventually, it became clear that the centre would not hold the international community found it convenient to deal with the Soviet Union by treating it as though it were an empire whose disintegration into its constituent parts could be understood as decolonization, thus leaving the conventional interpretation of self-determination intact. The main challenge to this hasty adjustment to international constitutional theory came on the one hand from Yugoslavia, whose communist government had avoided incorporation into the Soviet Empire, and on the other from the Council of Europe and the European Union, both of which had established democratic criteria for membership.

In the event, however, despite sending contradictory signals to the competing nationalists in former Yugoslavia, the Europeans colluded in heading off the challenge to the conventional interpretation that they themselves had mounted. Thus, although the European Union appointed the Badinter Commission to establish whether democratic practices had been put in place that would justify recognition of the Yugoslav successor states, Western countries first discouraged the break-up of Yugoslavia altogether and then recognized it precipitously, paying only lip-service to democratic principles. At the same time, the outside world went to great lengths to ensure that the internal boundaries of former Yugoslavia – like the boundaries of their own former colonies or the successor states those of the erstwhile Soviet Union – would define their international legal personality. From this point of view, the Dayton Accords represent a victory for the conventional interpretation. Admittedly, the Accords make provision for democratic elections as well as for territorial integrity. But whether, as a consequence, they will also mark the beginning of a new understanding of self-determination, in which acceptance of state borders is married to internal power-sharing, along confederal or consociational lines, remains to be seen.

Self-determination and Democracy

It is possible to construct a defence of national self-determination which is not linked to democratic values in the western liberal sense. Miller, basing himself on Plamenatz, argues, for example, that there was nothing absurd in the belief of Europe's colonial peoples that they would have a greater sense of control over their own destinies if they were ruled by local oligarchies rather than alien imperialists.[15] But it is unusual. Self-determination is more often understood to mean the exercise of political freedom in which a people expresses its identity by choosing its own government. The people, in other words, are the final source of state legitimacy; hence the concept of popular sovereignty, which can only be separated from the democratic ideal by an appeal to tradition or some collectivist sleight of hand. Whether people will always opt for democracy given the chance to do so, and regardless of the consequences, is a different question.

In any event, the democratic side won the Cold War. This victory ensured that claims for self-determination would henceforth have to be cast in democratic form. It did not, however, and indeed could not, resolve the underlying problem of political identity. Thus, to recapitulate: The right of all peoples to self-determination is a fundamental human right, but there is no secessionist

---

[15] See B. O'Leary, 'Insufficiently liberal and insufficiently nationalist', in Symposium on David Miller's 'On Nationality', *Nations and Nationalism*, 2 (1996), 450, note 4.

right of self-determination. It follows that existing states are assumed to reflect the relevant political identities of the world's peoples. In this sense, territory had triumphed over the social composition of the population in determining both statehood and sovereignty. Political language, with its emphasis on democratic rights and legitimacy, conjures up an image of culturally homogenous nation-states, whereas the reality is that most people live in multi cultural state-nations, as they have done ever since the end of the age of empire.

This is hardly an elegant solution to the problem of political identity, but it is the only one presently available. It may help to establish the practical obstacles to moving beyond the current position, and the options that face the inter-national community in seeking to revise it, if we review a range of traditional arguments on the relationship of self-determination, democratic government and secession, in the light of current circumstances.

The Democratic Case for and against Secession

First argument: that secession must be ruled out to avoid anarchy, and in the interests of public welfare. This was the position adopted by Abraham Lincoln during the American Civil War, and in a much-diluted form, it survives in Boutros Boutros-Ghali's *Agenda for Peace*. All citizens have the same funda-mental rights, grounded in the constitution and protected by law. The only way the minority can become the majority, on this view, is by persuading the majority to change their allegiance at the next election. Guaranteed rights of free speech and free association allow them, in principle, to compete on level terms with the government for the affections of the people.

The theory is attractive: there is no ground for holding that opposition will be regarded as treachery, and the government itself will be regularly held to account and will be changed following electoral defeat. The trouble is that at the end of the twentieth century, as in the middle of the nineteenth, it is not an accurate description of social reality in many parts of the world. In particular, as Beran has pointed out, it cannot deal with societies which are structurally deeply divided.[16] The argument that Jinnah advanced on behalf of the Muslim League fifty years ago was that Indian Muslims were a separate people, in a sense which would inevitably define and limit their political destiny. They could not see themselves as other than Muslims; and they could not hope to become the majority under any foreseeable circumstances.[17] On the basis of this argument the British were eventually persuaded to partition the country.

Whether this was a wise, or indeed a necessary decision, will no doubt continue to be debated amongst historians and nationalists in both India and Pakistan. The relevant point for the present argument is that until power was transferred at midnight on 15 August 1947, the British remained in control and were, therefore, in a position to take the decision. International society has no such authority to settle conflicts in societies where people insist on identifying

---

[16] H. Beran, *The Consent Theory of Political Obligation* (London, Croom Helm, 1987), pp. 39–42.

[17] Interestingly, Jinnah seems to have been mesmerized by the boundaries of British India. It was these that framed his political ambitions, not the fact that Indian Muslims were members of a world faith, which theoretically might have formed the basis of a much more radical territorial revision. Similarly, although Arab and African nationalists expressed their loyalty to wider pan-Arab and pan-African nations respectively, they concentrated their real efforts on taking over the colonial state within its existing boundaries.

themselves in ethnic or communal terms rather than as citizens. Nor has it shown any interest in acquiring it; or indeed in partition as an instrument of international conflict resolution.

The refusal to countenance secession under any circumstances has had predictably gruesome results. After the Croatian Declaration of Independence in 1991, the government wooed international recognition by passing legislation to protect Serb rights. The trouble was that Serbs were not reassured and continued to resist rule from Zagreb. A blind eye had to be turned towards the ethnic cleansing of the Krajina before Croatia would accept the American-brokered settlement in Bosnia. Similarly, when in 1994, the RPF began to close in on Kigali, the Hutu-dominated government of Rwanda launched a genocide rather than surrender power. In such cases, Lincoln's splendidly civic argument fails to address not merely the aspirations, but much more importantly, the fears of the people on both sides of the conflict.

The most obvious objection to allowing a secessionist right of self-determination is that partition invariably creates new minorities, groups stranded on one side of the line or the other, for whom the *status quo ante* was better than the new dispensation. Nationalists may say that you cannot make an omelette without breaking eggs, but that is of little comfort to the eggs. Beran's rational libertarian solution to this dilemma is to make the right of secession dependent on a principle of regressive self-determination. In other words the secession will be recognized if, and only if, the new government is prepared to extend the same right to minorities within its jurisdiction. That minority would then have to deal with its own population in the same way, and so on until the resulting territorial arrangements left no groups stranded and dissatisfied.

There are, in turn, two objections to this ingenious proposal. First, in practical terms, it is extremely difficult to believe that governments anywhere would take it seriously, even though its operation would probably act to keep the lid on the Pandora's Box of claims and counter-claims which they so fear. It would, for example, make the secession of Quebec from Canada impossible unless the PQ was prepared to grant the same right to the 'first nations' who have already declared their opposition. Establishing such a right in advance of any particular claim would be viewed as an open invitation to dissident groups to de-stabilize the government; would involve endless litigation about the division of assets; and would require a level of rational debate about competing claims, the absence of which is normally the hallmark of secessionist conflicts.

Second, even if these problems could be overcome, there is a theoretical objection to the proposal. Once the process has started, those who preferred the *status quo ante* because it allowed them to maintain multiple identities – for example, to be both a Quebecker and a Canadian – or merely to occupy a private space within a multi-ethnic state, will find themselves forced to declare for one group or another, as the Yugoslavs were forced to do after 1991. Under cover of rational argument, one form of contingency will have been substituted for another. The defence would have to be that it would make the international commitment to democracy more credible. Perhaps. Whether the world would be a more peaceful or a more tolerant place is more doubtful.

Second argument: that democracy will be subverted and political freedom destroyed, where two or more powerful national groups compete through the ballot box to capture the state. This is the instrumental, as distinct from rights-based, defence of partition advanced by Mill in *Representative Govern-ment*. Written in the 1860s, it can be read as an almost uncanny prediction of what happened in Yugoslavia in the early 1990s. Mill's argument is implicitly historicist: a non-national or civic national democracy will only emerge if peoples of different nationality have grown accustomed to living together – and being governed under a single authority – prior to the era of both nationalism and democracy. However, if national self-consciousness and a desire for 'free institutions' emerge together, the absence of an over-arching political culture will ensure that democracy will act as a source of conflict rather than of legitimacy.

The merit of Mill's argument is its concern with practical outcomes rather than collective rights in any abstract sense. His primary concern is how to protect human freedom; his advocacy of partition under certain circumstances is directed to the same end, not the conservation of particular national cultures or forms of life, as ends in themselves. For those committed to the latter objectives, it is Mill's indifference to minorities which are not sufficiently numerous to strike at the democratic foundations of the state, that most weakens his argument's appeal. Except in this limiting case, Mill was as opposed to secession as Lincoln, and his assimilationist assumption that minority discontent could be overcome by education, while benign in intention, and possibly true in some cases and over the very long term, has been falsified by events in many parts of the world.

Something of use, in my view, can still be salvaged from Mill's brief but percipient observations about nationalism and democracy. Because there is no satisfactory *a priori* criterion for settling state boundaries, international society has settled for investing those that actually exist with an absolute status which belies their contingent origins. It also belies the fact that in those cases where boundaries do change, the new map quickly becomes as sacred, and conse-quently as unnegotiable, as the old. When we contemplate the levels of destruc-tion and human suffering that have frequently resulted from the defence of these boundaries, it might be prudent for statesmen, scholars and lawyers to adopt a more open-minded approach to territoriality than they have customarily done. Despite the minority and identity problems which invariably follow from secession, a second best solution may sometimes be preferable to no solution at all. If this is not conceded, a bleaker and more traditional option remains.

Third argument: that while the existence of a nation is a pre-requisite for democracy, nations will come into being, in the future, as in the past, only through a process of struggle and self-assertion against other forms of imposed imperial sovereignty. This argument, which was advanced in the aftermath of the Cold War, by the veteran British politician, Enoch Powell, rests on a com-pelling but not necessarily ethnic logic. The essence of representative demo-cracy, Powell argued, is majority rule. No matter how consociational the constitutional arrangements, there will always be some party or interest that is left out of the ruling coalition. So what is it that persuades the minority to put up with rule by the majority? Lincoln had suggested that it was the opportunity to change the government by swinging public opinion behind the opposition. But, why should they be prepared to wait, particularly if the odds on success are long and there is a better chance of influencing events by taking the law into their own hands? Powell's answer is that the minority will only put up with majority rule, if there is some overarching community sentiment which is stronger than the conflicts of ideological, economic or political interest that customarily divide people on a daily basis.

It is not clear that a community of this kind can be engineered, at least from outside. But we know that most, if not all, well established nation states develop democratic institutions only after a prolonged period of power struggles and feuding at home and abroad. Even the USA had to fight a civil war to prove to themselves that they were one people and not two. Collective amnesia, as Renan famously remarked,[18] as much as shared memories, or invented traditions, is a defining characteristic of most nations. Whether it is true that behind every great fortune there is a great crime, it is difficult to think of great nation (or even a small one for that matter) that does not rest on great cruelties and/or injustices – in the past.

The difficulty posed by this argument is only too apparent: on the one hand, as an account of how the democratic world came into being and maintains itself, it is plausible; on the other hand, in so far as it condemns us to live – indeed to define ourselves – by the sword, it is morally repellent. Moreover, it is not merely liberals, but governments of all ideological persuasions, which have accepted the legal prohibition on the use of force except in self-defence. The twentieth century world wars, on this view, were fought, at least partly, to replace the rule of the sword with that of the constitution, internationally as well as nationally. This process was interrupted by the Cold War, but there is no evidence to suggest that the popular hunger for self-government that erupted after 1989 was an aberration. If, as this paper has so far attempted to establish, it is impossible to devise rational rules for redrawing the political map to accommodate the aspirations of all self-conscious groups, it remains to ask whether there is an alternative way of interpreting self-determination within international society.

Revision and Re-interpretation

We enter here on uncharted waters, so it is not surprising that governments seem determined not only to proceed with extreme caution but also even refuse to acknowledge that change is either necessary or desirable. And it is true, that from one point of view, not much has changed. The conventional interpretation of self-determination as de-colonization referred to international recognition, not always to the situation on the ground. Thus, for example, Chad or the Lebanon were at times over the past 50 years effectively partitioned, even though, at the international level, their sovereignty and territorial integrity were maintained. Many countries in Asia, Africa, and Latin America were also never pacified in the sense implied by the theory of internal sovereignty, that is they were in a constant state of armed rebellion with whole regions where the writ of the central government did not run, sometimes for years on end. Yet, in virtually no case, were rebel forces able to challenge the legitimacy of the government at the international level.

So far, the post-Cold War expansion of international society has been accommodated by treating the disintegration of the Soviet Union and the collapse of Communism as a form of de-colonization. Armenia and Azerbaijan have been recognized as independent states, but Armenia's military occupation

---

[18] E. Renan, *Qu'est-ce qu'un nation?*, M. Snyder (trans.), (Paris, Calmann-Levy, 1882).

of Ngorno Karabach has not been recognized any more than was Israel's occupation of the Golan Heights after the 1967 war. In both cases occupation was accepted as a strategic reality by those involved, but from an international and legal perspective, these occupations were regarded as anomalies and remained on the political agenda as outstanding problems awaiting resolution.

Similarly, the international community followed Russia in recognizing the sovereignty and independence of the former Soviet Socialist Republics – as a generation earlier it had followed Britain and France in recognizing their transfer of power to nationalist governments in the former colonies. The analogy can be pressed further. During British and French de-colonization, the activities of Corsican separatists or the provisional IRA were never viewed as part of the anti-colonial movement. The British and French governments occupied permanent seats on the Security Council, and so were in a strong position, to resist any attempt to internationalize these 'internal' demands for self-determination. But, amongst anti-colonialists, there was no sustained attempt to argue that the 1960 United Nations' Declaration on De-colonization (General Assembly Resolution 1514) should apply in such cases. Apart from other considerations to have pressed such a claim would have implied that the principle of *uti possidetis* would have been undermined at the very point when vigorous efforts were being made to establish it as an unnegotiable international norm in the context of de-colonization.

In the post-Cold War world, the Russians were not immunized quite so effectively from international criticism of their handling of the crisis in Chechnya. But such criticism stopped well short of any international pressure on Moscow to concede the Chechynan right to an independent state. In sociological and empirical terms a strong case could be made that Chechnya had a better claim to independence than, say, Belarus, but as an autonomous region in the Russian Federation, it did not have the pre-existing legal credentials to fit easily into the conventional interpretation. Recognition would, therefore, not merely have been resisted by Russia, which like Britain and France occupies a permanent seat on the Security Council, it would have been regarded by the international community generally as setting a dangerous precedent.

Three other considerations may help to explain the underlying reasons for the reluctance of governments to re-open the question of self-determination. Each illustrates a different aspect of the theoretical problem. The first is the obvious difficulty in reconciling the principle of self-determination, however conceived, with the deliberate use of force to change an international boundary. Historically, this was one of the principal ways that the political map had been re-drawn, but after 1945 the UN Charter rejected the right of conquest. The new constraint was, so to speak, the flip side of the principle of *uti possidetis*. It was all right for the governments of both established states and successor regimes to accept this principle, because inheritance could be assumed to have originated prior to the emergence of democratic self-consciousness or the awareness of universal human rights. It is a different matter altogether to try and put the clock back and to create a new right – namely possession – by what has come to be accepted as a wrong – namely an act of territorial aggression.

It was precisely because the attempt to transform the political landscape in Bosnia by force challenged the normative framework of international society at its most vulnerable point that the major powers acted as they did. The uneasy peace that was eventually brokered at Dayton, Ohio, in 1995, and which has been kept precariously in place by NATO peace-keeping forces, showed the extraordinary lengths to which the major Western states were prepared to go to maintain the principle of territorial integrity. It was impossible to return all territory that had been conquered, ethnically cleansed, and then re-populated in the preceding four years, to their original owners. Indeed it remains doubtful whether, even the loose confederal arrangement that was negotiated, could survive without the continued presence of international forces. So long as they remain, however, the future of Bosnia's political identity and territorial integrity will be maintained and may, in time, constitute a new reality. If this is the outcome, the international community will have successfully asserted its right to determine the internal constitutional arrangements, as well as the external boundaries, of states which seek international recognition. I shall return to this issue shortly; here it is sufficient to reiterate that with regard to territorial self-determination the Dayton Accords reinforce, rather than modify, the conventional interpretation.

A second aspect of the theoretical problem is how to prevent a successful bid for international recognition spilling over into, or otherwise destabilizing, the wider region in which the claimant's state is embedded. The doctrine of *uti possidetis* was formulated in nineteenth century Latin America as a means of putting an end to a destructive and potentially unending cycle of irredentist conflicts. Since 1945, the doctrine has been promoted in particular by the African states whose governments feared that conceding the legitimacy of any secession would open a Pandora's Box of claims, from which none of them could escape. The doctrine was therefore built into the foundations of the OAU at an early stage. Neither of the major revisionist states in contemporary Africa – Morocco which until 1969 claimed Mauritania and continues to claim large sections of the Western Sahara, and Somalia which claimed the Ogaden, Djibouti and the north eastern province of Kenya – have ever been able to breach the solid wall of diplomatic opposition to their claims.[19]

Nor, at least openly, were the Eritreans able to obtain diplomatic support for their secession from Ethiopia, to which they had been attached, with scant regard to their wishes, in 1952.[20] That they were eventually successful has less to do with the emergence of new criteria for recognizing the legitimacy of self-determination claims than with the power vacuum following the Soviet Union's abandonment of its client regime in Addis Ababa in 1991.

The predominantly Tigrean government that moved into this vacuum was itself allied to, and heavily dependent on, the Eritrean Peoples' Liberation Front (EPLF). Since its defeat of its rival in the 1970s, the EPLF had kept the Ethiopian army pinned down in Eritrea and made the country ungovernable, at least after dark. The new Ethiopian government was not in a position either morally or practically to resist Eritrean independence. Even so, other African governments continued to be nervous in case a precedent was being set which would lead to the unravelling of the OAU's territorial settlement.

They need not have worried. The Eritreans had always argued, without success but with some justice, that by demanding an independent state of their

[19] See J. Mayall, 'The OAU and Self-Determination', in I. M. Lewis (ed.), *Nationalism and Self-Determination in the Horn of Africa* (London, Ithaca, 1983), pp. 57–63.

[20] See S. Healey 'The Changing Idiom of Self-Determination in the Horn of Africa', in Lewis, *Nationalism and Self Determination in the Horn of Africa*, pp. 101–3.

own, they were upholding, not attacking, the conventional interpretation of self-determination as de-colonization. Unlike Ethiopia, whose government itself had taken part in the nineteenth century scramble for Africa, Eritrea has been colonized by Italy and then administered by Britain in the Second World War, only being attached to Ethiopia by the General Assembly when the great powers could not decide amongst themselves about what to do with the territory after the War.[21] On this view, Eritrean independence has merely brought the situation into line with the OAU orthodoxy that only ex-colonies can claim statehood. There are very few other potential claimants that can meet this criterion. One such is the self-proclaimed Republic of Somali land, which comprises the former British protectorate, but Eritrea has been no more sympathetic to its claims than other African governments.

When Eritrea was finally admitted to the United Nations and OAU in 1993 it was after 99.8% of the population had voted for independence from Ethiopia in a referendum which was heavily observed by international organizations. As the referendum was a condition of recognition, as in the Bosnian case, it may be cited as evidence of a new democratic standard for entry into international society. Maybe. It is possible, perhaps more likely, that the referendum should be regarded as a rite of passage, which tells us little about the future trajectory of the new state. The Eritrean plebiscite not only failed to give minorities in Eritrea rights of self-determination but banned political parties for five years, after which they are to be permitted providing they are not based on ethnic, linguistic, or religious differences. After so massive a vote of confidence in the national plebiscite, one might wonder why such restrictions were considered necessary.

Meanwhile, the nationalist movement in East Timor, which like the EPLF, can plausibly claim to have the conventional interpretation on its side, has made little headway in its effort to reverse its forced incorporation into Indonesia. Despite a sustained campaign at the United Nations, support from Portugal and widespread international sympathy, possession remains nine-tenths of the law. The government in Jakarta is not dependent on an outside patron in the way that Mengistu's government in Addis Ababa was dependent on the Soviet Union: in these circumstances *uti possidetis* has a more traditional meaning.

The third problematic aspect of self-determination is how the implied principle of self-selection can be reconciled with rules of entry to international society. The insistence in the Charter on territorial integrity, as a logical entailment of the principle of sovereignty, commits the United Nations against unilateral secession, not against secession *per se*. There has never been any objection, in principle, to the break up of existing states providing separation is negotiated, as it was between Norway and Sweden in 1905, the Irish Free State and the United Kingdom in 1921, Malaysia and Singapore in 1965, and Slovakia and the Czech Republic in 1993. Nonetheless, while such negotiation may open a pathway to international recognition (this was presumably what Boutros Boutros-Ghali had in mind in suggesting, that the UN had not closed its doors to new members), even democratic governments are reluctant to invite peaceful territorial challenges to their authority.

---

[21] For an account of the UN negotiations on the Italian colonies, see P. Calvocoressi, *Survey of International Affairs, 1947–48 and 1949–50* (Oxford, Oxford University Press, for RIIA), pp. 121–3 and 539–55.

Where such challenges appear imminent – as in Canada from Quebec – the authorities are more likely to invoke the conventional interpretation in an attempt to head it off at the pass. Thus, in 1996, the Canadian government referred three questions to the Supreme Court of Canada. These were respectively, 'whether there is anything in Canada's constitution or in international law that would give the National Assembly, legislature or government of Quebec the right to declare Quebec's independence unilaterally', and in the event of a conflict between the Canadian constitution and international law on these questions, which would take precedence?[22] But the two international experts consulted by the federal government concluded that 'outside the colonial context, there is no recognition of a *right to unilateral secession* based on a majority vote of the population of a sub-division or territory, whether or not that population constitutes one or more 'peoples' in the ordinary sense of that word.[23] It is true that both experts hedged their bets by suggesting that 'there may be developments in the principle of self-determination according to which not only colonialism but also flagrant violations of human rights or undemocratic regimes could lead to a right of unilateral secession', but they are firmly of the view that these putative developments are not relevant to Quebec.

Democratization

How seriously should we take the view that the exercise of sovereignty is now conditional on a commitment to multi-party democracy? A glance at the way in which the fall of Suharto was handled in Indonesia, or at how China continues to deal with the USA and other permanent members of the Security Council without having to make serious concessions over human rights, might suggest a sceptical answer. However, even if democracy cannot rank with sovereignty as one of Europe's most successful exports to the rest of the world, its appeal should not be discounted altogether. In an era of rapid global communications, ideas can spread with the speed of an infectious virus, even if they are also liable to mutate in the process.

It was probably inevitable that Western Europe and North America would set the agenda for the post-Cold War world. The ancient way of settling disputes about fundamentals, that is those that lie beyond the formal order, where there is neither pattern nor rules, was trial by combat. This idea has survived into the modern world, albeit in an unacknowledged and somewhat emasculated form.[24] The Western democracies won the Second World War and by this victory earned the right to determine the shape of the new order. It is no accident that the Charters of the major post-war international organizations – above all the Charter of the United Nations – were drafted in the parliamentary idiom of liberal constitutionalism. The west European countries are also the only regional group of states to have succeeded from the beginning – first in the Council of Europe, then in the European Community/Union – in basing their

[22] Department of Justice, Canada, Backgrounder, 27 February, 1997.
[23] The two experts were Professor James Crawford, Whewell Professor of International Law at the University of Cambridge, and Professor Luzius Wildhaber, of the University of Basel who is also a judge on the European Court of Human Rights.
[24] J. Huizinga, *Homo Ludes, a Study of the Play Element in Culture* (London, Temple Smith, 1970), pp. 110–26.

own co-operation on a shared adherence to democratic principles from the start. With the collapse of communism there was no other large-scale ideological vision left in the political market place. Nonetheless, democratic triumphalism after the Cold War was unfortunate: it suggested that all that was necessary to secure a democratic world order was a commitment to solidarist principles, multi-party elections and an act of political will. There was a tendency to gloss over the very high price the Europeans had paid (and inflicted upon the rest of the world) in establishing their own version of the democratic peace.

It is also far from certain that the Western powers as a whole have abandoned the pluralist conception of international society which was the most lasting legacy of the Westphalian settlement. When Henry Adams was sent as ambassador to France, he failed to secure French agreement to create a revolutionary concert supported by a completely open transnational market. The French were more interested in negotiating, on the traditional basis of inter-governmental reciprocity, monopoly trading rights in and out of Boston harbour.[25] Two hundred years later, Margaret Thatcher and Francois Mitterand reacted angrily when the USA attempted to extend its jurisdiction extra-territorially in an unsuccessful attempt to prevent British and French participation in the construction of the Friendship gas pipe line from the Soviet Union to Western Europe.[26] Even amongst democratic allies, non-interference continued to be regarded as the essential aspect of sovereignty, in the context of international co-operation. Without it, governments would have no defence against more powerful states, acting outside agreed alliance objectives, when national interests were perceived to conflict.

These observations suggest that when the former UN Secretary General called for democracy within 'communities, within states and within the community of states', in the passage quoted earlier, he was talking of different, if overlapping, phenomena. 'Democracy within communities' presumably referred to entrenching fundamental human rights and providing for participation in local affairs on a non-discriminatory basis. 'Democracy within states' clearly referred to the constitutional arrangements under which the people freely choose their own government, and have a regular opportunity to replace them. 'Democracy within the community of states', on the other hand, is a more ambiguous phrase. Traditionally, it has meant respecting the sovereign equality of states, regardless of the relative power, except where by agreement certain states were given special rights and responsibilities, as in the Security Council with its permanent veto-wielding members. But, in the context of the discussion of self-determination in the *Agenda for Peace*, the implication is that democracy is to be treated as one of the fundamental, and hence defining, values of international society.

If the traditional interpretation is adopted then there is little, if anything, beyond exaltation, that can be done at the international level to bring about local or national democracy where it does not already exist. The equal rights of all members of the United Nations protect them from external interference in their domestic arrangements. If, on the other hand, self-determination is to be re-interpreted as democratic government within existing borders, as a

---

[25] F. Gilbert, 'The new diplomacy of the eighteenth century', *World Politics*, 4 (1951), 1–38.

[26] See D. Baldwin and H. Milner (eds), *East-West Trade and the Atlantic Alliance* (New York, St Martin's, 1990), chs 4, 7.

fundamental value of international society, we have to ask what the international community should do to promote democratization.

There are two possible courses of action, corresponding very broadly to the measures envisaged in chapters 6 and 7 of the UN Charter in the context of peaceful conflict resolution and enforcement. First, where requested, international organizations can and do provide technical assistance in facilitating the transition from military or authoritarian government to an open system. Such assistance is provided not only by the United Nations itself, but by regional organizations and by the Commonwealth. Secondly, where, the transition turns out to be a source of conflict rather than its solution as a result of ethnic or communal conflict, the international community may be drawn in militarily to protect the victims.

The first of these interventions is less problematic than the second. Re-training the judiciary in the habits of independence, introducing legislators to best practice in parliamentary procedure, drawing up electoral roles, monitoring elections and providing their outcome with a seal of approval, all this can be criticized for mistaking appearance for substance, or for allowing unscrupulous or opportunist leaders to repackage their regimes in order to cling onto power and win international approval; but it is difficult to believe that it does much harm and it may do some good. Shame and honour should not be lightly dismissed as the supports of a new democratic standard. Leaders may choose to flout values espoused by their peers, but they would usually prefer not to. Democratic culture may also have to develop indigenous roots, but in the meantime the need to meet certain minimal standards of good governance may purchase them some time in which to do so. And if it saves some relatively innocent people from persecution, torture or worse, in a non-ideal world, the exercise will surely have been worthwhile.

Military intervention, where there is no clear political objective, is another matter. In the series of so-called 'humanitarian interventions' in the early 1990s, there was a depressing tendency for the Security Council to will the end but not the means. But this failure to overcome the resource problem[27] disclosed a more fundamental indecisiveness about what to do in civil conflicts. This indecisiveness reached its climax in 1994 when the Security Council pointedly refused to invoke the Genocide Convention in relation to Rwanda, and reduced the size of the peacekeeping force at precisely the time when, in the view of the UN Commander on the ground, a stronger force could have checked the slaughter if not prevented it altogether.

It is true that the technical capacity of the United Nations to deal with complex emergencies has been greatly improved as a result of the experience of 1990s. A recent report by a high level group, commissioned by United Nations Association of the USA, has also made further recommendations on this score.[28] But – as its authors readily admit – capacity building, at the UN, or within regional organizations or elsewhere, can do little to address the underlying problem of political will, or more accurately its absence. The

---

[27] See J. Mayall (ed.), *The New Interventionism, United Nations Experience in Cambodia, Former Yugoslavia and Somalia, 1991–94* (Cambridge, Cambridge University Press, 1996), pp. 1–24.

[28] International Task Force on the enforcement of UN Security Council Resolutions, *Words to Deeds; Strengthening the UN's Enforcement Capabilities*, Final Report (United Nations Association of the United States of America, 1997).

international community has shown little inclination to establish a new system of trusteeships for collapsed states. Without state authority, how can the democratic right of self-determination within existing borders be protected, let alone the people secured against systematic human rights abuse? Judging by the Commonwealth's efforts to transform itself into an association of democratic states, and to persuade military regimes, such as those in power in Nigeria and Sierra Leone, to conduct elections and implement the Harare Declaration, there is no obvious answer.[29]

An international society reconstructed on the solidarist principles of respect for human rights and democratic government would come close to being a world empire achieved by consent, or in Kantian terms, a self-policing *Perpetual Peace*. A world of this kind would not need the apparatus of imperial rule. If a democratic world order cannot be brought about by military intervention, and if it cannot be upheld – even in extreme cases of anarchy – by imperial means, however benign their intent, what sanctions can or should be applied to bring delinquent states to their solidarist senses? This is a normative question posed by the prospect of internationally sponsored democratization.

The practical problems with imposing sanctions are well-known: they seldom achieve their stated primary objectives, they are difficult to police effectively and it is virtually impossible to achieve universality in the face of the strong national interest which some states will always have in breaking ranks in order to profit at others' expense. But beyond these familiar arguments, there is a more fundamental normative objection to using sanctions to bring about democratization. They only really make sense when a democracy already exists and therefore the target government can be assumed to be responsive to pressure from below, and, just as important, the population, along with the government, can be assumed to be guilty as charged.

By contrast, if the target is a tyrannical government, and the objective is to force it to recognize the human and democratic rights of its people, it will have no compunction in making them suffer. Indeed the tyrant may gain some legitimacy in their eyes, since his control of the media and flow of information, will allow him to throw the blame onto those who are imposing the sanctions and who appear to be impervious to the suffering of innocent women and children. Even when sanctions seem successful in helping to return a country to democracy, as in Haiti in 1994, they remain morally extremely dubious. In that case, they undoubtedly increased the level of suffering of the population, but were considered necessary as a prelude to the Security Council resolutions authorizing military intervention, which in turn helped to restore the legitimate and elected government to power.[30] It is difficult to square such actions with the Kantian injunction to treat people as ends in themselves and not merely as a means to some end, however desirable. As an international policy the promotion of democratization through coercive action, whether military intervention or sanctions, thus seems mired in contradiction.

[29] See J. Mayall, 'Democratising the Commonwealth', *International Affairs*, 74 (1998), 379–92.
[30] See D. Malone, Decision-Taking in the UN Security Council, 1990–96: The Case of Haiti (Oxford, Oxford University Press, 1999).

Indigenous Peoples and Minority Rights

In the contest between the solidarist and pluralist conceptions of international society, it seems that the pluralists still hold the ascendancy. This is a long way from saying that solidarist arguments have been driven from the field. It merely indicates that any expansion of international co-operation, beyond the law of coexistence and inter-state reciprocity, can only be achieved by consensus, and therefore, almost certainly, also incrementally. In these circumstances the attempt to reinterpret the right of all peoples to self-determination as democratic self-government has focused attention on minorities for the first time since 1945.

The reason is straightforward. To recapitulate the argument from the earlier sections of this paper: if many societies are, as a matter of observable and experienced fact, deeply divided, the transition to democracy will abort for the reasons so accurately foreseen by Mill.[31] Yet the creation of new states by secession or partition can rarely be achieved without unleashing ferocious conflict, and not often even then. Why this should be, is, ultimately, mysterious, but it seems to have something to do with the sacralization of territory under conditions of popular sovereignty. The case for accepting the new, non-statist, definition of self-determination is that there is no escape from the arbitrary and contingent nature of political boundaries. It follows that what is required is constitutional engineering to reassure minorities that they will not be discriminated against and that their interests and identities will be protected.

The first attempt to build a principle of minority protection into the constitution of international society foundered between the two World Wars. This was partly because it was not universally applied – and those countries whose membership of the League of Nations was dependent on their signing treaties guaranteeing minority rights understandably resented being treated differently than other states – and partly because, as Jennifer Jackson-Preece has noted, the principle was discredited after it was used by the Third Reich 'to justify the dismemberment of Czechoslovakia in 1938, the transfer of southern Slovakia and half of Transylvania to Hungary in 1940, and the creation of Slovak and Croat puppet states'.[32] After 1945 international concern for minorities was largely replaced by, and subsumed within, the Universal Declaration of Human Rights and its supporting covenants.

The second attempt, after the Cold War, was a significant if limited improvement. The 1992 UN Declaration on the Rights of Persons Belonging to National or Ethnic, Religious and Linguistic Minorities was proclaimed by the General Assembly and was, therefore, in principle applicable to all states. By adding to the rights stipulated in Article 27 of the International Covenant on Civil and Political Rights,[33] the right of minorities 'to participate in relevant national and regional decisions, to establish and maintain associations, and to have contact both within and across international frontiers', it also constituted

---

[31] See Malone, Decision-Taking in the UN Security Council, p. 487.

[32] J. Jackson-Preece, 'National minority rights v. state sovereignty in Europe: changing norms in international relations?' *Nations and Nationalism*, 3 (1997), p. 347

[33] Article 27 stipulated: 'In those states in which ethnic, religious or linguistic minorities exist, persons belonging to such minorities shall not be denied the right, in community with other members of their group, to enjoy their own culture, to profess and practice their own religion, or to use their own language.'

'a floor for international thinking on minority questions ... Other regional organizations – whether in Europe or indeed elsewhere – might agree on something better than this basic code ... but they could not go beneath it.'[34]

The improvement on earlier efforts to make minority protection an international norm is limited by the lack of enforcement measures.[35] And this weakness in turn reflects the determination of governments to give no encouragement to minority secession or irredentism. A close reading of this and similar texts suggests that any development of international society along solidarist lines, will only be entertained if it is explicitly balanced by prior commitment to maintain the pluralist compact.

In Europe, where the problem of reconciling national self-determination with minority protection first originated, considerable progress was achieved at the political level within the European Union, the Council of Europe and the OSCE. An impressive series of Declarations, Documents and Conventions was negotiated between 1990 and 1995. The OSCE also created the office of High Commissioner for National Minorities to monitor member states performance and to engage in preventative diplomacy. Significantly, however, although the High Commissioner is empowered to investigate any situation which he considers has a potential for conflict, and to make recommendations to governments based on his findings, once a conflict becomes violent, he is grounded. The reason, presumably, is that mediation in a violent civil conflict could be construed as equal recognition of the rights of the rebellious minority and the government.

While the 1993 Council of Europe's decision to draw up a Convention on National Minorities (which is open to all European states whether members of the Council or not) has been implemented, little progress has been made with their simultaneous decision to draw up a National Minorities Protocol to the European Convention on Human Rights. Two reasons are probably responsible for the reluctance of governments to pursue this initiative. The first is an intellectual difference over the nature of the minority problem and hence the appropriate legal instrument to overcome it. For those who believe that minority problems arise from discrimination by the majority, protection of individual rights, usually by entrenching them in the constitution, and the use of the law to prevent discrimination, is the necessary but also sufficient response. On the other hand, there are minorities who do not merely wish to be protected against discrimination but see the essence of the problem in their need to have their own cultural distinctiveness protected, and indeed bolstered by the State. They want not merely individual but group rights and entitlements. Secondly, attaching a protocol to the European Convention of Human Rights would de-politicize an issue over which governments are currently determined to retain control, regardless of which side they take in the philosophical dispute. Unless there was to be a public international agreement to re-interpret the right of all peoples to self-determination as a right to democratic self-government – an outcome which seems improbable at the present time – governments will continue to see the spectre of secession and irredentism in any attempt to make minority claims justiciable.

[34] Jackson-Preece, 'National minority rights', p. 349.
[35] 'Article 9 [of the 1992 Declaration] merely indicated that the UN system as a whole was expected to contribute to the fulfillment of the minority provisions', p. 360.

Paradoxically, it is because the organizations representing indigenous peoples have been careful to avoid offending official sensitivities on this score, that they have had more success in establishing self-determination as one of their human rights. The definition of an indigenous people is ultimately no more straightforward than the definition of a minority, and for much the same reasons. Neither have been authoritatively defined, but representatives of indigenous peoples insist that they are not minorities and are, in any case, nowhere in a position, numerically or politically, to demand external sovereignty.

On the other hand they have succeeded in having their special status recognized by the international community. The international Labour Organizations' Convention 169 referred to 'their rights to "ownership and possession" of the "total environment" that they occupy or use, as well as their rights to be protected from environmental degradation, involuntary removal and unwanted intrusion by outsiders'.[36] In 1992, the Rio Declaration on Environment and Development recognized 'indigenous peoples as distinct social partners in achieving sustainable development' and called on states 'to recognize and duly support their identity, culture and interests and to enable their effective participation'[37] towards this end.

These developments fell short of public acknowledgement of their right to self-determination as distinct 'peoples' – the Charter formula – rather than people requiring special treatment. This issue proved controversial at the UN World Conference on Human Rights held in Vienna in June 1993, for reasons which echo the problems of defining and entrenching minority rights. Nor have these problems been finally resolved. However, Article 3 of the 1993 Draft Declaration on the Rights of Indigenous Peoples is unequivocal:

> Indigenous peoples have the right of self-determination. By virtue of that right they freely determine their political status and freely pursue their economic, social and cultural development.[38]

On the assumption that the Declaration is eventually adopted by the General Assembly, it will still not be binding on states, although it will arguably become part of the corpus of 'soft international law' and will contribute to the process of international standard setting. Moreover, even if it is not adopted in its present form, it seems clear that indigenous peoples have asserted their rights of independent access to international forums, and to that extent have successfully challenged the state's monopoly on sovereignty. It is ironic, but apparently the case, that, outside the European Union, which uniquely straddles constitutional and diplomatic norms and arrangements, it is the world's most vulnerable peoples who have succeeded in keeping alive the solidarist conception of a wider international society in an otherwise pluralist age. By avoiding the quagmire of definition, the representatives of indigenous peoples made significant political gains. But three aspects of their campaign suggest that the battle is far from over.

First, it is no accident that the campaign was initiated by indigenous groups in North America and other countries of European settlement. Many of these

---

[36] Quoted in R. L. Barsh, 'Indigenous peoples in the 1990s: from object to subject of international law', *Harvard Human Rights Journal*, 7 (1994), 44–5.

[37] Barsh, 'Indigenous peoples', p. 46.

[38] UN.Doc.E/CN.4/Sub.2/1993/3/26(1993).

groups ceded sovereignty to their conquerors under treaties which, theoretically, guaranteed them in the ownership of their lands and the rights to maintain their traditional customs and institutions. Such treaties were notoriously more often honoured in the breach than in the observance, but their existence meant that once a Western-educated elite emerged, well-versed in the political theory of both property rights and self-determination, they were well-placed also to press their claims in the appropriate political idiom and on the basis of pre-existing title.

In practice, these claims were usually for compensation in respect of the requisition of land, but it was a short step to the demand for political recognition. At the first meeting of the UN Working Group in 1982 the representative of the Micmaq Nation was quick to expose a fundamental weakness in the conventional interpretation of self-determination as de-colonization:

> We must be careful not to apply the principle of self-determination to the wrong people in a colonial situation. It is not de-colonization but a cruel deception, when self-determination in a colonized country is considered the exclusive prerogative of the colonists.[39]

Secondly, there continues to be strong resistance from India and other Asian countries to the proposition that tribal peoples in their countries – the most numerous group of indigenous peoples worldwide – are covered by the term. As Edward Keene has convincingly shown there is a long-standing, if contested, European tradition of resolving the tensions that inevitably arise between civil society (with its roots in the institution of private property) and the state by dividing sovereignty.[40] It was perhaps this tradition that lay behind the British imperial practice of indirect rule and their willingness – as in Buganda or Barotseland – to countenance the idea of a protected state within a colony. In practice a state within a state is what the majority of indigenous self-determination claims amount to. They may, indeed, be intractable problems in meeting these demands, but if they are overcome, there are no insuperable theoretical or constitutional obstacles to constitutional experimentation of this kind within Western political traditions.

There is no reason to believe that the west has a monopoly of constitutional wisdom. All the same, it was sovereignty, in the monarchical and Hobbesian sense of final and exclusive authority, rather than democratic power sharing or division, which proved the most successful Western export to the rest of the world during the age of imperialism. Consequently, it is in Asia that solidarist arguments for eroding state sovereignty and territorial integrity are viewed with most suspicion. The same would, no doubt, be true of Africa, if the near collapse of so many states had not dramatically reduced their voice in international affairs. Certainly, even before the 1994 genocide, it would have been hard to conceive of the Tutsi in Rwanda or Burundi, conceding any special rights to the Hutu majority on the grounds that they were notionally the aboriginal population.

This fanciful hypothesis throws light on a final confusing aspect of the campaign to re-cast self-determination as internal self-government. Despite the

---

[39] Quoted in Barsh, 'Indigenous Peoples', p. 36.
[40] E. Keene, The Colonising Ethnic and Modern International Society: A Reconstruction of the Grotian Taradition of International Society (University of London, Ph.D., 1998).

political importance of treating minority rights and the rights of indigenous peoples as separate, it is clear that in practice indigenous peoples are thought of as minorities. But they are also identified by their distinct and pre-modern way of life, which has survived despite its inevitable penetration and erosion by a myriad of modern influences from contract labour to gambling casinos. The Hutu are disqualified by their majority status and because, despite the persistence of racial stereotypes, their way of life is indistinguishable from the minority Tutsi, many of whom were their neighbours, at the time of the genocide.

It will take more than constitutional engineering to solve the crisis between these two communities. It will need a gigantic transformation in their consciousness and self-identity. Indeed, there is a case for saying that it was premature, in the sense of ill-prepared, plans for power-sharing that triggered the genocide in 1994. But even where an indigenous population retains a distinct identity and culture from later immigrants with whom it shares the country and whose numbers are roughly equivalent, it is not clear that the principle of primordial title will be easy to square with the new conventional interpretation of self-determination as democratic self-government.

When indigenous Fijians staged a coup against the elected (Indian-dominated government) in 1987, their membership of the United Nations was not affected. Because, at that time the Government of India was prominent in the anti-apartheid campaign within the Commonwealth, they were forced out of that organization. A decade later – after much regional and Commonwealth diplomacy – they returned following the negotiation of a new constitution which aimed to reconcile their rights with those of the population as a whole.[41] This episode can be read two ways – either as symptomatic of a general trend towards defining the nation in civic terms and protecting ethnic and communal identities by constitutional means, thus in effect diluting the external sovereignty of the state, or, as the result of a unique conjunction of events and pressures from which it is impossible to draw any generally applicable lessons.

Virtual Sovereignty and Pre-existing Title

Time will show which of these readings is correct. In the meantime, the recent history of Fiji – as of many other countries that have been racked by civil conflict – suggests that the concepts of sovereignty and self-determination are as contested at the end of the twentieth century as they were at the beginning. Yet, the view persists that because it cannot be shown to have an unambiguous meaning in contemporary politics, the concept of sovereignty itself is an anachronism. Let us conclude, therefore, by returning to the claim advanced by Professor Falk and others that sovereignty is no longer relevant for the analysis of world politics. The charge is an old one, reflecting, in the final analysis, the tension between authority and power. The two concepts are clearly not synonymous, but whether it is possible to possess one without the other, and if so, for how long, is a moot point.

There are strong and weak versions of the attack on sovereignty. Those who reject the concept altogether claim that the state has forfeited its traditional and

---

[41] For background on recent constitutional developments in Fiji, see R. Alley, 'Fiji at the crossroads?'. *The Round Table*, 342, (1977), 245–56.

central role in international politics, becoming just one actor – and not often the most important – amongst many. In the weak version, it is argued, more plausibly, that the state has surrendered some of its attributes – for example its ownership and control of a national economy – but has retained others – for example its responsibility for the welfare of its citizens. On this view, the state does not lose its sovereignty, it merely has to adjust to a rapidly changing international environment, if it is to perform its essential functions.

The state has not withered away but its competence has certainly narrowed, in particular in the face of the globalization of the economy. To this extent it may be that the shift from the emphasis on empirical to juridical statehood within international society now has a wider application than when Jackson developed it in relation to post-colonial states.[42] But, the international legal order is still invoked to buttress the authority of the state, arguably to compensate for its dwindling capacity, but not to replace it. In the 1960s, the European imperial powers gave up any attempt to make economic viability a condition of independence – it was sufficient to be a colony with borders drawn by the imperial powers.

The world of virtual sovereignty differs from that of juridical sovereignty in so far as the requirement of empirical independence is increasingly being dropped for states generally and not just for post-colonial states. To this extent Professor Falk and other critics of sovereignty maybe right. Where they are wrong is to assume that its use serves no real purpose. Yet, just as the first iron-builders adapted the existing and familiar technology – building bridges with iron rather than wooden mortise and tenon joints – so the new world of global marketplace is being constructed by adapting rather than abandoning familiar concepts. Indeed as territorial borders become more easily penetrated by transnational economic flows and other forces, territory itself appears paradoxically to have become if anything more rather than less sacred. This is primarily, no doubt, because it is held to belong to the people. It is difficult to imagine a present day equivalent to the Louisiana purchase or the deal by which Alaska was transferred to American sovereignty. Modern Government, to paraphrase Burke, has been given over to 'sophists, calculators and economists', but the territory over which they preside – and the popular emotions that are identified with it – remains stubbornly beyond their control. In this context, pre-existing title is a major asset, if not in every case a prerequisite, for entry into international society.

Here again there seems to be as much continuity as change. In the 1970s, India allowed Bhutan to enter the United Nations, despite retaining *un droit de regard* over its foreign policy, in recognition of historic title, a concession which was not extended to Sikkim, which had been more fully integrated into British India. In the early 1990s, as the Soviet Empire disintegrated into its constituent parts, two west European micro states – Andorra and San Marino – whose international personality had previously been expressed largely through their postage stamps, slipped into the United Nations almost unnoticed.

In the post-Cold War world there are both economic and political reasons for making such adjustments in the membership of international society. Globalization has reduced the plausibility of List's ideal of national political

---

[42] R. Jackson, *Quasi-states: Sovereignty, International Relations and the Third World* (Cambridge, Cambridge University Press, 1990), pp. 18–21.

economy,[43] but not the appeal of national political autonomy. It is noticeable, for example, that amongst the resurgent nationalist parties in Eastern Europe and the former Soviet Union, there are few advocates of national protection, let alone autarky. Rather, self-determination is more likely to be interpreted as the right to compete in the deregulated market for inward investment. In contrast, in Western Europe, where the European Union has created a regulatory framework beyond the state but between it and the world market, there has been a resurgence of nationalism in state-less regions which nonetheless have a historic political identity. Those who speak for such regions, from Catalonia to Scotland, often see positive advantages to being directly represented in Brussels rather than, or in addition to, state capitals. By the same token, the existence of the European Union may allow national governments to be more flexible and accommodating in dealing with internal demands for devolution or decentralization in the name of self-determination.

There are obvious dangers in assuming that Western Europe is a model for other parts of the world, where the state has evolved from different antecedent conditions and along different trajectories. On the other hand if, as Millwood has argued,[44] the European community should be understood not as a proto European state but as a mechanism created by the States themselves to ensure their survival, there is no reason why sovereign authorities in other continents should not prove equally resourceful and inventive.

---

[43] F. List, *The National System of Political Economy*, S. S. Lloyd (trans.), (New York, Longmans Green, 1904).

[44] A. S. Millwood, with the assistance of G. Brennan and F. Romero, *The European Rescue of the Nation State* (London, Routledge, 1992).

The Sharing of Sovereignty:
the European Paradox

WILLIAM WALLACE

No government in Europe remains sovereign in the sense understood by diplomats or constitutional lawyers of half a century ago. Within the 15-member EU mutual interference in each other's domestic affairs has become a long-accepted practice. Its extra-territorial jurisdiction extends across Norway, Switzerland and Iceland, states which recognize the supremacy of EU rules as an unavoidable consequence of their dependence on open access to its economic and social space. West European security is managed through NATO, an integrated alliance with joint commands, a (small) common budget and a number of multinational units. European security is managed through the Organization for Security and Cooperation in Europe, whose rules requiring 'transparency' in military forces and deployments are reinforced by the intrusive inspection procedures agreed under the Conventional Forces in Europe Treaty.

The legitimate units within these institutions remain states. Representatives of Luxembourg and Denmark take their place round the table in NATO ministerial meetings, in EU Councils, and in the extensive network of committees through which these and other European institutions operate; representatives of Scotland and Bavaria do not. Yet the interaction of these thousands of representatives, engaged in multiple continuous negotiations, information exchange, coalition-building, informal trade-offs among like-minded officials and ministers in different governments, is of an entirely different quality from the monolithic external sovereignty of the nineteenth century European state. Ministers' diaries are filled with multilateral meetings, and with rounds of bilateral consultations to prepare for them. Officials from every major department within national governments travel abroad, up to 2–3 days a week, to sit together in committees and to consult informally.[1] Military and police officers, customs and immigration officials train together and work together. To a remarkable degree, the processes of government in Europe overlap and interlock: among different states, between different levels of governance below and above the old locus of sovereignty in the nation-state.[2]

States, furthermore, are not the only significant actors within these institutions. The secretariats and parliamentary assemblies of NATO and WEU play

---

[1] W. Wessels, 'An ever-closer fusion? A dynamic macropolitical view on integration processes', *Journal of Common Market Studies* (1997), 267–299.

[2] Fritz Scharpf's article, 'The joint decision-trap: lessons from German federalism and European integration', *Public Administration* (Autumn 1988), 239–76, provides the classic statement of this interlocking – and – 'interblocking' – pattern of governance.

only auxiliary roles in moderating relations among governments – though the status and influence of the NATO Secretary-General, who chairs the NATO Council as well as its Defence Planning and Nuclear Planning Committees, should not be underestimated.[3] The Council of Europe's Commission, and Court, of Human Rights hear cases from individual citizens, and may overrule the decisions of member governments and national courts. Within the EU, however, states in the Council of Ministers (if the different representatives of competing national ministries, often operating in transgovernmental coalitions, can be described as representing the coherent interests of states) work alongside an autonomous European Commission and a directly-elected European Parliament, with a European Court of Justice interpreting Community law. Ministers, and members both of the European Parliament and of national parliaments, work also through the trans-national networks of European party federations; operating as informal caucuses before major Council meetings, providing a framework for coalition-building and for mutual support in domestic political campaigns.[4] Trans-national lobbies, of industrialists, farmers, environmentalists, universities, maintain offices in Brussels so that their members can press their case both at the national and at the Community level.[5]

Paradoxically, the governments of former socialist states in central and eastern Europe have celebrated their regained sovereignty by declaring their determination to join all these sovereignty-constraining West European institutions. They already submit to the scrutiny which the Council of Europe and the Organization for Security and Cooperation in Europe impose on human rights and democratic standards within member states. The eleven states accepted as applicants to the EU have struggled to fulfil the preconditions imposed, completing in 1996 a vast questionnaire from the EC Commission which probed national legal and administrative practices, financial and economic institutions, social and budgetary policies; after which the Commission assessed their suitability for early accession to membership in a series of 'Opinions' published in July 1997.[6] They sit as associates alongside the members of the Western European Union in the 'WEU Forum', and alongside NATO members in the Euro-Atlantic Partnership Council; accepting NATO standards as the criteria against which their armed forces must be judged, with training missions from NATO member states to help their forces reach them.

In terms of the criteria for sovereignty which Alan James sets out in his companion article, European states thus present a deeply ambiguous picture. The distinction between states which have an international capacity and those which do not remains clearly drawn, though the Westphalian principle of sovereign equality has given way within the EU to differential representation

---

[3] There is unfortunately no recent study of the role and influence of the NATO Secretariat as an institution. Recent NATO Secretary-Generals have been drawn from the ranks of foreign and defence ministers within member states.

[4] J. Gaffney (ed.), *Political Parties and the European Community* (London, Routledge, 1996); S. Hix and C. Lord, *Political Parties in the European Union* (London, Macmillan, 1997).

[5] S. Mazey and J. Richardson, *Lobbying in the European Community* (Oxford, Oxford University Press, 1993); J. Greenwood *et al.*, *Organized Interests in the European Community* (London, Sage, 1992).

[6] *Bulletin of the EC*, Supplement 5–15, 1997. For the evolution of the EU's negotiations with these states from 1989 to 1995, see U. Sedelmeier and H. Wallace, 'Policies Towards Central and Eastern Europe', in H. Wallace and W. Wallace (eds), *Policy-making in the European Union* (Oxford, Oxford University Press, 1996), ch. 14.

and weighted voting in a significant number of areas.[7] National territory remains clearly defined, though border posts and border guards – those symbols of the nineteenth century European state – are vanishing from the EU's internal frontiers. The people of Western Europe act in their daily lives as citizens of separate states; though for some purposes they now have rights as 'European citizens', including the right to vote in local and European elections when resident in another member state. Government remains primarily national, though significant aspects of governance now operate above (and below) the nation-state level. In the last resort, the principle of constitutional independence could still be reasserted through withdrawal from any or all of these European institutions. But it is striking that no member state has withdrawn from any; the costs of withdrawal, in terms of lost status and influence within the European order as well as lost economic advantages, would be very high.[8]

European states, it can be argued, are recognized by their neighbours as full participants in Europe's international order through acceptance into membership, or association and potential membership, of European institutions. Marginal examples illustrate this point. Successive governments of Turkey, a NATO member for 45 years, have insisted that any relation with the European Union short of the clear promise of membership represents explicit exclusion from 'Europe'. Swiss governments in the 1990s have balanced unhappily between their citizens' unwillingness to accept European institutional constraints and their own awareness that Swiss interests (and prestige) are damaged by their self-exclusion, leaving them to bargain over European rules and regulations from a position of weakness. Russia and Ukraine, on the edge of the developing post-Cold War European order, have both signed formal agreements with NATO, and Trade and Cooperation Agreements with the EU.

Over the past fifty years, as the Westphalian principles of sovereign statehood have spread from Europe across the former territories of European empires, European states have thus been moving towards a new interpretation of statehood. The nature of that re-interpretation remains both unclear and contested. Post-Cold War NATO has wavered between American hegemony and Atlantic partnership, committed in principle to a 'European Security and

---

[7] Sovereign equality was breached within the ECSC and EEC Treaties by the allocation of two Commissioners to large states and one to small; the move to qualified majority voting breaches sovereignty principles further. The distinction between states with international capacity and those without is blurred in the case of Europe's several micro-states. The Vatican, Liechtenstein, Andorra and San Marino have been accepted as members of the Council of Europe. Liechtenstein succeeded in 1995 in raising its status within the European Free Trade Area from associate to full member, but only after three of EFTA's six member states had joined the EU. Monaco, which James describes as sovereign, is not even a member of the Council of Europe. Luxembourg, with 400,000 citizens, is tolerated as an anomaly within the EU. The prospect of similarly-sized Malta applying for membership however provoked a debate about the limits of sovereign equality which abated only when the new Maltese government froze its application in 1996.

[8] The French Government withdrew from NATO's integrated military structure in 1966, without however withdrawing from the political framework of the alliance. It is an open secret that many within the French military and Ministry of Defence have wished to rejoin since the mid-1980's; moves towards rejoining, in 1995–6, however broke down over the reallocation of NATO commands. Greenland and the Faroe Islands have formally withdrawn from the EU; but both of these constitute territories under the Danish crown. Greek and Turkish membership of the Council of Europe was suspended during periods of authoritarian government, but neither withdrew; their democratic successor regimes regained full membership.

Defence Identity' which all member governments hesitate to pursue. The European Union held three 'Inter-governmental Conferences' between 1985 and 1997: revising its constitutional treaties, transforming itself from a 'Community' to a 'Union', reforming its procedures and expanding its policy competences. The 1997 Treaty of Amsterdam nevertheless left many constitutional questions unresolved, putting off to another 'conference of members of governments of the Member States' the 'comprehensive review of the provisions of the Treaties on the composition and functioning of the institutions' needed to cope with further enlargement from 15 members to 20 and beyond.[9]

West European governments have sought since they rebuilt state structures in the aftermath of the disasters of the Second World War to strike a careful balance between regained sovereignty and shared prosperity and security. 'The tension between the nation state and international integration', I wrote in the immediate aftermath of the Maastricht Inter-Governmental Conference (IGC) of 1991, 'is central to any discussion of the development of the European political system since the Second World War'.[10] Since then the outlines of the post-Cold War European system have become clearer. Multilateral institutions and conferences have proliferated further, while established institutions are expanding. The interpenetration of national administrations has extended, most markedly in matters of police, justice and 'interior' affairs.[11] The signature of the Treaty of Amsterdam has posed a fresh challenge for EU governments of how to persuade their reluctant electorates to pool further elements of domestic sovereignty with their neighbours.

Sovereignty has not been transferred to a state-like federation, as enthusiasts for a United States of Europe hoped for in the years after the Second World War. But sovereignty is increasingly held in common: pooled among governments, negotiated by thousands of officials through hundreds of multilateral committees, compromised through acceptance of regulations and court judgements which operate on the principle of mutual interference in each other's domestic affairs. In many of the central responsibilities of national government, European states can do little without the acquiescence and approval of their neighbours. It is an inherently untidy and inefficient system, built on sustaining the illusion that governments can themselves provide their voters with benefits – security, prosperity, regulation of economic and social interchange – which can in practice be won only through common action with others. In that sense the European political system after the Cold War is postmodern: resting upon a shared discourse which the participants prefer to understand from different perspectives, and which they interpret in different ways to different audiences.

---

[9] Protocol on the Institutions with the prospect of enlargement of the European Union, *Treaty of Amsterdam* (London, HMSO, Cm 3780, October 1997).

[10] W. Wallace, 'Rescue or retreat? The nation state in Western Europe, 1945–1993', *Political Studies*, special issue on 'Contemporary Crisis of the Nation State?' 42 (1994), p. 52.

[11] Figures on the rise in British government involvement in multilateral cooperation in the 1990s are given in *Dealing with the Third Pillar: the Government's Perspective*, 15th Report of the House of Lords Select Committee on the European Communities, Session 1997–8 (London, HMSO, HL 73, February 1998).

The Transformation of Western Europe

The West European state system was rebuilt after the Second World War on the basis of compromised sovereignty: compromised both by the conditions the American Administration attached to Marshall Plan aid and to the provision of security through the Atlantic Alliance, and by the closer institutional integration through which a semi-sovereign (West) Germany was accepted back into the regional system. Within this dual framework of Atlantic and West European institutions, West European states rebuilt their national legitimacy and identity through the provision of stable government, welfare and prosperity to their citizens.

Several competing narratives have been developed to explain this development. Enthusiasts for European integration described an almost Manichaean struggle between those committed to moving beyond the nation state towards a European federation and the benighted defenders of nationalism and sovereignty.[12] Realists emphasized the centrality of the United States, in imposing order and thus removing the threat of mutual insecurity from Germany and its neighbours.[13] Revisionist historians have traced the ambiguity of commitment to integration within even the most 'enthusiastic' governments, seeking to use the economic benefits which integration provided to support national reconstruction and so to 'rescue . . . the nation state'.[14]

The reconstruction of Western Europe between 1945 and 1970 allowed for the parallel development of common institutions and rules and of recovered sovereignty and legitimacy. American theorists were later to label this delicate balance between incompatible objectives 'the supranational compromise': the creation of a new level of administrative governance, leaving national governments with all the symbols of sovereignty – and with most but not all of the substance.[15] The European Economic Community, despite the federalist hopes of the first Commission President, exercised supranational legal competences over only a small and carefully-limited field of international economic relations.[16] The Americans would have liked to push their European allies further, into a European Defence Community within which a rearmed Germany could safely be contained. After the collapse of the EDC proposals in 1954, however, security and foreign policy integration was pursued through NATO, with the WEU a weak European grouping within this Atlantic framework.

---

[12] R. Mayne, *The Community of Europe* (New York, Norton, 1962); W. Lipgens, *A History of European Integration, 1945–47: The Formation of the European Unity Movement* (Oxford, Oxford University Press, 1982). J-B. Duroselle, *Europe: a History of its Peoples* (London, Viking, 1990) extends this narrative back into the distant past.

[13] J. Joffe, 'Europe's American pacifier', *Foreign Policy* (Spring 1984), 64–92. G. Lundestad, *'Empire' by Integration: the United States and European Integration, 1945–1997* (Oxford, Oxford University Press, 1998) provides as excellent survey of recent research on the US role.

[14] A. Milward, *The European Rescue of the Nation-State* (London, Routledge, 1992).

[15] L. Lindberg and S. Scheingold, *Europe's would-be Polity* (Englewood Cliffs NJ, Prentice Hall, 1970), p. 16.

[16] W. Loth, W. Wallace and W. Wessels, eds., *Walter Hallstein: the forgotten European?*, (London, Macmillan, 1998). The EEC at its formation in 1958 was one of three Communities, with the European Steel and Coal Community (launched in 1950) and Euratom. A merger treaty of 1965 combined these into 'the European Communities', which became by common usage in the 1970s the European Community (EC). The Maastricht Treaty of 1992 brought this together with the inter-governmental mechanisms for cooperation in foreign policy and in justice and home affairs into a three-pillar European Union (EU). Usage in the text corresponds to usage during the period referred to.

The problem of Germany was central to the construction of this compromised-sovereignty order. The balance of power principles on which the Westphalian order was built depended upon the fragmentation of the German lands of the Holy Roman Empire; French, Dutch and Swedish negotiators in 1648 were determined to entrench this.[17] The unification in 1871 of Europe's geographically central power, with its largest population (west of Russia) and strongest economy, created an imbalance unresolved by two continent-wide wars. The post-1945 European international order was built upon the division of Germany, and on the dual hegemony of the USA and USSR over the divided state and continent. Even within US-led Western Europe, Germany's neighbours were only persuaded to accept the economic and political rehabilitation of this shrunken federal state by constraining it, with them, within sovereignty-limiting institutions: an integrated NATO structure, a WEU with specific limitations on German arms production, and Communities to integrate coal and steel, atomic energy, and industrial and agricultural markets. The reunification of Germany in 1990 made integration even more vital to European stability, the problem of imbalance even more acute. The withdrawal of Russia, and the partial withdrawal of the USA, left Poland and the Czech Republic with interests as strong as France and the Netherlands to embrace Germany in order not to have to confront Germany.

President de Gaulle's defiance of American security leadership, and his challenge to the integrationist hopes of the European Commission in the Luxembourg crisis of 1965–6, appeared to reassert the sovereign intransigence of the French state. Its plausibility however depended on the continued integration of West Germany within the twin frameworks of the Atlantic Alliance and the EEC. American security provision and German compliance with external constraints allowed the French government to free-ride on the security provided, and to seek to harness German economic resources to French political ends through the integrated structures of the EEC.

No sooner had de Gaulle's block on further formal integration been removed by his resignation than a succession of external shocks – the impact on the world economy of US involvement in Vietnam, the suspension of dollar convertibility, sharp rises in oil and raw material prices – brought to an end the benign conditions of steady economic growth on which the supranational compromise had floated. Under conditions of recession, member governments retreated into zero-sum arguments about costs and benefits. The ambitious plan to move on from the achievement of a common market to full economic and monetary union by 1980 collapsed as European currencies moved apart. The period between 1966 and 1985 appeared from across the Atlantic, in Stanley Hoffmann's famous phrase, as the 'dark ages' of European integration, between the bright dawn of the early 1960s and the revival marked by the Single European Act and the 1992 Programme.[18]

Yet paradoxically this period saw some remarkable developments in the sharing of sovereignty and in the extension of shared policy-making, largely outside the supranational framework of the EC. The wavering of the American commitment to provide substantial ground forces in central Europe sparked

---

[17] This perspective on the Treaty of Westphalia is clearly presented in the permanent exhibition in the Munster City Museum.

[18] S. Hoffmann, 'The European Community and 1992', *Foreign Affairs*, 68 (1989), 27–47.

closer cooperation in defence among West European governments: first with the Eurogroup, launched on the initiative of the British and German governments in 1969, later with a number of bilateral and multilateral arrangements for joint forces, from the Dutch-British Marine Amphibious Force to the Standing Naval Force Channel.[19] In 1982 the French and Germans relaunched the project for defence integration which de Gaulle had unsuccessfully floated in 1963, and in the following year on British initiative a new effort was made to build European military cooperation through the Western European Union.[20]

The launch of 'European Political Cooperation' at the 1969 Hague summit, alongside the commitment to economic and monetary union by 1980, was a half-thought-through compromise between Gaullist French pursuit of an inter-governmental European Political Union and the efforts of other EC members to hold to the division between foreign policy and security issues, coordinated through NATO, and economic interests shared through the supranational framework of the EC. It rapidly proved a convenient vehicle through which West European governments could coordinate their approach to the Conference on Security and Cooperation in Europe – and through which the West German government could ensure multilateral support for the delicate diplomacy of its Ostpolitik. Cooperation among the nine foreign ministries in the EC mushroomed during the 1970s, extending out from the Helsinki process to cover the Middle East, southern Africa, central America and south-east Asia. Little was achieved in moving towards common policies, in the face of determinedly different assumptions within national political and media elites. But the working practices of national officials – diplomats – were transformed. Networks of committees were established, direct secure communications links set up, cooperation among embassies in third countries and among delegations to international organizations developed.[21]

Discreetly, with parliaments or publics entirely unaware and uninformed, the 1970s also saw the development of closer cooperation among European governments in some of the most central and sensitive aspects of domestic sovereignty: policing, border controls, intelligence, even judicial cooperation. *Groupe Pompidou* was launched in 1971, under the auspices of the 19-member Council of Europe, as a framework for cooperation in combatting the international trade in drugs. The *Trevi* group was initiated in 1975, within the framework of European Political Cooperation, to strengthen cooperation among European governments in grappling with the growing problem of trans-national terrorism. Other *ad hoc* groups, on immigration, asylum and refugees, and customs, followed. The five-country Schengen Agreement of 1985, and the 1990 Schengen 'Implementing Convention', moved a further crucial step forward by committing its members to the abolition of internal border controls

---

[19] William Wallace, 'European Security: Bilateral Steps to Multilateral Cooperation', in Yves Boyer *et al.* (eds), *Franco-British Defence Cooperation: a New Entente Cordiale* (London, Routledge, 1989), ch. 15.

[20] R. Rummel and P. Schmidt, 'The Changing Security Framework', in W. Wallace (ed.), *The Dynamics of European Integration* (London, Pinter 1990), ch. 15; W. Wallace, 'European defence cooperation: the reopening debate', *Survival*, 26 (1984), 251–61.

[21] P. de Schoutheete, *La Cooperation Politique Européene* (Brussels, Labor, 1986); S. Nuttall, *European Political Cooperation* (Oxford, Oxford University Press, 1992); T. Garton Ash, *In Europe's Name: Germany and the Divided Continent* (London, Cape, 1993).

and their replacement by common rules and procedures.[22] It was not until the 1991 Maastricht Treaty of European Union and the 1997 Treaty of Amsterdam that much of this by-then extensive network of trans-governmental cooperation was brought within the integrated structures of Community law and regulation; though the Maastricht Treaty on European Union regularized these *ad hoc* procedures into a 'Third Pillar' alongside the Community itself and the 'Second Pillar' of foreign and security policy, giving them only slightly greater visibility and political respectability.

The European Community itself was increasingly preoccupied during this period of economic adjustment and slow growth with the attempted management of surplus capacity and the policing of national subsidies. Community competition policy extended its scope, against strong opposition from a number of governments. The perceived costs of unstable currencies within an increasingly-integrated regional economy led to the establishment of the European Monetary System in 1979. The UK Government dropped out of the negotiations at an early stage, largely on the grounds that such a collaborative arrangement would limit its economic sovereignty, leaving France, Germany and their immediate neighbours to move ahead. The 'revival' of formal economic integration represented by the Single European Act and the 1992 Programme in the mid-1980s did not therefore come out of the blue; it followed from increasing frustration, among governments and private actors, at the difficulties of agreeing necessary rules among European governments – and from rising insistence that such shared regulations were needed.[23]

The most radical infringement of the accepted concept of sovereignty which developed in these years was however the effective establishment of the supremacy of Community law. Case by case, the European Court of Justice extended its interpretation of the Treaties; and national courts accepted and implemented its judgements, even against their own national administrations. As the Court had declared in its landmark 'Costa versus ENEL' judgement of 1964:

> By creating a Community of unlimited duration, having its own institutions, its own personality, its own legal capacity and capacity of representation on the international plane and more particularly, real powers stemming from a limitation of sovereignty or a transfer of powers from the States to the Community, *the Member States have limited their sovereign rights, albeit in limited fields ... the Treaty carries with it a permanent limitation of their sovereign rights* ...[24]

By the 1980s, the European Community was operating with an effectively federal system of law.[25] The Treaties had thus become constitutional

---

[22] Three of the five signatories, Belgium, Luxembourg and the Netherlands, already constituted a common travel area; the Schengen Agreement extended this to France and Germany.

[23] D. Allen, 'Managing the Common Market: The Community's Competition Policy', and M. Hodges, 'Industrial Policy: Hard Times or Great Expectations?', in H. Wallace *et al.* (eds), *Policy-making in the European Community* (Chichester, Wiley, 1983), chs 7 and 9; R. Tooze and S. Strange (eds), *The International Politics of Surplus Capacity: Competition for Market Shares in the World Recession* (London, George Allen & Unwin, 1981).

[24] Case 6/64, *European Court Reports*, 1964, p. 585 (italics added).

[25] E. Stein, 'Lawyers, judges, and the making of a trans-national constitution', *American Journal of International Law*, 75 (1981), 1–27; F. Mancini, 'The making of a constitution for Europe', *Common Market Law Review*, 26 (1989), 595–614; R. Dehousse and J. Weiler, 'The Legal Dimension', in W. Wallace, *Dynamics of European Integration*.

documents, subject to negotiated revision through inter-governmental conferences. The Council of Europe, WEU, NATO, the looser CSCE, all remained
recognizably international institutions. The European Community, however,
was something else: less than a federation, certainly, but much more than an
institutional intergovernmental regime.[26]

What were the underlying dynamics which pushed West European governments into sharing previously sovereign powers over policy in the 1970s and
1980s? The integrationist narrative of European international politics has
focused on the arrival of another strong Commission President, Jacques Delors,
as a major factor in the revival of regional integration in Europe.[27] But this fails
to explain why so much intergovernmental cooperation had developed in the ten
years *before* M. Delors took office in 1985, and why so much of the practice of
shared sovereignty after 1985 continued to be managed through intergovernmental mechanisms beyond the competences of the EC and its Commission.
Changes in Europe's external environment provide a partial explanation.
Increasing concern for European 'competitiveness' in responding to Japanese
advances in high technology and successes in capturing 'key' European markets
was a contributory factor in building the coalition of public and private actors
which led to the 1992 Programme.[28] Loss of confidence in American political
leadership at the end of the 1970s, in particular in Germany and Britain, fuelled
the further developments in European Political Cooperation which led to the
London Report, the Genscher-Colombo Plan and the closer association of EPC
with the EC through the Single European Act.[29]

It was the transformation of Europe's economy and society between 1965 and
1985, however, which generated many of the pressures to which governments
responded. Economic recession in the 1970s also marked a period of economic
adjustment: in which international companies moved from national to transnational manufacturing, in which improving communications allowed the
development of Europe-wide marketing, and in which previously-nationally
based services began to extend across national boundaries. Improvements in
physical communications, combined with rising affluence, sparked a parallel
surge in individual border-crossing – short-term and long-term, for pleasure,
for work, for study and for retirement.[30]

The transformation of European economic and social space to which the
interlinked technological, managerial and communications revolutions of the

[26] W. Wallace, 'Less Than a Federation, More Than a Regime: The European Community as a
Political System', in H. Wallace et al., *Policy-making in the European Community*.

[27] G. Ross, *Jacques Delors and European Integration* (Oxford, Oxford University Press, 1995);
C. Grant, *Delors: Inside the House that Jacques Built* (London, Brearley, 1994).

[28] M. Green Cowles, 'Setting the agenda for a new Europe: the ERT and EC', *Journal of Common
Market Studies*, 33 (1995), 501–26.

[29] W. Wallace, 'Political Cooperation: Integration Through Intergovernmentalism', in H. Wallace
et al., *Policy-making in the European Community*, ch. 13.

[30] F. Romero, 'Cross-Border Population Movements', in W. Wallace, *Dynamics of European
Integration*. British figures for arrivals of nationals from other European countries rose from
1.8 million a year in 1960 to 6 million in 1970, 12 million in 1980, 17.2 million in 1990, and
27.5 million in 1997. Arrivals at British ports of entry of British nationals, largely from elsewhere in
Europe, rose from 18.3 million in 1980 to 51 million in 1997 (*House of Lords* Written Answers,
28 July 1998). The scale of increase in border crossing between the 'core' states of Western
Europe – France, Germany and the Benelux – must have been even higher, as affluence rose and
trans-border road and rail links were improved. The Dutch government estimates that one third of
its population leaves the country in the first week of August, at the start of its peak holiday season.

1970s and 1980s led reflected the same underlying dynamics of economic and political change which observers of international trends have labelled globalization. The question must therefore be posed whether European experience over the past generation is more than simply a regional case study in the dialectical process of globalization and governmental responses to globalization.[31]

Three special characteristics of Western Europe however deserve particular attention. First, resolution of Western Europe's security dilemma – through an American-led alliance, within which a security community among European alliance members had evolved, and through an emerging consensus that the Soviet Union was a superpower in decline rather than an active threat – removed one of the most fundamental concerns of sovereign states from the regional agenda. It has been argued above that resolution of Europe's underlying security dilemma – the containment of German hegemony – had from the outset been the foundation for West European integration, and continued to motivate initiatives for further formal integration in the 1970s and 1980s, and beyond.

Second, Western Europe's geographical and population density – a dozen sovereign states in the 1980s, with a population of over 300 million, squeezed into an area comparable to the north-eastern corner of the United States – made for a particularly intensive experience of the shrinking of distance and the declining relevance of state borders to economic and social interaction. One of the pressures which contributed to the Schengen Agreement and the launch of the '1992' Single Market Programme came from the 1984 strike of French truck drivers, blocking border crossings around France in protest against the delays customs officials were imposing on what had become their regular trans-border routes; so preventing the elite of Paris and Brussels from reaching the Alps as the winter sports season got under way.[32] Globalization plus geography, plus Germany, explains why the evolution of shared sovereignty among West European governments has moved so much further than in any other part of the world.

Thirdly, European governments as they faced the unanticipated challenges of this technological and social transformation benefitted from established frameworks of institutions through which to respond. None of these institutions were particularly efficient in the 1970s. The European Community, by far the most developed both in institutional capacity and in policy competence, was characterized by the slowness of its decision making and the deep reluctance to reopen any aspect of its established *Acquis*. The Council of Europe was preoccupied largely with the harmonization of marginal and technical aspects of inter-state transactions. WEU was virtually a redundant organization for much of the 1960s and 1970s, its secretariat stirred into action by its member governments when they attempted to reopen the difficult dossier of European defence integration. But the habits of consultation had been established; the institutions and basic rules were in place. As member governments addressed

[31] A. Bressand, 'Beyond interdependence: 1992 as a global challenge', *International Affairs*, (1990); Bressand, ' Regional integration in a networked world economy', and M. Sharp,'Technology and the dynamics of integration', in W. Wallace, *The Dynamics of European Integration*, chs 2 and 3.

[32] Jacques Pelkmans and Alan Winters, *Europe's Domestic Market* (London, RIIA/Routledge, 1988), pp. 29–30.

new issues, they found it convenient to work through, and adapt and extend, existing multilateral frameworks.[33]

As these governments painfully worked out common rules in response to such new challenges, so other European governments recognized the advantages of being around the table while common rules were under negotiation. More than this, elites within excluded states came to identify inclusion within this network of regional institutions – including NATO as in effect a European institution – as constituting full recognition as European states within the European regional system. First Greece and Spain and Portugal, emerging from authoritarian government, were incorporated into institutionalized Europe (Spain and Portugal into the Council of Europe – from which Greece under the military regime had been suspended, all three into the EC, Spain also to join the other two within NATO, Spain and Portugal – and later Greece – into WEU). The neutral (or semi-neutral) democratic states of the European Free Trade Area attempted during the 1980s both to cling to their formal sovereignty and to gain greater access to EC decision making: negotiating a series of association agreements which never quite reconciled these contradictory objectives, leading the majority of EFTA members as soon as the Cold War was over to apply for full EC membership.[34] Meanwhile, behind the iron curtain, the struggling regimes of socialist states attempted to use the CSCE framework to assert the idea of a 'common European home', while dissident elites looked to 'rejoining Europe' through taking their place around the various tables at which democratic European governments coordinated their interests and extended their oversight over each others' domestic affairs.

A Deeper Pool? The Interpenetration of European Governments since the mid-1980s

The Single European Act, the 1992 Programme, the renewed commitment to monetary union in 1989 and the Maastricht Treaty of European Union (TEU) were heralded by enthusiasts for a united Europe as a second golden age of institutional development and commitment to common policies. In 1997, after the third lengthy Inter-Governmental Conference in 12 years had ended, one can only remark how ambiguous the further compromises between sovereignty and integration struck by heads of government in the endgame of each IGC process have been. Realists, defenders of sovereignty as the guiding principle for inter-state relations, must on the other hand be astonished by how much ground has been yielded, how close to the core of national sovereignty common rules and policies now come. The Maastricht TEU committed member governments to a single currency, managed by a European Central Bank, with strict conditions for common oversight of national economic policies. The Amsterdam Treaty failed to make much progress on either of the two sovereignty-sensitive issues passed on to it by exhausted negotiators at Maastricht: transition from cooperation to common policies in foreign policy and defence, and institutional and policy adjustments to prepare for further enlargement. But it marked some

[33] This argument is developed at greater length in W. Wallace, *Regional Integration: the West European Experience* (Washington, Brookings, 1994).

[34] H. Wallace, ed. *The Wider Western Europe: Reshaping the EC-EFTA Relationship* (London, Pinter, 1991).

potentially major changes in justice and home affairs, bringing immigration and asylum matters within the supranational Community framework and incorporating the Schengen conventions and their accumulated *Acquis* into the Treaty.

The end of the Cold War transformed Europe's geopolitics. The Soviet Red Army retreated – and disintegrated. 200,000 of the 300,000 American troops in Europe were withdrawn within three years. Realists like John Mearsheimer predicted that the traditional pattern of power politics among mutually suspicious sovereign states would re-emerge from under the superpower domination of the previous 45 years.[35]

Across Western Europe, however, governments cut defence budgets and force strengths, moving towards each other through institutional enlargement and policy innovation rather than back towards an attempted balance of power. The interpenetration of Western Europe's national economies, societies, and above all governments and administrations, had developed an impetus that was self-sustaining. Habits had grown up, patterns had developed. An entire generation had grown up within Western Europe's extended space. Most national officials by 1990 had worked throughout their careers within this multilateral context, taking it for granted to pick up the phone to their opposite numbers before they briefed their ministers and to carry their briefcases from office to airport to conference room once or twice a week.[36] Executives had long learned to define their businesses as 'European companies operating in a global market'; their younger recruits expected to move among European countries as their careers progressed. The exclusive claims to sovereignty and loyalty, economic interest and political legitimacy to which nineteenth century nation states had aspired had been diffused – though not entirely dispersed. Globalization plus geography, plus the *engrenage* which had grown up over a generation of administrative and elite interaction, thus held European governments together through the mistrust and reopening of old nightmares which might well have been provoked by the reunification of Germany.[37]

Little research has been undertaken on cross-border social integration of Western Europe in recent years.[38] Anecdotal evidence suggests that elite interaction has expanded across the range: intermarriage, study abroad, second

---

[35] J. Mearsheimer, 'Back to the future: instability in Europe after the Cold War', *International Security*, 15 (1990), 5–56.

[36] For those within the core of Western Europe, improvements in surface communications have meant that airports do not come into the equation. Fast trains now make it comfortable to travel between Brussels, Paris, London, The Hague and Bonn and return the same day. Hans-Dietrich Genscher as German foreign minister was notorious for his preference for travelling by car between Bonn, Brussels, The Hague and Paris, talking incessantly on his car phone as he went. EU enlargement has weakened this easy intensity of interaction among member governments. It should nevertheless be noted that nine of the fifteen national capitals of EU member states are within 90 minutes' flying time from Brussels, and that only Lisbon, Helsinki and Athens are much more than two hours away. Among current applicants, Prague is closer to Brussels than is Vienna; Warsaw and Budapest are as close to Brussels as is Rome.

[37] Students of Karl Deutsch will recognize that I largely accept his premise that rising interactions, provided they are relatively balanced and are perceived as offering mutual benefits to the large majority of those involved, lead to growth of security communities. K. Deutsch, *Political Community and the North Atlantic Area* (Princeton, Princeton University Press, 1957).

[38] The pioneering study was J. E. Farquaharson and S. C. Holt, *Europe from Below: an Assessment of Franco-German Popular Contacts* (London, Allen & Unwin, 1975). F. Romero, 'Cross-border population movements', in Wallace, *Dynamics of European Integration*, ch. 10 provides some invaluable statistics on flows in the late 1980s.

homes in second countries, multinational careers in multinational companies.[39] Several hundred thousand British, German, Dutch, Belgian and Swiss now own second homes in France. Substantial retirement colonies of northern Europeans have grown up in Spain and Portugal. Winter patterns of air traffic between northern and southern Europe resemble those between the north-eastern USA and Florida, as the affluent elderly move towards the sun.[40] Mass interaction is more limited; though 50,000 British were working in the Netherlands in the early 1990s, and the flow of British and Irish building workers into Germany both before and during the post-unification building boom was substantial enough not only to attract the attention of governments and trade unions but also to form the basis for a popular television sitcom.[41] Mass tourism makes for vast summer migrations across Europe, by charter aircraft, rail, bus and car. Mass violence within Western Europe is threatened only by the migration of football supporters following the various Europe-wide club competitions, against which national police forces share information and coordinate actions. If (as Alan James argues) a state is defined by its territory and by the people who live within it, then one indication of the declining centrality of the state within the contemporary European order is that so many of its people live across a wider social and economic space.

Cross-border mergers, in industry, financial services, even in areas such as air transport, telecommunications and electricity supply which were until recently state-owned, have extended: both encouraged by the pressures of global competition and assisted by the rules developed and enforced by European authorities. Cross-border economic integration has become an everyday consideration in national economic management. National governments bid against each other to attract multi-national investment, subject to regulatory oversight from the European Commission. Economic regulation, as Jacques Delors predicted in 1988, has shifted decisively from the national to the European level, leading some analysts to define the EU as 'a European regulatory state'.[42] Fiscal policies take into account the erosion of revenue threatened by substantial differences between national tax rates; governments negotiate with each other about how much further fiscal harmonization might in time need to extend.[43] Regional authorities negotiate with Brussels and with their counterparts across national boundaries to lessen their dependence on national benevolence and to pursue their own advantage – leading some observers to discern the development of

---

[39] This is not of course a uniquely European phenomenon; the argument here is that it has become much more commonplace within Europe than within other international regions. US-Canadian social interchange may in some ways be comparable; within East Asia elite interchange is however qualitatively less intensive (except among the transnational Chinese community).

[40] Information from the British Civil Aviation Authority.

[41] 'Auf Wiedersehn, Pet', BBC. The building boom in London in the mid-1980s attracted German architects to British firms; post-unification reconstruction in Berlin and the former East Germany reversed the flow, with younger British architects moving to Germany.

[42] Delors as Commissioned President angered Margaret Thatcher by predicting that within ten years some 80% of economic and social regulations applicable within member states would be of European origin. Only four years later the French Conseil d'État reported that less than 25% of new French legal texts were emerging without consultation or agreement with the Brussels institutions. G. Majone, 'A European Regulatory State?', in J. Richardson (ed.), *European Union: Power and Policy-Making* (London, Routledge, 1996), p. 265; see also G. Majone, *Regulating Europe* (London, Routledge, 1996).

[43] C. Radaelli, *The Politics of Corporate Taxation in the European Union* (London, Routledge, 1997).

patterns of multi-level governance which undermine the centrality of the nation state.[44]

These largely informal trends in economic and social integration would not have developed so rapidly without the formal institutional framework of common rules and removal of internal barriers which constituted a trans-national European economic and social space. National governments in turn have responded to these trends by negotiating new rules and establishing new patterns of cooperation to manage their consequences. Behind the grandiose rhetoric of the preamble to the Maastricht Treaty, declaring the establishment of a European Union, were gathered the overlapping concerns of national ministries and domestic and transnational lobbies, seeking to impose their preferred versions of common regulations on policy arenas no longer contain-able through national regulation alone. Alongside the political commitment of the French and German governments to monetary union were to be found European companies, and trade union leaders, persuaded that the costs of monetary turbulence within such a highly-integrated regional economy were greater than the benefits of sustained national monetary sovereignty.

Monetary union represents the most visible, potentially irreversible, move away from the traditional functions of the nation state currently on the European agenda. On most other areas of European integration, governments can work together through committees alongside the Commission, the Council Secretariat, NATO or WEU, without having to address a definitive transfer of authority. But here it is hard to avoid the choice. The Werner Report on Economic and Monetary Union, in October 1970, bluntly spelt out the political implications of EMU:

> the realization of economic and monetary union demands the creation or the transformation of a certain number of Community organs *to which powers until then exercised by the national authorities will have to be transferred.* These transfers of authority represent a process of fundamental political significance which implies the progressive development of political cooperation. Economic and monetary union thus appears as a leaven for the development of political union, which in the long run it cannot do without.[45]

Thirty years later, the member governments of a far more developed European Union are nevertheless approaching monetary union without directly addres-sing the extent of the transfer of sovereignty involved. They have agreed to exclude much of the economic agenda which Werner and the earlier studies of EMU considered an essential complement to a central bank, including the question of further enlargement of the Community budget beyond its current limit of 1.27% of EU GDP.

The rapid expansion of cooperation under the 'Third Pillar' during the 1990s illustrates the dilemmas and contradictions involved in pooling sovereignty without moving towards an explicit confederation. Fears over immigration, over transnational organized crime, drug-smuggling and people-smuggling,

---

[44] L. Hooghe, *Cohesion Policy and European Integration: Building Multi-Level Governance* (Oxford, Oxford University Press, 1996); B. Jones and M. Keating (eds), *The European Union and the Regions* (Oxford, Oxford University Press, 1995).

[45] Werner Report, definitive text, *Bulletin of the European Communities* (Brussels, EC), Supplement 11/1970 (italics added).

increased with the dismantling of the iron curtain, opening Western Europe's eastern borders at the same time that pressures for immigration across Europe's southern borders were also increasing. The intensity of interaction among national agencies sharply increased, with the creation of a new European agency, EUROPOL, to improve the efficiency of joint actions and information exchange. This radical departure from the domestic basis for policing, evidence and law has so far remained largely unreported to national parliaments; no formal transfer of jurisdiction is argued to be involved. But large questions of constitutional safeguards, of civil liberties and of judicial oversight – the stuff of democratic constitution-building – lurk just beneath the surface. The negotiation of conventions providing for easier provision of evidence across national jurisdictions, and for common rules on divorce and child custody (a necessary consequence of increased crossborder marriage), also takes the process of pooling sovereignty among governments further towards the core of domestic law.[46]

The Treaty of Amsterdam registers the contradictions of a European political system which has moved far beyond traditional concepts of sovereignty without developing a consensus on what is emerging in its place. The Treaty extends the declared objectives set out in the Maastricht Treaty to include common 'attachment to fundamental social rights', to 'take into account the principle of sustainable development . . . and of reinforced cohesion and environmental protection', and specifically sets out the objectives:

> to strengthen the protection of the rights and interests of the nationals of its Member States through the introduction of a citizenship of the Union; to maintain and develop the Union as an area of freedom, security and justice, in which the free movement of persons is assured in conjunction with appropriate measures with respect to external border controls, asylum, immigration and the prevention and combatting of crime . . .[47]

Part of this sensitive area of shared citizenship and common criteria for entry and residence is transferred under the Treaty from the Third to the First Pillar, into which the bulk of the Schengen Convention and its accumulated *Acquis* are also to be incorporated – thus in principle subjecting them to the shared oversight of the European Court of Justice and European Parliament. But the relative authority of national constitutions and this developing – but only half-acknowledged – European constitution is left unclear, in spite of post-Maastricht challenges before both the French and German constitutional courts.[48] The confusion about underlying objectives embedded in the Treaty is also reflected in the 51 attached Declarations 'adopted by the Conference', and the further 8 'Declarations of which the Conference took note': setting out a

---

[46] J. Monar and R. Morgan (eds), *The Third Pillar of the European Union* (Brussels, European Interuniversity Press, 1994); M. Anderson *et al.*, *Policing the European Union* (Oxford, Clarendon, 1995); G. Barrett (ed.), *Justice Cooperation in the European Union* (Dublin, Institute of European Affairs, 1997). A number of reports from the British House of Lords European Communities Committee in 1997–8 explored the problems of accountability in this field.

[47] Article 1, Treaty of Amsterdam, 1997.

[48] R. Ladrech, 'Europeanization of domestic policies and institutions: the case of France', *Journal of Common Market Studies*, 32 (1994), 69–88; G. Ress, 'The Constitution and the Maastricht Treaty: between cooperation and conflict', *German Politics*, 3 (1994), 47–74.

succession of domestic reservations and exceptions, from the British opt-out from provisions on the abolition of internal frontiers to the German insistence on protecting the role of publicly-owned credit institutions.

The European state system in the later 1990s thus represents an extraordinary picture of collective policy-making combined with autonomous domestic politics, of governments which have grown into each other and Parliaments which scarcely interrelate. National economic management has given way to European-level regulation; national monetary sovereignty is giving way to the European Central Bank. Internal borders have largely disappeared, without more than the common European passport and the new signs dividing Schengen residents from other EU and EEA citizens and from aliens at EU entry points to mark this effective transfer of national authority to the European level. Civil servants transfer between national and European institutions, even among national administrations.[49] Governments have so far managed to share sovereignty without fully admitting to their domestic publics the extent to which this involves the loss of national autonomy. It is open to question how much further governments can move without the underlying contradictions becoming apparent.

Post-modern States, Post-sovereign European Order?

Students of European integration and international politics struggle to characterize a state system in which constitutional independence has thus been ceded, sovereign equality modified, economic autonomy long since deeply compromised, security managed through an integrated alliance, internal borders opened and external borders managed through a common regime, monetary sovereignty shortly to yield to a single currency. The EU is *not* a federation; though it now displays a number of federal – or at least confederal – characteristics.[50] It is widely agreed to constitute a political system, a framework for governance with some statelike qualities above the state level.[51] Some would

---

[49] I am not aware of any comparative studies of exchanges of civil servants among national governments in the 1990s. The most extensive appear to have been taking place between Paris and Bonn, among the three Benelux states, and among the Nordic states. In 1997–8 there were at any one time some half-dozen diplomats from France, Germany and other EU states serving in the British Foreign Office, including in its Security Policy Department and Planning Staff.

[50] The German Constitutional Court, in its judgement on the Maastricht TEU, described it very carefully as neither a Bundestaat (a federation) nor a Staatenbund (a confederation) but a Verstaatenbund (a potential federation). Ress, 'The Constitution and the Maastricht Treaty', *German Politics*, 1994. But note that the American federation in its first half-century was in many ways weaker than the EU today: D. Deudney, 'The Philadelphian system: sovereignty, arms control and the balance of power within the American states-union, 1787–1861', *International Organization*, 29 (1995), 191–228.

[51] For recent surveys of the literature, see: W. Wallace, 'Government without Statehood: the Unstable Equilibrium', in H. Wallace *et al.*, *Policy-making in the European Union* (Oxford, Oxford University Press, 1996), ch. 17; J. Richardson, 'Policy-Making in the EU: Interests, Ideas and Garbage Cans of Primeval Soup', in Richardson, *European Union: Power and Policy-making* (London, Routledge, 1996), ch. 1; T. Risse-Kappen, 'Exploring the nature of the beast: international relations theory and comparative policy analysis meet the European Union', *Journal of Common Market Studies*, 34 (1996), 53–80; S. Hix, 'The study of the European Union: the new governance agenda and its rival', *Journal of European Public Policy*, 5 (1998), 39–65.

describe it as a 'quasi-state', or as an 'international state'; or as a post-modern pattern of government in a post-modern European order.[52]

The modern state (as Alan James notes) was defined by its unitary character. Post-modern European states operate within a much more complex, cross-cutting network of governance, based upon the breakdown of the distinction between domestic and foreign affairs, on mutual interference in each other's domestic affairs, on increasing mutual transparency, and on the emergence of a sufficiently strong sense of community to guarantee mutual security.[53] The absence of external threat, once the Red Army had retreated, has contributed to this partial deconstruction of the European state. There is, after all, in the late 1990s no rational argument for maintaining a Belgian army, or a Dutch or Danish air force, *except* to contribute to joint European forces or to offer small contingents to 'out-of-area' operations where vital questions of national security and interest are not at stake.[54] If West European states were again to be seriously threatened around their borders, or if the USA were to abandon its commitment to provide security and foreign policy leadership, then further awkward choices would have to be faced: perhaps taking an enlarged EU towards a more directly federal structure, with an effective common foreign policy and common defence. So long as US-led NATO provides a convenient alternative framework, however, European states will be able to avoid this further concession of formal sovereignty.

This emerging European order has a relatively clear core, an extensive periphery, and undefined external boundaries. Its core consists of the states around the Rhine valley and delta, locked together by absence of natural frontiers, dense concentrations of population and economic activity, and by shared values learned through bitter history.[55] These five states have accepted that their security and prosperity hang irrevocably together, that the defence of sovereignty is a zero-sum game while the pursuit of mutual trade-offs provides positive sums. For less politically and geographically central states within the EU – for the United Kingdom, Denmark, Sweden, above all Greece – the balance of advantages is less clear, with much resistance to accepting the trade-off between lost autonomy and enhanced influence. Four of the fifteen EU members – Ireland, Austria, Sweden and Finland – do not belong to the parallel integrated security framework of NATO. The applicant states of central and eastern Europe currently form a further peripheral grouping, pressing to be permitted to enter the EU and NATO but still coming to terms with the

[52] W. Streek and P. Schmitter, 'From national corporatism to transnational pluralism: organised interests in the Single European Market', *Politics and Society*, 19 (1991), p. 159; J. Caporaso, 'The European Union and forms of state: Westphalian, regulatory or post-modern?', *Journal of Common Market Studies*, 34 (1996), p. 33; R. Cooper, *The Post-modern State and the World Order* (London, Demos, 1996); C. Coker, 'Post-modernity and the end of the Cold War?', *Review of International Studies*, 18 (1992), 189–98.

[53] I am following here the definition in Cooper, *The Post-modern State and the World Order*. This short pamphlet was originally written as a paper for the British Foreign Office Planning Staff.

[54] This argument was made by a senior Belgian diplomat at a conference in Brussels in 1994, explaining why Belgium wished to contribute both to the Eurocorps and to the NATO Rapid Reaction Force. On current developments in defence cooperation, see J. Howorth and A. Menon (eds), *The European Union and National Defence Policy* (London, Routledge, 1997).

[55] The historically-inclined can travel down the Rhine valley from Basel to Rotterdam from one battlefield to another, before returning through the war cemeteries and memorials of Belgium and northern France.

intrusive quality of European governance and the mutual interpenetration of each other's domestic politics involved in playing the European game. Beyond them stretches a further periphery – Russia, Ukraine, Turkey, Albania, the successor states to former Yugoslavia: members of some European institutions, observers in others, conscious of their dependence on the European core but uncertain of what relationship they can or would like to develop with it.

The partial deconstruction of the European state is also evident in the strengthening of sub-state governance, even the echoes (in Britain and Spain, in Italy and Belgium) of subordinated 'peoples' (to use James Mayall's definition) demanding restoration of self-government. The modernizing state provided national security, protected the national territory and managed the national economy. But Flanders no longer needs the Belgian state to provide it with military protection; while Scotland rebuilds its prosperity through foreign investment, its leaders eyeing the economic advantages which Ireland and Denmark have won from their state-entitled bargaining capacity at the Council table. The German Länder have asserted their right to sit in on Council meetings when matters which encroach on their powers and interests are under discussion.[56] The Welsh Labour Party declared in the summer of 1998 that one of its top priorities for the new elected government of Wales in 1999 would be to appoint a senior 'minister for Europe' to build direct links with Brussels.[57] In the six-monthly European Councils of heads of government, in the annual NATO summits, states still speak to each other through the single voice of their sovereign's chief representative. Between these, however, the business of European politics and government is conducted across state boundaries by a great many other actors and agencies.

One of the greatest achievements of the nineteenth century model of the European nation state was its ability to bring together identity and order, legitimacy and community, national economy and national welfare within a single framework. The weakest dimension of the emerging post-sovereign European order is that it loosens the ties which bind elites to masses within nation states, and the links between policy outcomes and political account-ability, without providing any substantial sense of shared identity, of repre-sentation or of accountability at the European level. European institutions were designed for administrative elites, for networks of experts and specialists; it was part of the supranational compromise to present the European level of governance as technical administration, leaving political representation through national governments.[58] The post-sovereign European order is characterized by disaggregated policy networks and disjointed and opaque policy-making processes, without any of the symbols, myths or rituals through which modern-izing national governments built up a sense of national solidarity and virtual representation.

Post-modern elites may flourish with multiple identities, moving from state to state and from work to leisure. European masses have experienced a diminution

---

[56] E. Bomberg and J. Peterson, 'European Union decision-making: the role of sub-national authorities', *Political Studies*, 46 (1998), 219–35.

[57] 'Minister unveils plans to help Wales with EU funds', *Financial Times*, 11 August 1998.

[58] K. Featherstone, 'Jean Monnet and the "Democratic Deficit" in the European Union', *Journal of Common Market Studies*, 32 (1994), 149–70; W. Wallace and J. Smith, 'Democracy or technocracy? European integration and the problem of popular consent', *West European Politics*, 18 (1995), 137–57.

in the capacity of their states to offer them welfare, employment and personal security, without appearing to have gained much that is valued – or understood – in return. The narratives of national history from which integrating national governments forged shared loyalties and identities a century ago are disintegrating, except in south-eastern Europe. Yet no coherent European narrative is emerging, sufficient to generate a legitimizing community of shared identity at this new, diffuse, level of governance. Governments have attempted to maintain national welfare, national symbols, national interpretations of statehood and sovereignty, while transferring an increasing proportion of policy-making to the intricate network of Councils and committees which manage their shared sovereignty. The central paradox of the European political system in the 1990s is that governance is becoming increasingly a multi-level, intricately institutionalized activity, while representation, loyalty and identity remain stubbornly rooted in the traditional institutions of the nation state. Much of the substance of European state sovereignty has now fallen away; the symbols, the sense of national solidarity, the focus for political representation and accountability, nevertheless remain.

Sovereignty and the Third World State

CHRISTOPHER CLAPHAM

The Third World Sovereignty Regime

Third World states – here broadly taken to correspond to the formerly colonial states of Africa, Asia, the Pacific and the Caribbean – enjoy a paradoxical relationship to the international regimes which have been devised to regulate the global system, and especially to the core institution of state sovereignty. Like all international regimes, that of sovereignty was created and imposed at the instance of the dominant states of the international system, which were exclusively of European origin. It was used, not merely to regulate relationships between the European states themselves, but in the process also to entrench their domination over other regions of the globe. The Treaty of Westphalia, in establishing the European sovereignty regime, simultaneously created the template for the division of much of the rest of the world between European powers. Though European colonialism, notably in the Americas, had existed for a century and a half before Westphalia, that treaty codified the principle that territories belonged to states, and that only states, thus, had an unquestioned right to possess territories.[1] Given that 'states' encompassed only those entities which were admitted by tacit consent to the international state system, and that these in turn were overwhelmingly European, Westphalian sovereignty provided the formula under which territories which did not 'count' as states according to the criteria adopted by the European state system could be freely appropriated – subject only to their capacity to conquer the incumbent power holders – by those which did count. For more than two centuries, from the Treaty of Utrecht in 1713 to that of Versailles in 1919, territories were then transferred between one European state and another as bargaining chips in the resolution of European conflicts.

On the other hand, the post-colonial states have, since their independence in the decades following the Second World War, emerged as the most strident defenders of Westphalian sovereignty in the international order. This transformation obviously rested on the extension of the rules of membership in the international community, with the creation of a 'new sovereignty regime', the development of which has been analysed by Robert Jackson.[2] It required in particular the articulation of new conceptions of nationalism and

---

[1] There have, of course, been cases where effective territorial jurisdiction has been exercised by entities other than states, such as the Honourable East India Company in India, the 'white rajahs' of Sarawak, the American Colonization Society in Liberia, and the Charter Company in Rhodesia; all of these, however, came under the tacit protection of states, and their position was eventually regularized, either by takeover by the protecting state, or in the case of Liberia by independence.

[2] R. H. Jackson, *Quasi-states: Sovereignty, International Relations and the Third World* (Cambridge, Cambridge University Press, 1990), ch. 2.

self-determination, in which the 'nation' was equated with the inhabitants of any territory created by European colonialism, rather than – as had happened, say, with the dissolution of the Austro-Hungarian, Ottoman and in some degree Russian empires – with peoples who could claim at least some measure of distinct cultural or linguistic identity.[3] With this change, however, the newly independent governments took to Westphalian sovereignty like ducklings to water, and as participants in the post-1945 international order, their concern was overwhelmingly to protect rather than to subvert it. The charters of international organizations formed among Third World states, for example, characteristically formulated a more rigid and defensive attitude towards sovereignty than that of the United Nations, which had been created under the aegis of the victorious great powers. A classic example, the Charter of the Organization of African Unity adopted at Addis Ababa in 1963, allowed none of the concessions to supranationalism permitted by the United Nations. There was no Security Council or other executive committee which might give some states greater status than others, or any provision for the organization as a whole to take decisions which were in any way binding on individual states which disagreed with them. Instead, the Charter emphasized the sovereign equality of member states; non-intervention in their internal affairs; respect for the sovereignty and territorial integrity of each state, and its inalienable right to independent existence; the peaceful settlement of disputes; and an unambiguous condemnation of subversive activities carried out by one state against another.[4] Any pretensions on the part of the secretariat to supranational prerogatives were depressed by giving its head the deliberately lowly title of 'Administrative Secretary General'. The one significant derogation from the rights of sovereignty was the exclusion of territories under colonial rule, and those (initially South Africa, but from 1965 to 1980 also Rhodesia) which because of white minority government did not meet the criterion of 'majority rule' which constituted the moral charter of independent African states, and justified their claim to sovereignty.

Third World states even sought to extend sovereign rights into areas of international relations beyond the scope of territorial integrity and non-intervention. Given their economic weakness, and the penetration of their economies by trading networks (and notably transnational corporations) dominated by the developed capitalist states, the most important of these was understandably economic management. The Charter of the Economic Rights and Duties of States (CERDS), adopted by the UN General Assembly in December 1974, amounted in essence to an uncompromising assertion of the sovereign rights of states, and a call for a global economy regulated by states, as against a 'liberal' conception of the global economic order in which 'private' actors, and notably corporations, could operate in a relatively unconstrained manner across state frontiers.[5] Critical provisions of CERDS included the assertion of permanent sovereignty over natural resources within state territory, the right to form

---

[3] See J. Mayall, *Nationalism and International Society* (Cambridge, Cambridge University Press, 1990), ch. 7; cf. B. Davidson, *The Black Man's Burden: Africa and the Curse of the Nation-State* (London, James Currey, 1992), for a comparison of state formation in eastern Europe and tropical Africa.

[4] Charter of the Organization of African Unity, Art. III.

[5] For a supportive assessment of CERDS, see C. Thomas. *In Search of Security: The Third World in International Relations* (Brighton, Wheatsheaf, 1987), pp. 64–70.

producer cartels to regulate primary product prices, and potentially most sub-versive of all, a demand for the indexation of prices for globally traded commodities. Like the demands for a New International Economic Order (NIEO), with which it was closely associated, CERDS was very much a product of the period which followed the first OPEC oil price rise of 1973, and became little more than a historical curiosity by the 1980s, but it accurately reflected the attempt by Third World states to extend the range of sovereignty. Its eventual failure resulted, not simply from the inability of Third World states to assert control over corporations which enjoyed the protection of the dominant states in the international order, but much more basically from the collapse of statist projects of economic management in the industrial world, and of the ideologies that had sustained them. Indeed, the more successful Third World states, and notably those of east and southeast Asia, had little use for CERDS, and benefitted from precisely the integration into global markets that it sought to restrict.

Still more ambitious was the attempt by Third World states to institute a New World Order for Information (NWOI), articulated at the Colombo summit of the Non-Aligned Movement in August 1976, which became a major source of conflict at the UNESCO General Conference in Nairobi in November that year. This sought to bring the global dissemination of information under the control of states, the critical clause in the draft declaration proposed at Nairobi stating that 'states are responsible for the activities in the international sphere of all mass media under their jurisdiction'.[6] Though this demand was successfully challenged by capitalist states, in the name of freedom of information, it was still more radically undermined by the capacity of the electronic media to escape from the control of any state. In short, the inability of Third World states to assert sovereign rights over information and economic management was essen-tially the result, not of the powerlessness of Third World as against developed industrial states, but of the problems faced by the international state system as a whole in confronting the range of changes that have generally been lumped together under the heading of globalization, and the ideological shifts which reflected these changes.

Though it was certainly paradoxical that Third World states should have become such fervent supporters of the sovereignty regime which had been the means of subordinating their own peoples and territories to the major global powers, it was by no means contradictory. These states were themselves the creation of the colonial sovereignty regime, and their commitment to it rested on a perfectly valid perception that they remained dependent on the international order for their continued survival. They consequently needed to do whatever they could to maintain the stability of the state system, and to ensure that it was, so far as possible, run in accordance with their own interests. As Jackson has shown, their 'quasi-statehood' rested on a tacit recognition by the international system (or, in effect, by its major powers) that they should be permitted to enjoy the formal privileges of membership, despite the fact that they were often unable to meet what had hitherto been the empirical criteria for entry. Militarily, they were often (though not always) incapable of defending themselves against any serious assault. Economically, they even on occasion depended on external aid,

---

[6] For a hostile assessment of the NWOI, see R. Righter, *Whose News? Politics, the Press and the Third World* (London, Burnett, 1978), esp. chs 4 and 5.

not only for the capital investment needed to raise them from their current poverty, but for the wherewithal to pay their own bureaucracies. As conditions of public order deteriorated, states such as Afghanistan, Burma or Cambodia in Asia, or Angola, Chad or Ethiopia in Africa, were quite unable to exercise even minimal control over much of their ostensible national territory. In these circumstances, 'juridical statehood' – the fact that they were recognized as sovereign states by international organizations and the major powers – became a critical resource in the hands of their rulers.

'Sovereignty' is thus not merely a technical term used to denote the formal criteria for membership of the international system; like other political concepts, it is essentially contested because it confers power on some people, and removes it from others. As Philpott points out, the concept is by its nature Janus-faced: it looks both to an international system in which recognized sovereign statehood serves as the admission ticket to the 'premier league' of international actors, accorded a status denied to non-sovereign entities; and to a domestic political order in which, as Vincent pointed out, 'state sovereignty fulfills an analogous function to that of a "No Trespassing" sign standing at the perimeter of a piece of property held under domestic law.'[7] Scholars of international relations understandably tend to emphasize the first of these elements, which formally defines the membership of the international order with which they are primarily concerned. Nor is this aspect of sovereignty irrelevant to Third World states: the ability to participate in international activities on a level formally at par with the superpowers and their own former colonizers strikingly indicates their arrival on the global scene, and provides a source of endless gratification to their rulers. It is however the contention of this paper that the second element is critical: what matters about sovereignty is not mere formal recognition of independent statehood, but rather the power which it confers on the rulers of states, through its denial of the right of other states and external agencies to 'interfere' in their own exercise of domestic power. In the domestic as in the external sphere, sovereignty is very different from autonomy: there are considerable constraints on the freedom of action of all states, even the most powerful ones, and an assertion of sovereignty is not refuted by the evidence of such constraints. The relationship between sovereignty and autonomy is however the precise equivalent for states of that between rights and liberty for individuals. Sovereignty is however a claim to autonomy in specific respects, and a state which lacks any autonomy in these respects can no more be said to be sovereign, than an individual who lacks any liberty can be said to enjoy rights.

The key claim which the rulers of Third World states use the language of sovereignty to assert is one to unfettered control over their internal affairs, and notably over their own domestic populations. This is an aspect of sovereignty which readily escapes attention in developed liberal states, where the relationship between governments and citizens is at least relatively unproblematic. Third World rulers' use of sovereignty as an ideology of internal state consolidation, and their assertion of international autonomy as a tool for the entrenchment of domestic political power, is nonetheless precisely analogous to

[7] R. J. Vincent, *Nonintervention and International Order* (Princeton, Princeton University Press, 1974), p. 331.

the role of sovereignty in early modern Europe.[8] The doctrine of sovereignty enabled rulers (or 'sovereigns') to protect their territories against external threats, the better to bring about the unrestricted imposition of their internal power, and what went in this respect for Henry VIII or Louis XIV applies equally to Sukarno or Nkrumah. In neither case, even though sovereignty came in the nineteenth century to serve as the instrument of mass nationalism, was there any necessary link between external sovereignty and domestic democracy. Once 'self-determination' had (in most cases) been validated by a charter election which established the status of the newly independent government, the requirement that the sovereign ruler should 'represent' the people of the state in any way which involved effective accountability to them was rapidly allowed to lapse. Nor was the claim to sovereignty seriously affected in cases where the incumbent government had never been elected at all: monarchies, military regimes, and single-party states which governed their peoples with varying degrees of brutality enjoyed precisely the same status.

Sovereignty was, moreover, far more critical as an instrument of state consolidation for Third World states in the Cold War era, than it had been even during its heyday in early modern Europe. European rulers generally sought only the forbearance of their fellow sovereigns, while they imposed their power through artillery and bureaucracy on potentially rebellious subjects. They had at the same time to defend their territories against external attack, far more than has generally been the case for the rulers of Third World quasi-states, and this involved some form of accommodation, at least with the most important of these subjects: the establishment of a sovereignty regime in Europe did not always involve the imposition of a centralized autocracy.[9] Third World rulers, on the other hand, were often heavily dependent on the outside world both for their artillery and for their bureaucracy, as also for the economic resources which correspondingly depended on the rents which could be extracted from international trade; and sovereignty was all the more important as a device for asserting a measure of autonomy from the very external states and other international actors to which they were subordinate. Their claim to sovereignty was thus very far indeed from being a mechanism for cutting themselves off from the world – a strategy followed only, with disastrous results, by a very small number of states such as Burma and Khmer Rouge Cambodia. It was,

---

[8] This process predates Westphalia by over a century, and its classic expression is to be found in the preamble to the legislation by which, in 1533, King Henry VIII of England asserted his independence from the Roman Catholic Church:

> Where by divers sundry old authentic histories and chronicles, it is manifestly declared and expressed that this realm of England is an Empire, and so hath been accepted in the world, governed by one supreme Head and King ... (Statute in Restraint of Appeals, 24 Henry VIII, ch. 12; cited from J. R. Tanner, *Tudor Constitutional Documents*, A.D. 1485–1603, (Cambridge, Cambridge University Press, 1940), p. 41).

All of the core elements of sovereignty are to be found there, including external recognition ('accepted in the world'), domestic supremacy ('supreme Head and King'), and the articulation of a (largely fictitious) historical charter.

[9] C. Tilly, *Coercion, Capital and European States, 990–1900* (Oxford, Blackwell, 1990), provides an interesting overview of alternative forms of European state formation and their determinants, and the way in which these sometimes involved some kind of 'deal' between rulers and their more important subjects.

rather, a means of engaging in global relationships on extremely discriminatory terms, as between different groups within the domestic society.

In essence, then, sovereignty was a device through which those who controlled Third World states sought to maintain exclusive jurisdiction over exchanges across state frontiers. 'Arbitrage' over such exchanges was critical to every aspect of political life in the quasi-state. At its most basic, the success with which rulers could establish it might determine the continued existence or non-existence of the state itself. The capacity of the state to survive any military challenge turned on its ability to secure the support of a sufficiently powerful patron, who would supply the diplomatic backing, armaments, and in extreme cases (such as South Vietnam and Afghanistan) the military forces needed to protect it against its challengers. Still more important in most cases was the state's ability to police its economic frontiers. The great majority of Third World states gained a very high proportion of their income by using a variety of devices which ultimately depended on sovereignty, in order to extract surpluses from the flow of resources between the domestic and international economies. Some of these devices, such as the establishment of state marketing boards with a monopoly over the purchase and resale of cash crops grown by African peasant producers, formally fell within the realm of domestic regulation; but they were actually used (by colonial as well as by independent governments) in order to enable the state to cream off the difference between an artificially low domestic price determined by the state, and an international price determined by the market. The royalty payments imposed by states on international mining companies fell more explicitly into the international realm, but served essentially the same purpose; the function of CERDS, though justified in terms of a rhetoric of representation and development, was actually in large measure to assert the state's rights over revenue collection. The ability of states to establish an official exchange rate for their currencies, which was often wildly disproportionate to the rate which the currency could command on the open market, likewise generated revenues derived from the difference between the two rates, as well as securing cheap imports for urban elites, and enabling selected individuals with political connections to make monopoly profits through the grant of import licences. The need for physical control over the frontier itself was imposed, in most cases, not so much by the requirements of 'national defence', but in order to prevent those who did not control states from evading, through 'smuggling', the exactions of those who did. In just the same way, the New World Information Order was an attempt to prevent the 'smuggling' of information both into the state (where it might subvert its control over domestic populations), and out of it (where it might weaken its capacity to cut international deals). In some parts of the Third World, notably Central America and the Caribbean, sovereignty generated funds through the opportunities that it provided for collaboration with the international trade in narcotics, not just through the provision of facilities for the physical transfer of controlled substances to markets in the USA, but through offshore banking and the laundering of drugs-related funds.

The ways in which, and the extent to which, sovereignty could be used in order to enhance the power and wealth of Third World governing elites has varied between regions of the Third World, in accordance partly with the place of the regions concerned in the global political and economic order, partly with different conventions of statehood governing relations within the region itself.

During the Cold War, there was a marked difference between zones of hegemony which were effectively controlled by a single superpower, zones of confrontation between the superpowers, and zones of relative indifference to which superpowers were reluctant to dedicate substantial resources. In zones of hegemony, such as the Caribbean and Central America, local governing elites could only assert claims to sovereignty against the hegemon (on which they were, in any event, often highly dependent) at considerable cost, as the cases of Cuba, Nicaragua, Grenada and indeed Panama very clearly indicate: the principle of sovereignty should not be confused with the ability to exercise substantive independence. In zones of confrontation, such as southeast Asia and the Middle East, the protection of one or other superpower was vital, and a transfer from one to the other was normally conceivable only as part of a major domestic upheaval in which the incumbent governing elite was swept away.[10] In zones of relative indifference, with tropical Africa as the obvious example, the governments of some of the feeblest states in the world enjoyed a remarkable and paradoxical ability to change patrons, or even to maintain a reasonable level of non-alignment between them.[11]

But differing regional conceptions of statehood, and levels of state capacity, also had a substantial impact. While 'sovereignty' was always available as a device through which Third World states could seek to protect themselves against extra-regional powers, regional rules to some extent applied to their relations with one another. Both the states of tropical Africa and the Arab states of the Middle East, for example, articulated ideals of statehood which excluded the regional pariahs of apartheid South Africa in the one case, and Israel in the other; to these, the conventions of sovereignty did not apply. But the conventions governing relations between accepted states in each region varied. 'Arab unity', notably, could be used by a Nasser, a Qadhafi or a Saddam to appeal directly to populations within other Arab states in a way that would have been regarded in tropical Africa as an unacceptable interference in the domestic political affairs of their neighbours: 'African unity' was not permitted, despite Nkrumah's aspirations, to play an equivalent role. For revolutionary Iran, as for some other Islamic states, the concept of the *umma* overrode, or at least challenged, conventions of territorial statehood. Attitudes towards frontiers also differed, notably as between those states whose identity depended on their territoriality (as was notably the case with most post-colonial African states), and those which possessed an alternative idea of statehood which could be used to challenge their existing frontiers. In southeast Asia, relations between the states of Indo-China were on a different plane from their relations with other parts of the region: although Cambodia and Thailand both formally enjoyed the status of sovereign states, a Vietnamese attack on Cambodia did not attract anything resembling the reaction that would have been excited, regionally as well as globally, by an attack on Thailand.

[10] Egypt's switch under Sadat from the Soviet Union to the USA is the obvious exception. See S. R. David, *Choosing Sides: Alignment and Realignment in the Third World* (Baltimore, Johns Hopkins University Press, 1991).

[11] I have examined this paradox in C. Clapham, *Africa and the International System* (Cambridge, Cambridge University Press, 1996), ch. 6; at the same time, it should be noted that France exercised much the same constraints on effective sovereignty within its African *pré carré*, as did the USA in its Central American 'backyard'.

Most significant of all in accounting for regional variations in the effectiveness of sovereignty were the varying fortunes of ruling elites in different parts of the Third World in constructing viable domestic states and economies. While all such elites acted to a significant extent as intermediaries between the domestic and international spheres, the terms on which they were able to do so differed markedly. At one extreme, rulers in southeast and east Asia were generally able to form effective states and to devise successful economic strategies which – at least until the upheavals of late 1997 – enabled them to combine engagement in the global economy with a substantial level of domestic political autonomy. It can very plausibly be argued that the enhanced autonomy conferred by sovereignty on these states enabled them to manage their economies far more effectively than would have been the case had they been subject to the direct control of an international economic system dominated by the established capitalist powers. Latin American elites generally controlled effective states, but were (for a variety of reasons, both domestic and international) far less successful in devising economic strategies to match them. Middle eastern 'rentier states' combined fragile political structures with a profitable though perilous association with global markets, whereas African states, both politically and economically weak, had the most dependent position of all. In south Asia, the combination of the powerful bureaucratic and military elites inherited from British imperialism, with both domestic and international insecurity and a generally weak economic performance, helped to promote a particularly strong commitment to ideologies of state autonomy, of which sovereignty formed part. A great deal more can certainly be done to sort out the different resulting patterns of sovereignty than is possible in this paper.[12]

Regardless of its regional variations, however, the post-independence Third World sovereignty regime served the dual functions of protecting the territoriality (and in some degree the autonomy) of the state itself, and of providing international backing for the entrenchment of state control (and the power of the regime currently in office) over the rest of the domestic population. Although actual levels of accountability of Third World regimes to their people varied appreciably, such variations derived almost exclusively from differences in domestic political structures, to which the international system was largely indifferent, except on those occasions when these structures directly related (notably as between 'communist' and 'non-communist' regimes) to the major lines of cleavage within the international system itself. The sovereignty of a democratically governed India rested internationally on the same basis as that of a militarily governed Pakistan.

The Failure of the Third World Sovereignty Regime

This use of sovereignty as an ideology for maintaining state power was however inherently fragile, since it rested on a combination of domestic and external circumstances which could not be expected to continue indefinitely, and which indeed carried within them the seeds of their own destruction. Externally, it

---

[12] M. Ayoob, *The Third World Security Predicament: State Making, Regional Conflict and the International System* (Boulder CO, Lynne Rienner, 1995), approaches these issues in a way which reflects his own South Asian experience, and an implicit acceptance of the validity and viability of the state-building enterprise.

depended on the willingness of major states to accept constraints on the exercise of their own power, which were in practice kept in place to an appreciable extent by the conventions needed to regulate their competition with one another. Domestically, it sometimes rested on the willingness of populations to accept (or their inability to resist) a level of autocracy and misgovernment which rapidly undermined the legitimacy which the governments of newly independent states had generally enjoyed at the outset. The self-confidence of Third World governing elites in their own mission, reinforced as this was by statist ideologies (and notably 'socialism' in its various forms) which they happily adopted from the industrial world, readily led them into ambitious programmes for 'nation-building' and economic transformation, which were not only impossible to sustain, but proved to be counterproductive. Resting as it did on the ability of state elites to control exchanges across the domestic-international divide in a way that was beneficial very largely to themselves, the sovereignty regime was highly vulnerable to any means by which external actors on the one hand, and non-state domestic ones on the other, could forge their own exchange mechanisms in ways that cut out the middleman represented by the state.

Since in most of the Third World – excluding only a few obvious exceptions such as Afghanistan and Somalia – the formal attributes of sovereignty remain in place, it is easy to overlook the changes that have taken place in the power relations which the ideology of sovereignty has been used to protect. Maps still (even for Afghanistan and Somalia) show the territory of the world as neatly divided between 'sovereign' entities, regardless of how little they tell you about what kind of government, if any, exists in the spaces thus demarcated. Most states continue to maintain formal representation at the United Nations and elsewhere. Most, though not all, of the mechanisms through which the autonomy of states in the international system has been reduced continue to operate in ways which respect at least the fig-leaf of national sovereignty, either because the formal consent of states has been obtained, or because they are undertaken by international organizations which have been established through agreement between states. In this way, to adopt Bagehot's useful distinction, sovereignty continues to form the 'dignified' part of a constitution of international society, the 'efficient' elements of which – at least in parts of the Third World – operate behind the legitimating screen which it provides.

In practice, the sovereignty regime provided no more than a breathing space, during which governing elites had to consolidate their statehood, before the relative freedom of action which they were generally accorded in the first few decades after independence came to an end. In doing so, of course, they faced the very variable, but often extremely intractable, conditions bequeathed to them by the arbitrary processes of colonial state formation. It cannot be assumed that there was always a viable state ready to be created from the collection of human, economic and territorial resources which the new governments suddenly found themselves having to make something out of. There is nothing in the history of the world prior to the twentieth century to support the contention that the whole of its land area could be regulated according to the principles of statehood devised in post-medieval Europe. At the very least, the idea of statehood presupposes that human beings can be organized into territorially-based hierarchies which they can be compelled or induced to accept, and that the economic resources will be forthcoming to maintain the rather expensive institutions which statehood entails. That such a form of organization can be made to work throughout the world is improbable; that it can be made to coincide with the territories often haphazardly bequeathed to newly independent governments by departing colonial powers, is staggering in its presumption. In some places, the enterprise was evidently doomed from the start; and in any event, the end of the Cold War has revealed an international landscape in which no clear distinction can be made between entities which do or do not correspond to 'states', on behalf of which corresponding claims to sovereignty can be asserted.[13]

Nonetheless, governing elites initially enjoyed at least some autonomy in deciding how to go about implementing the 'hegemonic projects' on which the creation of effective statehood depended;[14] on the whole, a relatively modest approach, in which they did not seek to monopolize either access to domestic political power, or the benefits to be extracted from international trade, generally worked the best, accompanied though this had to be by adroit manoeuvre within both domestic and external political arenas. In much of east and southeast Asia, at least (most obviously excluding Burma and the Indochinese states), this approach enabled local elites to manage the process of incorporation into the global economy under conditions that enhanced their own autonomy, and which should (again given adroit leadership and adaptation) enable them to survive even their current economic crises. In much of sub-Saharan Africa on the other hand, failures of both political and economic management left state elites very poorly placed to respond to the challenges produced by the combination of domestic alienation and dramatic changes in the international system.

Internationally, the sovereignty regime can now be seen as a device which served the interests of most of the states in the international system. The superpowers, paradoxically, were in many respects the main losers from a convention which emphasized the rights of sovereignty, since they were the states most obviously constrained by it. Superpower status nonetheless carried with it implicit rights of intervention in the affairs of other states, and the ideologies through which the USA and USSR sought to legitimate their global role (the 'free world' on the one hand, against 'proletarian internationalism' on the other) could be used to override the claims of independent statehood, at least in zones (such as central Europe or central America) which the superpowers regarded as vital to their own hegemony. For them, sovereignty was useful largely as a means through which to ensure that competition between themselves did not get out of control, carrying as it did a mutual recognition of the rights implied by alliance with the officially recognized governments of client states. This did not prevent subversion, but it did place certain limits on what could be done; it was permissible, for example, for the superpower to commit troops to the defence of the regime in a recognized client state, as the USA did in Vietnam and the USSR in Afghanistan; whereas it was possible only to provide covert assistance to the domestic opponents of such a regime. For Third World states, as already noted, the regime was almost entirely beneficial, though it did place constraints on the emergence of regional powers within the Third World;

---

[13] This is a theme which I have explored in C. Clapham, 'Degrees of statehood', *Review of International Studies*, 24 (1988), 143–57.

[14] See R. H. Jackson and C. G. Rosberg, *Personal Rule in Black Africa* (Berkeley, University of California Press, 1982), for an exploration of the alternative styles open to the rulers of sub-Saharan Africa.

small states which felt threatened by potentially hegemonic neighbours could to an appreciable extent avoid subordination by attaching themselves to extra-regional patrons. For the former colonial powers, whose interests were largely bound up with the maintenance of effective state structures within their former colonies, it was also generally welcome, even though it could be used to justify expressions of autonomy such as the nationalization of the assets of companies based in the former colonial metropole.

This convenient correspondence of interests between states on which the sovereignty regime depended was nonetheless eventually undermined by a two-pronged assault: a pincer movement created by the alliance between external organizations of every kind (international institutions, business corporations, non-governmental organizations, and some states whose commitment to the existing constitution of international society had for different reasons waned), and alienated domestic constituencies. The balance of the alliance varied from case to case, the initiative sometimes being taken by domestic groups which sought external allies, sometimes the other way round. Underlying it all, however, was an assault on the legitimacy of sovereignty: on the claim that the state and those who ran it represented the people within its territory, and sought to implement some idea of 'national interest'. Instead, the state was cast as a private or partial interest, representing not the citizenry as a whole against the outside world, but one section within the citizenry (a small one at that) against others. These two conceptions of the state, as something which serves a common interest on the one hand, and a partial interest on the other, are of course entwined in the long history of political thought, and in practice virtually all states embody some combination of the two. The legitimation of sovereignty in the modern world, in which the legitimacy of government is deemed to depend on the welfare (and preferably the consent) of the population, depends however on emphasizing the first rather than the second; and the moment this emphasis is reversed, the idea of sovereignty comes under threat. For a surprisingly long period, sympathetic Western intellectuals were prepared to acquiesce in the idea that Third World governments generally represented their peoples, and to support them against what they regarded as illegitimate attempts at external intervention and control. Some still do. As this viewpoint became progressively more difficult to uphold, however – and the activities of some Third World regimes became extremely hard to justify – so the balance not just of might but of right changed sides.

It was in the economic sphere that the sovereignty regime first started to crumble, once the oil price rises of the 1970s had fed through into the Third World debt crisis. This was an arena in which the Cold War made very little difference, since by the early 1980s the USSR and its allies were clearly in no position to offer any counterweight to the Western capitalist states, and the international financial institutions (IFIs) through which much of their policy was managed. It was also significant that the debt crisis coincided with a shift towards liberalization and away from statist solutions to economic problems within some at least of the major capitalist states. Third World and notably African states, which had acquired levels of debt which they could not con-ceivably expect to repay, and which needed access to further credit facilities in order to save their economies from complete collapse, were obliged to seek credit from IFIs (led by the World Bank and the International Monetary Fund) at whatever price these were prepared to provide it; and that in turn entailed the acceptance of conditions which would previously have been regarded as an infringement of the economic sovereignty of the states concerned. Many of these conditions, which were incorporated into packages that were generally known as Structural Adjustment Programmes or SAPs, regulated the interface between the domestic and international economies, and included the imposition of free market exchange rates (in place of official rates which were often heavily overvalued), and the removal of tariffs designed to protect domestic industries.[15] Others, however, intervened directly in issues that were formally at least of entirely domestic concern, such as the regulation of marketing and pricing mechanisms for food supplied by domestic producers to domestic consumers. SAPs made it brutally clear that indebtedness was incompatible with any plausible claim to the exercise of economic autonomy.

Third World regimes which sought to fend off the demands of structural adjustment found many sympathizers in the West: as between African governments on the one hand, say, and the IMF on the other, the balance of moral advantage was not always entirely clear. Like other assaults on sovereignty, however, structural adjustment was justified in terms of the benefits that it promised to exploited (and especially rural) producers in Third World states, and to the economic welfare of the population as a whole, as against the interests of state-centred elites who had manipulated the economy to their own benefit. In the next phase of the assault on sovereignty, which took the form of demands for democratization, good governance, and respect for human rights, the emphasis on the domestic legitimacy of external policy demands was much more overt. In some respects, this campaign carried on from that for economic reform: IFIs had to rely for the implementation of SAPs on the very governing elites whose interests were most directly undermined by them, and it was scarcely surprising that these should have accepted the money while doing their best to subvert the reforms that they had promised in exchange; elected governments which might be expected to represent the interests of the rural masses who voted for them could be regarded as part of the answer. In many cases, however, demands for participation by the alienated population (orchestrated though these often were by ambitious counter-elites) sprang up as soon as overt external support for repressive regimes was withdrawn. Although the relationship between the 'internal' and the 'external' is often virtually meaningless in such deeply dependent states, demands for democracy amounted at least in some respects to a domestic assault on an idea of sovereignty which had in practice enabled deeply unrepresentative regimes to be kept in power by external force.

The good governance agenda, and notably the campaign for human rights, also brought to the fore one of the most significant instruments in the assault on sovereignty: the Western-based non-governmental organization or NGO. Institutions such as Amnesty International and Human Rights Watch had long campaigned for the universal recognition of the rights entrenched (more or

---

[15] There is a massive literature on structural adjustment. See in particular R. van der Hoeven and F. van der Kraaij, *Structural Adjustment and Beyond in Sub-Saharan Africa* (London, James Currey, 1994); P. Mosley, J. Harrigan and J. Toye, *Aid and Power: The World Bank and Policy-Based Lending*, vols 1 and 2 (London, Routledge, 1991); and for a view sympathetic to African states, B. Onimode, *The IMF, the World Bank, and African Debt*, vols 1 and 2 (London, Zed, 1989). I have discussed the international politics of structural adjustment at greater length in Clapham, *Africa and the International System*, ch. 7.

less, at least) in Western liberal ideologies; but the end of the Cold War, which enabled Western governments (and especially the United States) to disengage themselves from the embarrassing support which they had often felt obliged to give to repressive regimes in the name of anti-communism, greatly enhanced their leverage. These were however only one example of the universalization of the values of Western civil societies in ways which challenged the sovereignty of Third World states.[16] A broader attack was mounted by the *droit d'ingérence* or right of intervention promoted by Bernard Kouchner, founder of Médécins sans Frontières and subsequently minister in successive Socialist Party governments in France, which claimed a general right to override sovereignty in the name of humanitarianism – a late twentieth century revival of the *droits de l'homme* of two centuries earlier. A similar approach was taken, albeit generally with far less publicity, by famine relief organizations operating in war zones, which developed a doctrine ('a starving child knows no politics') that justified the delivery of emergency aid through whatever organization controlled the territory concerned, even if this was an insurgent movement which was fighting against the nominally sovereign state, and which benefitted both materially and diplomatically from its recognition by the NGO.[17] Another significant contributor to the decline of sovereignty was the environmental movement, for which universal transcendental values likewise overrode the claims of statehood: the needs of 'the planet', or more specifically of threatened parts of it such as the rhinoceros, took precedence over the demands of the state.

Nowhere was the sovereignty regime more explicitly challenged than in the changing status of insurgencies. Certainly, both the independence struggles of 'liberation movements' against colonial regimes, and the role of insurgencies in Cold War confrontations such as those in Vietnam and Afghanistan, had given at least some insurgencies a measure of legitimacy against the rival claims of juridical statehood, a measure which Ronald Reagan sought to extend to the Nicaraguan Contras by describing them as 'freedom fighters'. With the end of the Cold War, however, the international status of insurgencies markedly improved, as these came to be regarded, not as rebellions which had to be suppressed by central governments in the name of state consolidation, but as evidence of misgovernment by the state itself, which needed to be resolved through some process of internationally supervised mediation. With greater or lesser degrees of success, this approach was then applied to conflicts such as those in Angola, Liberia, Mozambique and Rwanda in Africa, and Cambodia in south-east Asia.[18] In collapsed states such as Cambodia and Somalia, previously unacceptable forms of external intervention were implemented,

[16] Radical Islam, of course, likewise undermined sovereignty in some respects, even though it would be used to protect the sovereignty of Islamist states in others; any transcendental ideology, which upholds certain values as absolute and universal, is inherently threatening to a doctrine of sovereignty which ascribes legitimacy to institutions and procedures rather than to ultimate values.

[17] See for example B. Hendrie, 'Relief Behind the Lines: the Cross-border Operation in Tigray', in J. Macrae and A. Zwi (eds), *War and Hunger: Rethinking International Responses to Complex Emergencies* (London, Zed, 1994), pp. 125–38; W. DeMars, 'Tactics of Protection: International Human Rights Organizations in the Ethiopian Conflict, 1980–1986', in E. McCarthy-Arnolds (ed.), *Africa, Human Rights, and the Global System* (Westport CT, Greenwood, 1994), ch. 5.

[18] I have examined the peculiar tragedy of the application of the new 'rules' of conflict mediation to Rwanda, in C. Clapham, 'Rwanda: the perils of peace-making', *Journal of Peace Research*, 35 (1998), 193–210.

however temporarily.[19] New NGOs dedicated to conflict resolution, such as International Alert, came into being, exciting the suspicion of governments through their willingness to treat with, and hence give international status to, 'rebel' movements such as the Revolutionary United Front in Sierra Leone. Human rights organizations, which had previously publicized the transgressions of regimes from outside their territory, were supplemented by election monitors who enjoyed an internationally recognized role in supervising the conduct of governments from within it.

In the face of these challenges, Third World states and their supporters sought to retreat and regroup, erecting barricades around a more restricted, and more defensible, conception of sovereignty than the grandiose claims put forward at the height of the sovereignty regime in the 1970s. Pretensions to construct an entirely statist international order, represented by CERDS and the NWOI, dropped out of sight. Even the demand for unrestricted internal state control was modified. The Organization of African Unity, which from its foundation in 1963 had espoused sovereignty in its starkest form, came during the 1980s to sponsor the African Charter of Human and Peoples' Rights, a document which, while carefully worded in such a way as to evade any effective restriction on the power of states, nonetheless recognized at least in principle that control by states over their own citizens should be subject to some form of external supervision. The defence of state power in east and southeast Asia was in some degree moved out of the universalistic sphere of state sovereignty (to which states such as China nonetheless continued to subscribe) into the particularist realm of 'culture'. Scholars such as Francis Deng, a Southern Sudanese working in the United States, sought to erect a conditional doctrine of sovereignty, under the heading of 'sovereignty as responsibility', under which sovereignty rested on accountability to both domestic and external constituencies,[20] a formulation which bore an intriguing resemblance to the 'dual mandate' by which Lord Lugard had sought to justify British imperialism. In practice, it seems probable that a degree of autonomy will be permitted largely as a result of the indifference of hegemonic states, in parts of the Third World where they have few interests and where the costs of enforcement are high, rather than through any recognition of the inherent rights of sovereignty itself. The entire project of seeking to manage delinquent Third World states from outside, through mechanisms ranging from structural adjustment through the imposition of multi-party political systems to the extreme expedient of humanitarian intervention, has come to seem impracticable, in the face of the ability of local actors to frustrate and manipulate the would-be interveners.[21] As the missionary zeal imparted by the end of the Cold War declines, Third World states are likely to be left to sink or swim on their own.

At the same time, the decline of Cold War sovereignty regimes enhances the prospects for regional powers, as these gain the ability to create localized

[19] See J. Mayall (ed.), *The New Interventionism 1991–1994: United Nations Experience in Cambodia, Former Yugoslavia and Somalia* (Cambridge, Cambridge University Press, 1996).

[20] See Francis M. Deng *et al., Sovereignty as Responsibility: Conflict Management in Africa* (Washington, Brookings, 1996).

[21] This is a theme which I have explored in sub-Saharan Africa in C. Clapham, *Building Political Stability in Sub-Saharan Africa* (London, Wilton Park Papers, 136, 1997), and 'Running Africa from Outside', in K. King and S.M. McGrath (eds.), *Running, Reporting and Researching Africa* (University of Edinburgh, 1998).

hegemonies of a kind that would previously have been prevented by extra-regional patronage. A particularly striking example of this process has arisen in central Africa, with the collapse of the convention of non-intervention, and the engagement of Rwandan and Angolan military forces on the side of the victorious insurgents in the Congo/Zaire civil war of 1996–97, and the direct intervention of the Angolan army in the 1997 civil war in Congo-Brazzaville. It is paradoxical but not surprising that this should have happened in the region in which a formal commitment to the principles of sovereignty was most strictly upheld: the OAU's insistence on non-intervention was necessary precisely because states were so fragile, and their boundaries so artificial, that conflicts in one state always risked the involvement of their neighbours. Eventually, the dangers inherent in the fragility of African statehood were almost bound to break through the rules with which governing elites sought to contain them.

Conclusion

Some of the restrictions on effective state autonomy indicated in the previous section can be rendered formally compatible with the continued maintenance of a doctrine of sovereignty, whereas others cannot. A state which agrees to a Structural Adjustment Programme, under no matter what level of external pressure or desperate domestic need, is formally exercising its sovereign rights, as it is likewise when it accepts external monitoring of its elections, or adheres to an international convention which permits its citizens (or multinational companies operating in its territory) to challenge its jurisdiction in an extra-territorial court of law. A 'state' which, like Somalia in 1992, is subject to invasion by a military force authorized by the United Nations, but without agreement by any authority plausibly purporting to represent the Somali state, has conversely been subjected to an international trusteeship which places its sovereignty in abeyance. Numerous examples of intervention by other states, corporations, or non-governmental organizations, often in collaboration with insurgent movements, likewise derogate unambiguously from the principles of sovereignty, even though such activities may not be formally authorized by a body such as the UN. The argument of this article, however, is that such distinctions are not of the first importance: just as an individual who 'chooses' bondage in preference to death can scarcely be said to be free, so a state which accepts the external management of its economy or supervision of its domestic political arrangements, can scarcely be said to be sovereign. What matters is that the events of the 1990s have demonstrated that the functions which sovereignty has served for Third World governing elites can be achieved only when these are able to avert economic catastrophe and maintain an appropriate level of effective control over their domestic territories.

Nothing is more hazardous than attempting to look at the present from the viewpoint of the future. In retrospect, however, the kind of sovereignty regime erected in the Third World with the collapse of European colonialism may well come to be regarded as no more than a very temporary and artificial solution to the problem of incorporating new areas of the globe into the international system erected in the aftermath of Westphalia. This process has already passed through a number of fairly well-defined stages. First came a straightforward process of booty imperialism, exemplified by the conquest and looting of India and what became Latin America, and the enslavement of Africans to provide a labour force for a more systematic productive process in the Caribbean basin. Subsequently, formal colonialism expressed a need to extend administrative control into parts of the world which had previously been left largely to their own devices. The escalating costs of this control in the face of indigenous resentment and resistance, coupled with changes in the international system during the Cold War era, helped to induce the withdrawal of the colonial powers, and the erection in their place of a new state structure which was protected by the major powers through the post-1945 sovereignty regime. As this regime in turn comes under challenge, so the picture of the international system conveyed by multicoloured maps, in which each colour designates the territory of a different sovereign state, is becoming less and less adequate as the representation of a much more fluid and complex reality. The rules of juridical sovereignty offer no long-term security for quasi-states. Those states which succeed in maintaining effective control over their own territories, together with economic structures that offer them a stake in the global economy, will be able at least to assert their claims to a level of sovereignty which is shrinking even in the key states of the capitalist core. Other parts of the world, in which effective statehood is not maintained, are already reverting to a *terra nullius*, in which local warlords make deals with intermediaries of the global economy, in a manner little different from that employed in much of the Third World prior to the imposition of colonial rule.[22] The era of sovereignty as a universal organizing principle for the management of the global system has ended.

---

[22] For a study of this process in a number of African states, see W. Reno, *Warlord Politics and African States* (Boulder CO, Lynne Rienner, 1998).

The United Nations in the 1990s: Proactive Cosmopolitanism and the Issue of Sovereignty

Paul Taylor

Introduction

During the Cold War sovereignty was usually interpreted by United Nations members in the manner of traditional hard-line realists. The Charter was understood to mean that the rule of non-intervention was to be rigidly applied, and that what happened within states was no concern of outsiders. In the wording of the key paragraph, Article 2, para. 7, the word *essentially* was mostly overlooked as this would weaken the assertion of state exclusiveness. 'Nothing contained in the present Charter shall authorize the United Nations to intervene in matters which are *essentially* within the jurisdiction of any state or shall require the Members to submit such matters to settlement under the present Charter.' (author's italics) The predominant view of governments was that sovereignty was a private world into which the outside world was not permitted to enter. The only exception was operations under Chapter VII: 'this principle [exclusive domestic jurisdiction] shall not prejudice the application of enforcement measures under Chapter VII'. (Article 2 para. 7) Almost always the Security Council justified intervening within a state only when there was a threat to international peace and security, even when there had been gross infringements of human rights.[1]

But there was a contrasting notion of sovereignty: that it could be envisaged as having a licence from the international community to practice as an independent government in a particular territory. Such a licence could be granted by the act of recognition of that government by other states, and a consensus amongst them that this should be done could be interpreted as an expression of the will of the international community. After the end of the Cold War, however, more governments were prepared to demand that those amongst them whose internal policies were not up to international standards should change their ways, and those accused, however defiant, found it difficult to avoid making concessions to international pressure so that policies could at least be given a patina of respectability. The standards by which they were measured were increasingly those of the liberal democratic states.

There were also developments in the concept of the *international community*: in the earlier years of the United Nations the international community and its authority were seen as weak and discountable, but by the late 1990s they had become more substantial and hard to ignore. There were, therefore, two

[1] See J. Mayall (ed.), *The New Interventionism* (Cambridge University Press, 1996).

contrasting notions of sovereignty: that it was a private world, with weak international authority, and that it was an international licence to operate as an independent government, granted by the collectivity of states, which, it is argued here, formed the international community. This essay examines the interplay between these two notions and argues that there was a discernible move to the latter after the end of the Cold War. It sees no prospect for the abandonment of sovereignty but seeks to understand its adaptation to new circumstances.[2]

Traditionally a 'state' was held to be sovereign when there was no authority which had precedence over it: outside actors therefore had no right to be involved in its internal affairs. And sovereignty was an absolute unaffected by the circumstances of the time. But theorists such as Bodin held that there was indeed a superior authority – God. In a number of writings this notion took substantial form in the assertion of a general requirement for civilized behaviour as part of the divine order.[3] In more recent times the idea that there was something above the state was encompassed in the idea of the will of the international community, and, after the end of the Cold War, this was increasingly acknowledged, if not obeyed. There were also very few states that could avoid involvements from outside themselves through which pressures were channelled which could not be resisted by the actors targeted. What is proposed in this essay is that there was after the end of the Cold War an expression in more utilitarian and secular terms of the ancient qualification of sovereignty as an absolute: there was a stronger form of the international community which was a modern equivalent of the divine order.

Sovereignty cannot be considered in exclusively theoretical or philosophical terms, but always needs to be related to the current circumstances of the state, including prevailing expectations about its emerging role. The changing circumstances after the end of the Cold War included, first, developments in the way in which international organizations sought to protect international peace and security; second the further evolution of a system in which laws made outside the state required compliance within it, especially in the world of business and commerce – they imposed upon the state (in this the European Union was the most advanced illustration of a general development); third was the extension of the range of mutual involvements through which common standards, such as democratization, were promoted; fourth, a rudimentary global watch – a full time system of surveillance of states – to identify crisis points, linked with the development of mechanisms for more rapid response, was being set up; and, fifth, the international community had set about establishing mechanisms for rehabilitating and restoring states that had failed.

These various developments reflected and promoted moral interdependence. For instance the idea of increasing international surveillance to detect incipient crises assumed that obligations to assist extended beyond the state, and that there was moral solidarity which took precedence over a community's right to privacy. This implied that efforts to deal with collapsed states, Somalia,

---

[2] The essay is entirely consistent with the arguments in defence of sovereignty which are well developed in M. R. Fowler and J. M. Bunck, *Law, Power and the Sovereign State: The Evolution and Application of the Concept of Sovereignty* (University Park, Pennsylvania State University Press, 1995).

[3] A. Murphy, 'The Sovereign State as Political-Territorial Ideal', in T. Biersteker and C. Weber (eds), *State Sovereignty as Social Construct* (Cambridge, Cambridge University Press, 1996), pp. 81–120.

Cambodia, Bosnia, etc. were not *just* a series of special cases, reflecting the special interests of the Great Powers, but were also expressions of the evolving norms. Discussion of these various circumstances runs through the primary framework of the essay which is chronological.

Before turning to this discussion it is necessary to explain *proactive cosmopolitanism*. There were two contrasting views about how a cosmopolitan community might arise: first that it could emerge from what was imminent and general, as was the case with the realization of Kantian categorical imperatives or the principles of natural law; and secondly, in a positivist fashion, that it was the approximation of the values and behaviour of diverse groups to the values and behaviour of a particular group. In the latter view a cosmopolitan community was established either by conversion, as, for instance, in conversion to Christianity or Islam or to the principles of western liberal democracy; or by empowering those who shared the preferred values and behaviour in the diverse communities.[4] In this view it was argued that there was in different communities a sufficient mutuality as to agree about what such notions as *fairness, justice* and *liberal* meant with regard to behaviour. These notions were not confined to particular communities, and, on the contrary, were universal – there were always people who understood them and reflected them in their behaviour, whatever the religion or ideology – and what was needed to create the cosmopolitan community was practical measures to increase the influence of such people.

The term proactive cosmopolitanism as used in this essay therefore has two components: a deliberate attempt to create a consensus about values and behaviour – a cosmopolitan community – among diverse communities; and the reflection and promotion of cosmopolitan values through specific new activities in international organizations such as the United Nations. This was a modern version of the Kantian strategy of encouraging the specific instruments of hospitality and commerce as well as the actualization of moral imperatives.[5] What it excluded was the imposition of such values from outside. However the United Nations and the European Union, with increasing energy and openness, increasingly pushed the civil and political values of Western Liberal states[6] in other parts of the world. In terms of the moral interdependence concept of Donelly there emerged a greater tendency to do something about the practices of other peoples, publics and elites, which seemed abhorrent, but also to promote western liberal values.[7] But this tendency was linked with the increasing penetration of the state by international instruments which were often

---

[4] See R. J. Vincent, *Human Rights and International Relations* (Cambridge, Cambridge University Press, 1986), especially pp. 37–57.

[5] See the excellent examination of the Kantian approach to peace in F. H. Hinsley, *Power and the Pursuit of Peace: Theory and Practice in the History of Relations between States* (Cambridge, Cambridge University Press, 1963), ch. 4.

[6] In the 1990s the Security Council regularly included in its mandates for peace-keeping operation proposals to advance liberal democratic solutions to internal conflicts and promote Western standards of governance worldwide; the Chinese went along with this! See P. Guillot, 'Human Rights, Democracy, and the Multidimensional Peace Operations of the United Nations', in Mortimer Sellers (ed.), *The New World: Sovereignty, Human Rights and the Self Determination of Peoples* (Oxford, Berg, 1996), pp. 273–304.

[7] See J. Donnelly, 'State Sovereignty and International Intervention: The Case of Human Rights', in G. Lyons and M. Mastanduno (eds), *Beyond Westphalia? State Sovereignty and International Intervention* (Baltimore, The Johns Hopkins Press, 1995), pp. 115–146.

organized through institutions like the United Nations, and such instruments could be regarded as the modern instruments of the Kantian strategy.

In a first section the development of the system with regard to peace and security arrangements is considered. The stress is upon both the way in which they increasingly involved intervening in the state and the changing norms which this reflected. (Parallel changes are also reflected in human rights arrangements, though these are not considered here.) In a second section attention is focussed upon reflections of cosmopolitanism in the expanding agenda of the United Nations regarding the maintenance of international order after the Cold War. In a third section the implications of the developments for sovereignty are discussed and proposals for taking forward the arrangements of proactive cosmopolitanism in the late 1990s are set out; this illustrates the direction of evolution of the agenda.

The Evolution of the System

The Changing Role of the UN and Peace Maintenance

A primary element in the circumstances of sovereignty in the 1990s was the emerging practice of the United Nations with regards to peace maintenance. It is necessary to give some space to discussing its development. Its scale and nature had greatly altered by the 1990s compared with its earlier forms and the changes were themselves symptomatic of deeper changes in the role of the UN. The rules of traditional forms of peace-keeping had emerged by the late 1950s.[8] They included the need for the approval of the host state for the location of the forces, and the requirement that the forces should be lightly armed; and that they should not be proactive in their use, but respond only if attacked first. They were to be placed under the command of the United Nations, with the Secretary General himself as their supreme commander, and UN field command, with the advice of a committee of the contributing states. And the forces would normally not come from any of the major powers. The various examples of peace-keeping before the late 1980s showed a number of variations with regard to these principles, but they were the norm.

The essential condition of all uses of peace-keeping was that they be placed between the forces of the parties to a dispute to encourage diplomacy between them. The indispensable assumption was that a compromise was possible. They were also intended during the Cold War period to help to exclude the super-powers from the conflict, though this was usually a cover for covert involvement by the United States. Without the support of the latter in materials and finance it is doubtful that much peace-keeping would have been done. Nevertheless the Soviet Union found it convenient to ignore this subterfuge and all but the first peace-keeping venture, in Suez in November 1956, derived from a Security Council mandate which necessarily required the approval of the five veto-holding powers. Suez was the exception in that it was set up by the General Assembly.

After 1989 – the end of the Cold War – peace-keeping forces were used more frequently and for a number of tasks that led them to face problems of a different order from those met earlier. As of early 1998, the time of writing,

---

[8] A useful overview of the development of peace-keeping is J. Sutterlin, *The United Nations and Maintenance of International Security: A Challenge to be Met* (Westport, Praeger, 1995).

about the same number of instances of their use – about twenty – had occurred since 1989 as in the entire period since their first use in November 1956, and at their peak the forces included around 75,000 troops compared with an average of under 10,000 in the 1980s. But these new instances were generally in circumstances that were even more difficult. They involved complex humanitarian crises, in which there were serious infringements of human rights and shortages of food and medicine, and, in addition, major security problems – usually in the context of civil war – with the accompanying intractable political disagreements. In these circumstances the security forces found themselves performing new tasks, especially helping to provide the essentials of life in the face of active opposition, and often they were of necessity more heavily armed, and given a mandate to be more proactive in the use of arms in order to get help through to the ill and starving. This meant that they were much more likely to attract the active opposition of the parties to the dispute. It was much more difficult for them to maintain the position of neutrality which they had sought on earlier occasions – though even then it had not always been possible, as with the experience of the United Nations Interim Force in the Lebanon (UNIFIL) in southern Lebanon after the Israeli invasion in 1982.[9] The forces also now often came from the great powers and even from the superpowers. The USA provided a major force for the operation in Somalia in December 1992, and later was involved in the operation in ex-Yugoslavia to police the Dayton agreement.[10] Major powers such as Britain and France became regular contributors to the forces, and Germany and Japan also became more involved, though not in the front line.

In these circumstances by 1998 peace-keeping forces had experienced a number of new problems. Because of the difficulty of maintaining their neutrality in the eyes of the combatants, the number of casualties was much greater, and contributing countries became much more reluctant to hand over command and control of the forces to the UN without reservation. The US President indicated this in a Presidential Directive, and there were a number of instances of participating forces double-checking with their own governments about whether or not they should follow instructions from UN officers. States also began more frequently to impose limitations on the uses to which their forces could be put by UN commanders. Command and control became an area of contention and too often led to uncertainty about who was in charge, with often damaging consequences, and escalating costs coincided with the reluctance of some states, principally the USA, to pay their allotted share. This led to a massive short-fall in contributions for peace-keeping, as well as on the regular assessed budget.[11]

A further problem concerned the supervision of the forces by the Security Council. Too frequently the original mandate of the Security Council, on which the role of the forces was based, was unclear about ends and means, and was also expanded without sufficient consideration, a process which became known as *mission creep*. There was a degree of ad hocery about Security Council

---

[9] A. James, *Peacekeeping in International Politics* (London, Macmillan, 1990), pp. 122–130.

[10] See Economides and Taylor, and Lewis and Mayall in Mayall, *The New Interventionism*, pp. 59–93.

[11] For a comprehensive account of these problems as they stood in 1997 see P. Taylor, S. Daws and U. Adamczick-Gerteis (eds), *Documents on Reform of the United Nations* (Aldershot, Dartmouth, 1997), Part II, pp. 65–169.

decision making: commitments were made without thinking through the strategic and logistic implications. The classic example of this was the decision to create the safe areas in ex-Yugoslavia, which led to populations being falsely assured that they were secure in UN protection.

The difficulties of the new peace-keeping were such that a few authorities, including Secretary General Boutros Boutros Gahli, were led by the mid-1990s to the conclusion that the more active form of peace-keeping was unsustainable. This was probably a premature conclusion. After the end of the Cold War it was necessary to find an alternative principle to the superpower standoff for the maintenance of international peace and security, and a more active form of peace-keeping was one of the options. But conditions which had to be met before the regular use of more active forms of peace-keeping was conceivable had to be identified and evaluated. It was necessary to sort out the financial arrangements; it was necessary to develop a system for the more rational development of Security Council mandates and to avoid 'mission creep,' it was necessary to ensure that Security Council mandates were clear and capable of being applied on the ground, and attention had to be given to the tactical imperatives of military operations: if there was the possibility of hot war UN personnel should not be located where they were likely to be taken hostage and used as human shields. It was also necessary to establish clear chains of command and control. These were difficult conditions to meet, but the costs of dealing with them were no greater than the costs likely to arise from keeping the mechanisms for maintaining international peace and security in a kind of time warp, and new peace-keeping was more in keeping with the pattern of the long term development of international society than would be a return to *ad hoc* balances of power, or spheres of influence, be they regional or global.[12]

Peace Maintenance in Longer Perspective

The development of peace-keeping was necessary because it coincided with the logic of the current phase of the development of the relationship between the global institutions and the state. The new peace-keeping was just one manifestation of a wider range of involvements within the state, and reflected a new concern to strengthen the state so that it was more capable of carrying out the necessary functions of statehood in modern international society. The new activism could be enhanced without compromising the traditional norms of intervention[13]: that it should not be directed at imposing an order founded on principles that were foreign to that state. It was, however, adding a new ingredient in implying that such a process of internal maturation need not be violent, but could take place within a framework of internal order under

[12] For a balanced evaluation of these problems, see A. Roberts, *Humanitarian Action in War*, Adelphi Paper 305 (London, The International Institute for Strategic Studies, 1996). Roberts concluded that 'The most promising approach to the role of the military in relation to humanitarian efforts is likely to be pragmatic one. While not denying a role for the UN peace-keeping forces, or for full-scale "humanitarian intervention" in cases of extreme emergency, such an approach also stress the importance of other forms of military protection and assistance. ... future attempts ...need to avoid the elements of ambiguity, verging on dishonesty, that have characterized many such efforts ...' p. 87.

[13] For an excellent examination of the concept of intervention and its variations see O. Ramsbotham, 'Humanitarian intervention, 1990–95: a need to reconceptualize?', *Review of International Studies*, 23 (1997), 445–468.

international supervision. It was possible for the international community to use greater degrees of compulsion in holding the ring within a state without compromising neutrality and without constituting intervention in the technical sense of seeking to impose precise forms of outcome from outside.

Just as a police force could remain impartial when using duress within the state, so long as the laws were generally known, and as long as the response of the police was proportional to the scale of the offence, so an active international peace-keeping force could appear neutral as long as the rules of engagement were clear to the parties to a dispute, and no partiality was shown in applying them. Being proactive in the use of force by peace-keeping forces need not jeopardize the principle of neutrality. It was, however, absolutely necessary that adequate means for upholding the rules were available, and could be seen to be available, so that the forces of order were not brought into disrepute by the observation of incapacity. It was also necessary that there should be an efficient and effective United Nations command and control system over such forces. This seemed impossible with enforcement, and the experience of more active forms of peace-keeping had not been encouraging. But some countries, such as Canada, were not as averse as others to accepting such international command, and it was not clear whether the problems hitherto had been ones of principle. The doubts were arguably more to do with a lack of confidence in the United Nations' procedures in this context in the 1990s, and such procedures could be improved. Trends would suggest that this was the preferable course: the difficulties, though serious, were by no means insuperable, and there were strong practical and moral arguments for tackling them.

The background was a trend towards a more general involvement of the UN system in the rescuing of failing states, as was reflected in the new mechanisms for providing assistance in humanitarian crises. But it also fitted into the pattern of the longer term evolution of the state, which had passed through a number of phases since the emergence of a primitive state system out of Medieval Christendom after the Thirty Years War in the early seventeenth century. The fact of this progression was itself evidence of the impossibility of staying with the arrangements as they had emerged in the Cold War and it underlined the point that the new forms of activity were as much about evolving norms as national interests.

- Before the Treaties of Westphalia in 1648 medieval Christendom had been a system of shifting and permeable territories under a variety of Princes, who continuously intervened in each others realms and were challenged by the Church's claims to secular power.
- Between 1648 and 1815 the state in Europe gradually consolidated its internal arrangements and established internal monopolies of force, taxation and administration. At the same time elements of international society emerged, such as a distinctive system of international law, and a body of less formal rules which applied to relations between states and the practice of diplomacy in international society. This was the period of the emergence of an international society more strictly defined as a set of actors – the states – which accepted a range of conventions of behaviour in their mutual relations.
- In the period after the defeat of Napoleon until well after the Second World War, the predominant concept of the state which emerged was that

of a national welfare state, with increasingly formal prohibitions on intervention internally. This was a natural corollary of the extension to the nations of sentiments of attachment which had been previously confined to relations between family members. The notion that such intervention was an infringement of a moral right to domestic privacy was reinforced: this development was linked with the positivist view of cultural relativity, sometimes called communitarianism. The right to privacy reached its high point in the period after the Second World War, and in particular in the insistence in the 1960 Declaration on Decolonization that the right to independence of peoples in states was unconditional.

- This period arguably extended into the mid-1980s and the first indications of change were the new approach by Soviet President Gorbachev and the resulting *entente* among the five permanent members of the Security Council initiated by the British. This was the basis of a growing international intrusiveness in the internal affairs of the UN member states.[14] The relationship between the state and international order was again altered as the idea of cosmopolitanism re-emerged. It was not that the state was challenged, but that its claim as a moral absolute was challenged. McCorquodale pointed out that 'a commitment to applying international human rights law to the right of self-determination reinforces the acknowledgement of states that their sovereignty is not absolute at least as far as the treatment of persons and groups on their territory is concerned'.[15] The challenge to cultural relativism and the re-emergence of cosmopolitanism was associated with the view that what went on within states was indeed of general concern.

A point that needs to be stressed, however, was that accepting obligations to citizens globally had to go along with acquiring a right to judge the behaviour of those citizens, and governments which claimed to speak for them: an increasing preparedness to undertake international humanitarian actions, and the linked use of proactive peace-keeping forces, was necessarily associated with the assertion of the right to judge. The new forms of peace-keeping had to be evaluated in the context of this new cosmopolitanism. The old kind was appropriate to the communitarian approach to inter-state relations: the new kind was a necessary adjunct of the new cosmopolitanism.

Peace-keeping forces were part of a spectrum of involvements in failing states each of which arguably reflected a degree of moral solidarity. This spectrum could be divided into four interrelated stages. First was the stage of using the forces to ensure that food was provided and disease controlled. At this stage the forces might be required to use force to get food through. Second was a stage at which the forces were involved in various kinds of pacification. Such activities had by the late 1990s been identified in a number of categories, including establishing safe areas, corridors of tranquillity, green lines, and the rehabilitation and resettlement of refugees. Activities at this stage might also include restraining the availability of arms to a civilian population and collecting and guarding heavy weapons. In a third stage the forces might be required to provide

---

[14] This argument is borrowed from D. Malone, 'The UN Security Council in the post-Cold War world: 1987–97', *Security Dialogue*, 28 (1997), 393–408.

[15] R. McCorquodale, 'Human Rights and Self-determination', in Sellers, *The New World Order*, p. 26.

back-up support for a range of activities related to the restoration of civil society. These included establishing an administration, civilian police forces, and supervising elections, activities which were becoming a regular feature of the business of the system. They might also involve helping to encourage the establishment of organizations such as forms of representation for workers and political parties – the process of democratization. A final category of activity was found throughout the spectrum and involved attempting to keep apart the armies of the parties to a conflict, and promoting negotiation.

There were of course dangers and difficulties which were typical of each of these activities. There was the risk that help might be diverted to help the warring factions and thereby prolong the conflict. This was a serious argument against humanitarian assistance. But it could not be regarded as a fatal impediment in the way of the development of a more moral community. Evidence from the violence in the Great Lakes area of Africa in the late 1990s was that although this had certainly been a problem in the refugee camps, it had become less so over time. Clearly every precaution needed to be taken to prevent this happening and to encourage the handing-in of weapons. Second, the question arose of whether such investment was worth while when it might lead to the hardening of the lines of division between communities as with the green line in Cyprus. The only response to this was that such a green line was very much cheaper than the prolongation of active war.

In any case the justification for extending the role of peace-keeping was part of a wider process of enhanced involvement in failing states, which derived from the characteristics of the present stage of evolution of international society. It is not here argued that these activities were merely an expression of the need to do good. That they reflected interest in the sense that the active states had specific and general gains – raw materials and security – was undeniable. But there was an admixture of moral imperative: governments could not tolerate undue suffering for a number of complex reasons, including the natural sympathy of their electors with the victims. That it occasionally had outcomes which were difficult to accept as a settlement or solution to a problem, and involved continuing commitment of money and resources by the international community, was no reason for refusing such involvement. It was part of a process of active order maintenance which was relevant to international society, as well as the individual states, which could best be described as pacific engagement. There were moral grounds for such activity, which were an aspect of the development of a cosmopolitan moral community, as well as more utilitarian calculations of costs and benefits.

The UN Agenda after the End of the Cold War

Attention is now focussed upon the evolving practices, and perceptions of new problems, in the 1990s. These are seen as reflections of cosmopolitanism, as well as responses to particular problems.

The New UN and Crisis Response

The skills of the UN in maintaining peace and security and providing humanitarian assistance were much improved in the late 1980s and 1990s in two main respects: information gathering and analysis and increasing capacity for speedy response. Again it is useful to place this account in the context of the overall development of the system for promoting peace and security through a global international organization.

- The first example of this was of course the League of Nations. In the original design its executive committee, the League Council was to be convened if a crisis was reported: it was not intended to be in permanent session. And the mechanisms for gathering information were primitive: they depended on ad hoc procedures such as whether states had noticed a crisis and were prepared to convene the Council. It was as if the fire brigade had to be put together when someone happened to notice a fire in the neighbourhood. In the first years more peace maintaining was actually carried out by the representatives of the powers that had been victorious in the 1914–18 war, acting outside the League framework, but this was not part of the design. The League also had no machinery either for setting up or for commanding military forces on a collective basis, though a number of efforts were made without success to correct this deficiency.
- The United Nations was a development from the League in that the Security Council was indeed a permanent institution which functioned continuously and not just when called into session, with special responsibility for maintaining international peace and security. The fire brigade was now on permanent standby, and the alarm could be sounded either by the member states or by the Secretary-General. The latter was given a new role in the Charter: he was asked in Article 99 to bring any dispute, which, in his opinion, might threaten the maintenance of international peace and security, to the attention of the Security Council. He could report the outbreak of fire anywhere in the world: the watch tower was permanently manned, and the response could be much more rapid. Article 99 proved far more important than it appeared at first sight as it was the legal basis for the gradual expansion of the Secretary-General's role with regard to investigating emerging threats to the peace and mediating between the parties. In order to evaluate the increased range of information a department was created in the Secretariat for the analysis of the information available to it. This was the Department of Political Affairs which worked alongside the Department of Peace-keeping Operations.
- Through the 1980s and 1990s a third phase of development of the global institution was observable. In the preceding phase, despite the enhancement of the United Nations' information collection and analysis capacity, there remained a random quality to the engagement of the Secretary General or states. In the new phase, however, the institution began what became known as a *global watch*. Its information gathering machinery was greatly enhanced, professionalized and on permanent duty, despite the difficulties made by some states.[16] It was not, as had earlier been the case,

[16] Perez de Cuellar set up an Office for Research and the Collection of Information (ORCI) which was abolished by Boutros Boutros-Ghali, its functions being then assigned to the new Departments of Political Affairs (DPA) and of Peace-keeping (DPK). Boutros-Ghali stated 'That Department ... is now organized to follow political developments worldwide, so that it can provide early warning of impending conflicts and analyse possibilities for preventive action ...' (A/50/60 – 1995/1, 3 January 1995, Para. 26).

that the organization surveyed the horizon in search of fire and then acted, but rather that increasingly a whole range of factors which were likely to encourage fire was regularly reported and analysed. Some of this was done in cooperation with the intelligence services of the great powers, but more was done through the United Nations' own resources, and there were advantages in working this way. A beginning was made with the use of satellite and computer technology, and information from local officers in various organizations was systematically collected. A special case of this was the creation of the arms registry, which collected data on the movement of arms around the world, of which a surprising amount was readily available in the public realm, in newspapers and specialist journals.[17] In the late 1990s the next step was to require that both governments and manufacturers should fully disclose the range of their wares and the customers they served.

This information was a help in identifying possible trouble spots. Troop movements could also be more easily spotted, and it was now more likely that a potential malefactor would be aware that his or her misdeeds would be known. The certainty of being found out was likely to be itself a deterrent: the intelligence services of the world's main military powers had the capacity to do this for years but there were advantages in going beyond this to a discrete UN capacity in this area. Information was less likely to be sensitive to political interest and more likely to be generally available in fact and to be believed to be available. Sophisticated information about a developing crisis would be placed firmly in the common realm. In this third phase it was as if the streets of the international neighbourhood were under constant surveillance by video cameras.

There were however two further difficulties in the way of using the information. The first concerned the capacity to respond quickly and to sustain that response. The second was how to bring the attention of the Security Council to a problem after the relevant information had been collected and evaluated by experts in or outside the Secretariat. With regards to the first difficulty there were a number of significant developments in the early 1990s. These included the professionalization of the Department of Peace-keeping Operations. The number of its staff was increased, and included more specialist military and political advisors. It was closely involved in the new system for information gathering. And it was placed on 24 hours operation. A great deal had been achieved, even though more needed to be done.[18]

With regard to the second difficulty there were in the late 1990s a number of proposals. It had been noted that the Security Council had been slow to focus on the Somalia crisis in 1992, and, later, on the crisis in Rwanda and Burundi. Some argued that the Secretary-General had deliberately contrived a row at the London Conference on Yugoslavia in London in the summer of 1992 in order to

[17] The United Nations Registry of Conventional Arms was created by the General Assembly in December 1991. Members states were required to provide data for the previous year on imports and exports of battle tanks, armored combat vehicles, artillery, combat aircraft, attack helicopters, warships and missiles and missile launchers, as of 30 April 1993. See J. Tessitore and S. Woolfson (eds), *A Global Agenda: Issues Before the 48th General Assembly of the United Nations* (Lanham, University Press of American, 1993), pp. 141–142.

[18] See *Command and Control of United Nations Peacekeeping Operations: Report of the Secretary-General*, GA, A/49/681, 21 November 1994.

attract attention away from the first world crisis to the worsening Third World crisis in Somalia.[19] There were many other reasons why attention might not be engaged with a crisis, including various kinds of fatigue or a shortage of resources. But the problem was that information about a developing crisis was not itself a guarantee that it would engage the Security Council's attention. One proposal was that a committee of high level experts should be set up alongside the Security Council which would help the Secretary-General to get an item onto the agenda, and advise about the realism of the response. At the time of writing this remained, however, a problem area.[20]

A parallel capacity had also been developed in the United Nations' arrangements for dealing with humanitarian assistance especially the DHA. It had set up a Humanitarian Early Warning System which drew upon the various early-warning mechanisms of other United Nations and non-United Nations organizations – including non-governmental organizations – and used computerized and satellite technology. It also collected information from officers in the field especially those working with the UNDP. A group had been set up to consider the further enhancement of this capacity. It was possible for it to predict from geographical, climatological and social indicators where crises were likely to arise. In the case of humanitarian action capacity to respond quickly, though not always adequately, had been developed. The DHA established teams of assessors from its own staff and other UN bodies, which were like the American DART teams, to go out to a threatened area quickly to assess the scale of a crisis and the response needed. 'These missions have been fundamental, first, in drawing the attention of the international community to the plight of affected populations, and, secondly, in assessing the needs of vulnerable groups for the subsequent planning, elaboration and implementation of humanitarian programmes' (A/51/172 Para 80).

Such teams also existed to assess natural disasters. With regard to so-called sudden-onset disasters the DHA was assisted by the United Nations Disaster Assessment and Coordination Team, with the participation of 18 Member States. In 1995 the DHA had provided assistance to 55 member states to support their efforts to cope with the impact of 82 sudden-onset natural disasters and environmental emergencies. The DHA did, however, point out that although 'each new catastrophe typically triggers close attention to mitigation measures, at least for the disaster type in question, such attention is often localized and short-lived and, as a result, the global socio-economic impact of disasters, measured in terms of the number of people affected by disaster, has continued to increase by about 6% per year' (A/51/172 para 87).

The DHA helped countries to properly assess their full spectrum of risks, to prescribe, on the basis of global experience, the most cost-effective disaster reduction measures, to coordinate external guidance, where needed, on how to apply those measures in the most vulnerable areas, and to stimulate wider

---

[19] See P. Taylor, 'Options for Reform' in John Harris, (ed.), *The Politics of Humanitarian Intervention* (London, Pinter and Save the Children, 1995), pp. 91–144, especially p. 96.

[20] For a useful account of the problems in the way of more effective peace-keeping see G. Evans, *Cooperation for Peace: The Global Agenda for the 1990s and Beyond* (St. Leonards, NSW, Allen and Unwin, 1993), pp. 70–80 and *passim*.

involvement and closer cooperation among the numerous international agencies with relevant technical and managerial expertise. Such risk assessment documents were on the same lines as the Country Strategy Notes developed by the UNDP. The WFP attempted to strengthen local capacities for disaster mitigation with field level vulnerability exercises. (A/51/172 para 59) Some individual countries, including Sweden and Britain, had also set up teams which could be called out at very short notice to evaluate the disaster in the field.

Under Resolution 46/182 the General Assembly had also established a Central Emergency Revolving Fund of $50 million which could help to finance the first efforts of the Agencies to help with a crisis. This fund was not without its difficulties, in particular that the money had to be repaid and could only be provided to assist with the financing of efforts partly funded from elsewhere, and it was too small. DHA also utilized *flash appeals* to ensure timely response to critical first phase emergency needs (A/51/172 para 46). A number of the Agencies had also agreed so-called service packages with governments and other organizations through which military and civil defence assets could be called on at times when the emergency response required reinforcement. UNHCR had such packages. And WFP had eight such logistic service packages in mid 1996 UNICEF was in the process of developing such arrangements. (A/51/172 Para 35)

One of the features of the evolution of UN arrangements in the 1990s was an increasing professionalization of work in a wide range of different fields including peace-keeping and humanitarian activities. A number of countries, led by Canada had started to train military personnel for such activities, and indeed Canada had set up a research institute on peace-keeping. There had also been a complex emergency training initiative led by the DHA and the UNDP, and a UN Staff College was established in Turin under the ILO. Warehouses for the storage of emergency supplies to help peace-keeping forces and humanitarian activities had also been established. The most important of these was at Pisa. In 1997 some functions developed within the DHA were to be located in other institutions, according to the plan outlined by the new Secretary General in July. But the achievement of DHA in this regard remained.

The picture which emerged from this discussion was that the United Nations system had gone through a period of astonishing change in the 1990s with regard to information collecting and evaluating and with regard to the enhancement of its capacity to respond quickly to crisis. The machinery had become more professional despite the continuing shortage of resources and the increase in the number and type of problems with which it had to deal. It is hard to see how the emergence of an enhanced moral solidarity could be excluded from an explanation of its development; this was an aspect of changing views about the proper relationship between the international community and states which was justified primarily in terms of the welfare of individuals. Of course some target states objected, but the increasing capacity to respond and to respond quickly was generally expected and generally required. This was no special plot of the Great Powers, but rather a product of collective obligation. But this was not anti-state: indeed, precisely the opposite – it was focussed upon strengthening the state. The international community could now be dimly discerned as a discrete agent of change, embodying an increasing cosmopolitanism, and enlarging the area of consensus about the norms which were appropriate within states.

New Types of Security Threat

In the late 1990s two patterns of involvement from outside were likely to interact in the state, one from legitimate and another from illegitimate agencies. The former was the increasing involvement of international organization, more evident in the Third World. The latter was a threat to the security of individuals, more often in the first world, from the new dangerous non-governmental organizations of international crime and state-sponsored terrorism. This was becoming increasingly visible, and was beyond the reach of either peace-keeping forces or enforcement procedures from outside the state, and from conventional police forces from within the state. Examples included the various Mafias of the old kind, and new kinds such as those from Russia and the Far East, which were often linked with the trade in illegal substances, but were increasingly operating in a more diverse range of areas, some legitimate. Another new illustration was the appearance of private mercenary armies, such as Executive Outcomes, which in the late 1990s had been hired by some governments in Africa to deal with internal military threats which they could not handle with their own armies.[21]

These various enterprises challenged the state's monopoly of force and were capable of enforcing codes of behaviour, and systems of private taxation, which were alongside or hostile to those of the state. They clearly challenged the security of individuals and threatened order within the states, and had an obvious international dimension. It was a special form of warfare: in some cases states orchestrated the use of violence in other states through groups or individuals which had been infiltrated into the territory of another state. Modern technology and sophisticated skills in evading recognition could make it very difficult for the target state to identify such individuals. The impact of such forces on the civil order, and life and property, in the target state could be very serious, and for the initiating state it would have the effect of war without the need to acknowledge responsibility. Of course comparable developments had occurred in earlier periods, such as the infiltration of Soviet Communist elements into capitalist countries which actively pursued the goal of fermenting revolution and the overthrow of the government. But the new practices were different in that they involved a preparedness to use deadly force in the pursuit of private gain and influence on a scale not seen before.

The nature of these problems indicated the need for strengthening international cooperation between police forces, and setting up unified transnational command structures if the problem required this. States and their individual police forces, assuming they themselves were not a part of the scam, were likely to find dealing with them separately and individually impossible precisely because they were transnational. The organizations were capable of withdrawing from one state and regrouping in others only to be reactivated in the target state later. It was also difficult for police forces in particular states to gain access to the command and control structures of the organizations in other states without themselves transgressing the rules of exclusive national jurisdiction. There were also some kinds of such operations, which were closely linked with government officials, or members of business or political elites in

---

[21] A similar organization was Sandlines which caused embarrassment to the British Foreign Office in 1998 because of its involvement in the war in Sierra Leone and the allegation that it had procured and supplied arms to the ousted government in defiance of UN sanctions.

another state, which needed the weight of an extra-territorial authority to be effective. In an extreme form, when they were directly controlled by another government, doing something about them which was effective could lead to war, either because the controlling government, when found out, reacted with more direct violence, or because the scale of the intervention was such that it could not be coped with except by attacking the source government. This was a problem which, therefore, raised the question of the civil order within states as well as that of maintaining peace and security. It was on a continuum extending from the problems of disorder within the state, and those dealt with by new forms of peace-keeping, to those security problems of a more traditional kind.

The appropriate form of such a force would include the capacity to deploy a range of specialist forces, which could be asked to operate in more open combat or in situations where SAS type skills were more appropriate. But the forces also needed to be linked with sophisticated investigative techniques which could work on an international basis, and which could if necessary demand answers from individuals who were close to governments. An effective arrangement for dealing with such problems therefore also assumed a range of features in the participating state. They would need to be prepared to tolerate the incursion of a transnational police force into their domestic arrangements, and to be open enough at least to accept this.

The European Union was one group of states where advanced police cooperation existed and in which a further enhancement of regional trans-national capacity was being actively sought in the late 1990s: the ability to create forces which were likely to be effective depended on the civil order within the state, but a variety of different forms of liberal domestic order could tolerate the kind of arrangement that was emerging in Europe.[22] But some states – generally those with intolerant and precarious regimes, quite probably at risk of internal humanitarian crisis – would not, and were likely to play the sovereignty card to avoid cooperation. The well-founded state sought after by the international community in the late 1990s was, therefore, also desirable from the alternative perspective of dealing effectively with new kinds of non-governmental threats to individual security. The problem clearly had an international dimension: it suggested the need to confederalize the mechanisms for protecting national civil orders. It was therefore a feature of international society after the Cold War that the range of conceivable force deployments to maintain order had been considerably broadened, compared with the earlier phases of international society, and that the earlier distinctions between national and international security had been blurred.

This implied in the late 1990s something quite startling: that the direction of development of the use of police and military was positively linked with the development of cosmopolitanism – that new peace-keeping was a step towards enhanced international civilian police capacity, and that this was only possible if the civil values of communities around the world become more similar and more liberal. The step beyond that would be a transnational cosmopolitanism linked with advanced forms of police cooperation dealing with crimes over a very wide

[22] According to the new Title VI of the Treaty on European Union. Andrew Duff concluded: 'For all the difficulties what emerges is a picture, in five years time, of an extensive and sophisticated web of police coordination throughout the European Union', A. Duff (ed.), *The Treaty of Amsterdam: Text and Commentary* (London, Federal Trust for Education and Science, 1997), p. 42.

spectrum. Like business and ideology, crime was also likely to become more transnational and to demand transnational response, and to create difficulties in deciding what kinds of crime were local, and the exclusive responsibility of national police forces, and which were transnational and therefore the proper responsibility of a higher police authority.

But at the other end of the scale there were in the late 1990s much stronger grounds to be fearful of rogue governments such as that of Saddam Hussein. It had become possible for a government to adopt an effective international criminal strategy on a scale that had never before been possible. Modern technology could give them the means of global destruction for relatively modest outlay. The dangers posed by such states to international society, to the citizens of the world as well as to governments, were sufficiently appalling to justify firm action against them. Such action could become an imperative if the government appeared to have nuclear, chemical or bacteriological weapons.

The scale of the problem was illustrated in the late 1990s by the response to Saddam Hussein's attempts to evade the UN inspectors appointed to locate and destroy his more dangerous weapons. The international community initially hesitated but eventually accepted the need for a firm response, though disagreement about whether or not to use force remained. One report was that the USA had been prepared to use a specialized nuclear device to penetrate and destroy bacteriological weapons bunkers and their contents. As never before the world could be held to ransom by irresponsible, corrupt or plain mad regimes possessed of such weapons. Once again the case for a strong transnational authority equipped to act appropriately to deal with such regimes was apparent. For the first time technology and custom had reached the point at which the removal of a dangerous government was justifiable simply because of the degree of damage which it could do. There was, of course, the need for satisfactory ways of licensing such action. But this was a revolutionary qualification of the concept of statehood, which happily coincided with the preponderance of the liberal states in the post-Cold War period. It demanded solidarity but it also supported the drive to achieve it.

Democratization and Globalization

In the mid-1990s the trend towards economic globalization had major implications for the circumstances of sovereignty. Globalization was in part a self-serving agenda for the economic forces of the developed world, and went along with the agenda of deregulation, and making the world free for multinational corporations.[23] The prevailing image was of a world which was becoming more interdependent, and more dominated by multinational corporations and global economic forces, such as more widely distributed direct foreign investment. This was seen by many as a positive development, and, in contrast, local attempts to impose conditions upon mutual involvement were seen as setting unacceptable limits upon the development of the common good. Furthermore, it was thought, they were unlikely to succeed: globalization was inevitable.

The opposite view, reflected in the arguments of the G77, the Non-Aligned, and the proponents of social democracy, was that the common good was not

---

[23] For an incisive critique of economic globalization see P. Hirst and G. Thompson, *Globalization in Question* (Cambridge, Polity, 1996).

served if deregulation was pushed beyond certain limits: certainly it was mistaken to see deregulation, and exposure to market forces in an open world economy, as necessarily beneficial. Liberal internationalism now risked rule by organizations which were hard to control by democratic forms of government and often led to the exploitation of the disadvantaged. Even for developed states like the members of the European Union globalization was an impediment in the way of pursuing social goals such as full employment. It was local organizations, in the state or region, that were more likely to pursue social purposes successfully; at least it was unlikely that global corporations would do this, since the more global they were the more it was likely that their inherent drive to profit would be untroubled by social purpose.

Global corporations were likely to pursue profit maximizing strategies at the expense of high levels of employment, effective welfare provision, and the promotion of democracy. The 'dynamics of globalization are gradually dis-embedding the domestic social contract between the state and society, which had become integral to the programme of welfare capitalism and social democracy,' and 'the state has itself been "globalized" or "internationalized", that is the policy orientation of the state has ben pulled away from its territorial constituencies and shifted outwards, with state action characteristically operating as an instrumental agent on behalf of non-territorial regional and global market forces, as manipulated by transnational corporations and banks, and increasingly also by financial traders.'[24]

A greater degree of deregulation of economic forces worked to the advantage of core regions, and within them of richer individuals and institutions, and perpetuated the disadvantage of peripheries and poorer elements within them – whether they were in the European Union or at the global level – unless deliberate measures were adopted to shape the global forces to local needs. In pre-democratic countries multinational corporations had no motivation for strengthening legitimate national controls, by tolerating or encouraging trade unions, or other forms of local participation in their decision-making. They were likely to be tolerant of non-democratic forms of organization, as long as they produced stability in the short term – the corporation's first political priority – and would circumvent democratic processes by helping to restrict the expression of opinions which did not reflect their interests, or trying to control host country leaders. There were of course exceptions to these generalizations, but the experience of business attitudes towards democratization in Hong Kong in the late 1980s and 1990s suggested that when successful multinational business faced a choice it preferred a comfortable authoritarianism to a challenging democracy.

Since the late 1980s, however, the UN had become more directly involved in helping the emergence of democracy. A letter from the European Union to the Secretary-General picked up a theme which was increasingly visible in UN and UN-related documents, namely support for enhancing the role of the UN in helping the development of a *civil society* in states that had experienced internal crisis.[25] The use of the term 'civil society' was striking: it was now often found in UN documents, but had rarely been found before the late 1980s. It appeared in

[24] R. Falk, 'State of siege: will globalism win out', *International Affairs*, 73 (1997), p. 131.
[25] Letter from the Presidency of the EU, at the Permanent Mission of Ireland to the United Nations, to the Secretary General, 16 October, 1996, Para. 21.

this case in the context of support for the recovery of states in which there had been serious humanitarian crisis, but it often had a wider reference: support for a proactive strategy on the part of the international community in promoting democracy.

In the late 1990s an unprecedented commitment emerged to the promotion of liberal pluralist arrangements as a condition of development on the part of the major players, the World Bank, the UN system and the EU: it encompassed the elements of a well founded civil society and democratization as well as such changes as improved credit and insurance arrangements. The head of UNDP stated in 1998 that 40% of the resources of his organization now went on governance improving activities. There was increasing evidence of UN agencies, 'and other international organizations' helping governments to strengthen democratic forms. Cases mentioned in the mid-1990s included Niger and Guatemala, where UNDP had adopted a more political role in supporting government reform. The point was made that in Latin America the UNDP was an active factor in democratization. This was a remarkable alteration in stress and its significance should not be underestimated: for the first time in the history of the United Nations the organization was directly addressing core structures in the state and even in the difficult continent – Africa – illiberal practices were increasingly being delegitimized. The Security Council's authorization in July 1994 (SC940) of armed intervention in Haiti to restore a democratically elected government was particularly striking: there had been no credible threat to international peace and security.[26] This surely contributed to the de facto dilution of the concept of sovereignty as earlier understood in the Council and elsewhere. UNICEF's strategy had also been rededicated: the new approach was to be 'rights based', meaning that it was to be derived from the Rights of the Child Convention.

The EU urged the adoption of a comprehensive approach in respect of non-military aspects of peace operations (including tasks such as democratization, police training, institution building, capacity building and delivery of humanitarian assistance), to help with the 'transition from humanitarian relief to long term planning, including in the context of support for *civil society*'.[27] The EU had also begun to impose *multiple conditionality* in its relations with the ACP countries: strings were attached to economic support which included democratization.[28] The change in this direction could be traced from the mid-1980s when Margaret Thatcher became the first European leader to attempt to build human rights conditions into provisions for European Community aid to African, Caribbean and Pacific (ACP) countries under the Lome Conventions. 'Although that attempt was initially rejected by ACP leaders as an unwarranted infringement on their domestic sovereignty, by the time of the Lome IV convention of 1990 an explicit reference to human rights in the context of EC aid could no longer be avoided.'[29] In fact the EU programme was broadened to include a requirement for a whole range of internal adjustments to promote

---

[26] D. Malone, 'Haiti and the international community: a case study', *Survival*, 39 (1997), 126–146.

[27] EU letter, p. 8.

[28] See J. Matheson, Multiple Conditionality and the EU, London School of Economics and Political Science, PhD. Thesis, 1997, unpublished.

[29] N. Wickramasinghe, 'From Human Rights to Good Governance: The Aid Regime in the 1990s' in Sellers, *The New World Order*, p. 311.

greater transparency and efficiency in using their aid. Although the mechanisms for dealing with human rights infringements in the international legal system remained flawed it was undeniable that in a number of ways the intrusions of the international community to promote minimum acceptable standards had been extended. The start made upon the setting up of an International Criminal Court in 1998 was an aspect of this. The revolutionary proposal was to bring international criminals to account, including the leaders of states.

The argument emerges that the promotion of well-founded states, which was now seen as essential for international order, was the appropriate counter-strategy to globalization. The weight of evidence in the late 1990s suggested that the assumption was false that development, democratization and globalization were positively connected. Globalization as an economic process contained elements which were corrosive of international order. It was a happy coincidence that its apparent progress coincided with the choice by a number of major actors of a deliberate strategy of democratization. By the late 1990s it was necessary, therefore, to have an agenda of statism, which was now a condition and a consequence of cosmopolitanism. It was necessary to make the world safe for sovereignty.

Changes in the way development was managed were also relevant to the process of democratization. For instance, funds now often went directly to programmes, rather than going through governments, who were thereby reduced in their ability to syphon off money for their own special reasons, the purchase of arms and other forms of indulgence. Since the late 1980s there had been a considerable enhancement of the role of the UN system with regard to the rehabilitation of failing states. The EU document mentioned above recognized and supported this involvement.

Similar arguments related to the proposal for a Multilateral Investment Agreement (MIA) made in the mid 1990s to the World Trade Organization by the EU, Canada and Japan, which was seen by the G77 as a way of guaranteeing the unrestrained right of multinationals to invest with minimum conditionality in their states. In the view of Southern economists, it was unlikely to benefit locals, and was more likely to lead to a further draining of resources to the richer parts of the world. 'Experience in the globalization episode of the last century does not really make out a case of laissez faire and free capital flows having promoted development. Rather it shows uneven global development associated with such flows'; the 'entire argument rests on the existence of efficiency enhancing effects of undistorted price signals – an assumption that draws theoretical support from the welfare principles of unregulated markets. "But" such an assumption is challenged by the reality that there exist market failures of one type or another'. Thus, *there are equally strong theoretical grounds that argue against unregulated markets*'. [my stress][30]

It was pointed out that only seven of the leading 20 host countries for FDI between 1985 and 1995 were developing countries, and that with the exception of China all were middle income countries with rapid growth. This pointed to the important conclusion that FDI was more likely to help a developing economy *once growth was well under way*, but that the usual range of benefits ascribed to FDI-technology transfer, strengthening local industries etc. – were

[30] Third World Network, *North South Development Monitor*, Interpress Service and South Centre, 28 October, 1996, pp. 2–5.

unlikely to accrue until take off had started. Thus it could be important for the poorest states to find a means of imposing conditions on multinationals who proposed investing in their territory, and of deciding what such conditions should be. To do this they needed allies in the international system. In the late 1990s one form of this was the reformed mechanisms of the UN's economic and social organizations. For instance the Country Strategy Notes were the first attempt at an authoritative definition of country specific policies and approaches for economic management and development, involving, as they did, inputs from the range of UN organizations involved in development, with advice from donor officials, and the participation and consent of the host countries and bilateral contributors.

In the late 1990s there was a fundamental opposition, not only between globalization and democratization, but also between development and globalization. The three primary agendas contained damaging contradictions which could only be overcome by an alliance between liberal developed states, acting within international organizations like the EU and the UN, to promote liberal and democratic social and political agendas. This implied in turn not only an active policy of building states which met these conditions, but also a strengthening of the arrangements between them.

But these are mere hints at underlying problems and their solution. State enhancement to counter the threat to international order posed by economic globalization was needed, and a beginning had to be made in the UN system on various new initiatives to achieve this. Proactive cosmopolitanism and state-enhancement were coincident and necessary to protect the international order against the corrosive effects of globalization.

Sovereignty and Cosmopolitanism in the Late 1990s: a Neo-Westphalian System?

The main themes identified in the introduction have now been discussed, with the exception of the development of a legal system within which laws made outside the state increasingly imposed within it. This has been discussed at length elsewhere, and in this essay it is more useful to give space to its implications, which is done below. But the development of mechanisms to protect international peace and security, the extension of the range of involvements to promote common standards, such as democratization, and the emergence of a global watch and more speedy response, have been discussed in their main phases. It is apparent, however, that under these headings only a selection of new interventions and involvements have been considered. Kant had proposed a strategy which stressed the importance of international discourse, commerce and hospitality.[31] By the late 1990s there had emerged countless illustrations of a modern equivalent of this strategy in the work of international institutions, in particular those of the UN system, of which Kant would doubtless have approved.

The point should be stressed again that the involvements and interventions were to consolidate the state, to protect its position and not to weaken or remove it. But by the late 1990s the international community, working through the United Nations system, and other international organizations, seemed to have considerably enhanced its authority compared with the period of the Cold

---

[31] Hinsley, *Power and the Pursuit of Peace*, pp. 65–7.

War. There was now a sense in which sovereign states were legitimized and sustained by such an authority to which they were in general terms accountable.[32] This accountability was the condition of states being regarded as ultimately responsible on particular matters, and their right to an exclusive domestic jurisdiction was increasingly questioned if their performance fell short in an expanding range of specific practical arrangements. This could be seen as a filling out, and translation into secular terms, of a feature of the Westphalian system: that even princes were subjects of a divine order. In the late twentieth century, however, such a higher authority could only exist in the context of the new cosmopolitanism.

Some reformulation of the act of creating sovereignty seemed to be indicated to reflect the expanding role of the international community in monitoring internal circumstances and rescuing failing states. Indeed there was a case for granting the United Nations primary responsibility for conferring sovereignty through the recognition process – i.e. multilateralizing the process – and for removing that right from states to act individually and separately. If states were to be monitored and rescued multilaterally should they not also be licenced multilaterally? Sovereignty was a goal of the international community deserving recognition in its procedures as well as its constitutive principle.

Popular support of statehood had often been looked for in earlier times as a condition of recognition, but publics and other states were coming to regard this as a starting point. The range of 'sovereignty creating acts' was in effect being expanded from seeing that territory was controlled with some reference to popular support at the time of recognition to a more comprehensive concern with the details of internal arrangements, so that the support would endure. A new condition of sovereignty was therefore now discernible, in addition to the traditional one that a territory should be controlled by a government: that the state was well-founded in the light of the standards of the international community. The terms of the granting of the licence to practice statehood were in the process of being enlarged and giving responsibility for awarding the accolade of recognition to the United Nations was a concomitant of this.

The recognition as states of the territories which had formed Yugoslavia was a fairly *ad hoc* business with unintended and disastrous consequences, driven by the interests of Germany, and imperfectly monitored by the Batinder Commission set up under the authority of the Commission on Yugoslavia;[33] it was unreasonable that the recognition process should be left to states individually and separately, but, as was increasingly happening, the UN[34] be left to pick up the pieces. The obligation of states to the international community to maintain acceptable internal standards needed to be underlined as their poor performance could lead to major costs for other states; there was a straightforward utilitarian justification.

The *ad hoc* character of the recognition of states, was matched by a corresponding 'ad hocery' about their derecognition, the removal of the acknowledgement of sovereignty. The lack of any general procedure for derecognition

---

[32] The elements of continuity in the state system are discussed in R. Jackson and A. James, *States in a Changing World: a Contemporary Analysis* (Oxford, Clarendon, 1993).

[33] Economides and Taylor, in Mayall, *The New Interventionism*, p. 91.

[34] See the excellent discussion of the issues raised here, including recognition by the UN, in J. Dugard, *Recognition and the United Nations* (Cambridge, Grotius, 1987).

increased the difficulty of intervening – meaning an involvement using force – as the states which separately continued to recognize a state were more likely to argue that the sovereignty of that state should not be breached. But as the cosmopolitan moral community was strengthened sovereignty would be weakened as an impediment in the way of intervention. Indeed the earlier relationship between intervention and sovereignty would be reversed: weight would increasingly be placed on the question of the justice of the state's claim to sovereignty rather than upon the nature of the justification for intervention. The question of which *precise* justification of intervention was proposed, be it a threat to international security under Chapter VII, or a gross infringement of human rights, (whichever happened to fit in with the prevailing interpretation of the Charter) would be of lesser significance as a liberal interpretation of either would suit the case. The logic of the situation was, however, that derecognition should also be a matter for the United Nations, with appropriate safeguard procedures, given the changing character of its role in maintaining international order. It should be done as a single multilateral act under the authority of the UN. This would clarify the point that sovereignty had a relationship with being well-founded, and that when intervention by the international community was judged necessary, a state entity could not be sovereign.

Sovereignty could be interpreted as being ultimately responsible – the buck stops with the sovereign, though paradoxically – as was argued above – being ultimately responsible could come to be the result of an enabling act from the international community. But sovereignty also meant having the right to do certain things: it involved having a role with regard to a range of specific functions. The question was whether this role had been affected by the changing circumstances of sovereignty. New problems in the way of legitimizing states by granting them sovereignty were matched by new problems about deciding what states should be able to do in order to remain sovereign.

Having a role, and doing something, involved being granted a *competence*, and was not the same as being ultimately responsible. In recent years the analytical distinction between these two questions – who was ultimately responsible and who had competence to act – was more frequently reflected in the practice of states and international organizations: the question of which body was ultimately responsible, was increasingly separated from that of which body was allowed competence.[35] The exercise of exclusive control over certain key functions, such as foreign policy and defence, used to be regarded as being central to sovereignty, and could not be allocated to other centres. But in the late 1990s the member states of the European Union could accept that the Union should have a role in their harmonized foreign policy, and that it might increase its involvement in the common defence. There was a majority for this among the Union's citizens, even in cautious states such as the UK. The question of taking decisions in these areas by qualified majority vote had even entered the agenda. This was an astonishing development which seemed to remove the dilemma, discussed *inter alia* by Rousseau, that responsibility for maintaining the peace could not be allocated to a higher, federal authority without fatally damaging the entity which it was designed to protect, namely the state itself.

---

[35] This issue is discussed by the author in his *The European Union in the 1990s* (Oxford, Oxford University Press, 1996), ch. 2.

Ultimate responsibility remained with the sovereign states, as a condition of their sovereignty, as long as they retained reserve powers, including the power to recover the competences, even though the grant of the right to exercise that responsibility came from the international community. Public opinion and governments could accept that such a transfer of responsibility for foreign policy and defence was not an infringement of sovereignty as long as the reserve power was kept! Something remarkable had happened: sovereignty was now a condition, even a form, of participation, in the larger entity. What was stressed in the role taken on by being sovereign was the right to be involved, to participate in the mechanisms of international society, and to represent there the interests of the state. It was even possible to imagine states which were sovereign but which normally exercised no exclusive competences.

The expectation was that the chances of the reserve powers' being utilized would be progressively reduced. Outside the European Union it was unusual for issues of foreign policy or defence to involve supranational authority. But it was common for other questions, previously regarded as essential to the exercise of national sovereignty, especially in the economic, social and other technical areas, to be handled elsewhere in whole or in part. The transfer did not always go smoothly and states were sometimes surprised by what they learned they had given away. For instance in the late 1990s individuals in the US Administration and members of Congress reacted with horror to judgements against the US made by the World Trade Organization. The general trend, however, was for issues to become less sensitive with regard to sovereignty: competences were now routinely exercised by international agencies in areas which would have been sacred to sovereignty in earlier times. But paradoxically the state's survival rested on the assumption that this transfer could not be guaranteed: the competences could still be recalled in principle even if this in practice was unlikely.

If the status of the international community was to be protected it would be necessary to avoid situations in which the reserve powers would have be used. The key to successful diplomacy was the avoidance of policies which could lead to having to make a choice between national interest and courses of action indicated by the agenda of cosmopolitanism, as in this case national interest would have to come first. This was the nature of international society and the state. A policy competence would have to be renationalized if, for instance, a state's ability to provide for the welfare of its citizens was likely to be damaged. The skilled diplomat would increasingly require a sophisticated grasp of paradox. But in a community of well-founded states it would be less likely that a choice would have to be made to repatriate a competence, as the interests of all states would be informed by the cosmopolitan ideology.

Lurking behind these points was another more important one: the dialectical relationship between the state and the international community, as it had emerged by the late 1990s, increasingly demanded that states should be acceptable as proper participants in the international civil order. There was increasingly the perception that unless they met certain conditions of probity and internal welfare they could not be full members. One illustration of this was that members of governments which fell short were more often regarded amongst the community of diplomats as unsuited to the exercise of public office in the institutions of the international community. If this tendency-norm were to evolve into a practice-rule it would be hard to deny that in this key area states had become unequal as citizens of the international community, and that this had grave implications for the question of whether they could be regarded as equal and, therefore, sovereign.

In effect: changes in the circumstances of sovereignty in the late 1990s suggested that it could come to depend upon being recognized as a fit member of international society. It could be ultimately responsible, exercise competences on behalf of its citizens, and play a full part in the community that sanctioned this, only if it complied with the conditions of both the international and the domestic community. It was a short step to seeing the unfit as the unsovereign.

The significance of the above can be underlined by a sketch of conceivable next steps. What was on the agenda of the reform of international organization and its relation with the state in the late 1990s. Where was the system headed? These items give a preliminary indication of a possible route. There were proposals which aimed at enhancing the accountability of governments to the international community; proposals for requiring qualifications of individuals and institutions as a condition of allowing them to operate international instruments (institutional development); and proposals which were aimed directly at improving the lot of individuals within states independently of the proposals aimed at national or international agencies. The proposals in normal type are those which appeared frequently in the literature in the late 1990s:[36] they amounted to expectations about next steps, which were as realistic a measure of what had been obtained by the late 1990s as a discussion of actual attainment. They were the other side of the line represented by the word 'now'. Subsequent steps linked with the proposals might also be entering the discourse and are placed in *italics*: this enhances the sense of the direction of movement.

Proposals under these various headings were:

A. Government accountability
Under this heading proposals appearing on agendas in the 1990s included:

1. Strengthen the War Crimes Tribunal and set up an International Criminal Court.
    A certificate of good housekeeping to be provided at the end of a government's period of office in all states by a designated agency of the UN as representative of the international community, with the power to freeze and sequestrate the assets of malefactors.
2. Tighten up the arms register arrangements and agree an international code for the supply of arms with effective policing. Make it compulsory to register and to apply an international code of manufacture and supply, *with direct access to manufacturers inventories and production facilities for the international arms authority.*
3. *A code of proper behaviour for political leaders to be agreed by the General Assembly linked with the publication of a register of corrupt governments by*

---

[36] The list draws on the wide range of reports on reform of the United Nations which were current in the late 1990s. Particular use was made of The Commission on Global Governance, *Our Global Neighbourhood* (Oxford, Oxford University Press, 1995); *A Report of the Independent Working Group on the Future of the United Nations*, appended to K. Huefner (ed.), *Agenda for Change: New Tasks for the United Nations* (Opladen, Leske & Budrich, 1995); G. de Marco and M. Bartolo, *A Second Generation of United Nations: For Peace in Freedom in the 21st Century* (London, Kegan Paul, 1997), especially ch. 10 and Annexe 1, Summary of previous proposals.

the UN. An index of governments rated with regard to corruption to be published by the General Assembly.
4.   More liberal formal procedures for intervention – based on the interests of peoples – Chapter 1, Article 1(3) in contrast to Chapter VII. *A code for the use of force (military or economic), as in Haiti, to restore democracy in the event of military take-over.*

B. Institutional development
Items included:

1.   Judicial review by the International Court of Justice of the decisions of the Security Council.
2.   Enhancement of the powers of the Security Council to include more sectors eg. Environment and human rights. The capacity to achieve cross-sector coherence in its decisions would be enhanced. *The ICJ could then be granted power to require that such coherence be maintained by the Security Council within and across sectors.*
3.   The ICJ to become active in resolving conflicts between acts of international legislation such as that between World Trade Organization rules and Multilateral Environment Agreements. (In 1998 WTO rules required that trade liberalization codes override tighter environmental requirements in the MEAs; there was often a straight contradiction between the two with no formal process of reconciliation.)
4.   A Commission of Experts to be created to bring the attention of the Security Council to new crises and recommend an appropriate response: *such a commission could also develop a role in determining the adequacy of resources with regard to SC mandates and their strategic and other implications for peace-keeping. It could be empowered to require that SC resolutions were technically efficient.*[37]
5.   *Responsibility for the recognition and de-recognition of states to be transferred to the UN and exercised under a special procedure.*
6.   *Exclusion of governments with a low index rating, as determined in the procedure in A4. above, from executive positions in international institutions including the UN – and from voting, or new memberships in international organizations in the UN system.*
     (In the Treaty of Amsterdam in the European Union states agreed that if a member was found guilty of offences against human rights it could be punished by having its voting rights in the Council of Ministers suspended.)[38]

C. Cosmopolitanism and citizens
Items included:

1.   All diplomatic relations and diplomacy to be linked to the promotion of human rights.

---

[37] The Report of the Independent Working Group, reproduced in Huefner, *Agenda for Change*, calls this a Security Assessment Staff.
[38] New Article F 1. Clause 2. Referred to the Council's right to 'suspend certain rights . . . including the voting rights' . . . of a member state found to be in serious and persistent breach of the principles . . . (including respect for human rights [Article F]).

2. *All states to have formal constitutions subject to international approval by a designated agency (see C3) which guaranteed civil rights and respect for minorities.*

3. A Commission for Constitutionalism and Due Process to be set up. The UN Human Rights Conventions to be incorporated into all national constitutions under its supervision on the model of the European Convention of Human Rights. (In 1998 the British government was considering such incorporation.)

4. States to be required to pursue a *civil rights first* strategy involving a range of obligations intended to maintain and promote civilized internal orders. These would include an obligation to avoid infringements of internationally recognized civil liberties. *The obligation could be extended to include an obligation to avoid excessive income differentials – mean income – not average – and exclude privileged access to social services, such as health, police, and education. Indicators of civilized society could rate poorer societies more highly than rich countries with, for instance, wider income differentials and uneven social service access.*

5. Removal of prohibitions on direct appeal to international courts and forums by individuals against governments.

6. *Instigation of rules requiring that development and investment strategies promote human rights, equity and environmental considerations.*

7. *The making of a list of recognized NGOs that could operate within all states as of right i.e. without requiring the explicit permission of governments.*

8. More 'mixed' representation in international institutions i.e. by individual, group, region as well as governments.[39]

9. Limiting certain new collateral effects of war upon individuals: e.g. by limiting the use of land mines, *and* damage to health from lack of proper precautions in testing, developing or storing chemical, bacteriological or nuclear weapons. An international mechanism for identifying and destroying redundant weapons.

Two kinds of implications of the changing circumstances of sovereignty were discussed in this section. First was the change in views about the implications of being sovereign, and ways of becoming sovereign. Second was the proposal for future developments which had become conceivable in the late 1990s because of those changes. Such proposals only acquired a veneer of credibility in the light of the changes in views about sovereignty.

Conclusions

The definition of sovereignty always had to take account of the circumstances of the time and of the place. It was an absolute which had to be constantly reinterpreted in the light of the actual limitations placed on state behaviour, and this produced continuous controversy and a steady stream of dissertations – which was hardly surprising in view of the logical impossibility of qualifying an absolute.

---

[39] See the excellent consideration of this question in D. Held, *Democracy and the Global Order: From the Modern State to Cosmopolitan Governance* (Cambridge, Polity, 1995).

One reason for this was that the traditional discussion of sovereignty worked from the state-actor, and its claims to sovereignty, to the compromises with the principle which resulted from membership of international society. This reconciliation was always unconvincing. Changes in the work of the United Nations since the end of the Cold War, and the implications of membership in the European Union, extended the list of anomalies with regard to the traditional view to breaking point: how could a 'state' be sovereign in the traditional sense when its people could appeal to a superior court, such as the European Court of Human Rights or the European Court of Justice, against its own government and when laws made outside the state apparently prevailed over those made within, as in the European Union? One response to the difficulties was to reinterpret the principle as a reflection of the constitutive role of the international community *as well as* an acknowledgement of the innate need of people for self-determination. In the past sovereignty had been seen as being made by the sub-systems, the states; a stronger appreciation was needed of the way in which the international community could constitute the state and express its sovereignty.

Developments in the work of United Nations system in the 1990s, and attitudes towards it, made it possible to identify somewhat more clearly this dialectical quality in sovereignty.

Aspects of this dialectic are brought out in the following summation:

- Sovereignty increasingly defined a unit of participation, and established a right to participate in the institutions and arrangements of the international community. Having the right to participate in the management of common arrangements with other states was a much more important consideration in sovereignty than the traditional right to exclusive management of any single function, even defence and foreign policy. (Luxembourg, but not Quebec, was a sovereign state in the 1990s, not because the former did more alone than the latter – arguably Quebec had more functional independence in Canada than Luxembourg in the European Union. It was rather that Luxembourg had the right to participate in the range of international forums with state members, whereas Quebec did not; and Luxembourg retained the reserve powers mentioned below to limit the competence of external agencies.)

- But: sovereignty increasingly came to be seen as conferring on states the obligation of being accountable to the international community. Being licenced to practice as a state carried with it the condition of its government's being prepared to demonstrate, to the satisfaction of the international community, continued adherence to the terms under which it held the licence i.e. being well-founded in the varying senses discussed above. The sovereign was the entity which was accountable to the higher unit, and states which evaded this obligation were increasingly seen as falling short of the standards expected in the state-citizens of international society.

- Sovereignty identified (a) the locus of responsibility in the state and (b) the focus of popular perceptions about which authority was ultimately responsible. The rights and obligations of sovereignty were vested in a government which was the ultimate guardian of the popular interest and which could not renounce that interest because it was sovereign. It was the focus of popular hopes and expectations.

- And: it was an embodiment of interest: its government, embodying the sovereignty of the state, had the right to determine a collective interest according to accepted procedures in the state.
- But: with regard to competence:

  a. Sovereignty embodied a grant to the state from the international community of the right to act on its own account in international society.

  b. It was also a grant of the right to extend competence to act to other entities such as international institutions, other states, or private organizations, within its territory or on its behalf in international society.

  c. Conversely the sovereignty of states meant that the system of which they were members necessarily left them with the right to limit that competence. By the late 1990s no form of majority voting in international institutions had limited this right. This was the equivalent in the circumstances of the late 1990s of the traditional right to exclusive domestic jurisdiction. It had, therefore, become less useful to see states as having exclusive domestic jurisdiction and more useful to see them as having reserved the right to limit the effects of legislation made outside. This was because of the development of an increasing capacity for making rules, with direct implications within states, in international institutions; the prime example of this, but by no means the only one, was the European Union.

- Sovereignty also carried the implication of a grant of the right to privacy for citizens. This was the perception that their behaviour among themselves was no business of others. But the limitations of this right included the requirement that practices should have general approval within the state and that they did not compromise the privacy of the citizens of other states. This right did not exclude the rights of others to argue against practices which they found abhorrent, and to promote intervention if a practice was contrary to a clear internationally held standard. But the assumption had to be made that any practice which turned one section of a community into the victims of another was necessarily abhorrent.

These perceptions of sovereignty arose in the context of the late 1990s. They included, in particular, extensions of the role of international institutions, especially the United Nations and the European Union, and the emergence of a more proactive cosmopolitanism which stressed an overlay on diverse cultures of universalizing values. All of this was in the process of *becoming*: it was a consequence of the happy coincidence that the end of the Cold War left the democratic liberal states in a position to push their values.

The entrenchment of cosmopolitanism, based on such liberal values, confirmed the right of outsiders to judge internal arrangements, and to act to ensure that acceptable standards were maintained. This was the essential condition of the grand underlying dialectic: the sovereignty of states obliged them to meet the norms of the international community but the norms of the international community were a product of the sovereignty of states.

Westphalia, Authority, and International Society

Daniel Philpott

The Peace of Westphalia, the 1648 settlement of the Thirty Years War, now eponymous among scholars for our system of sovereign states, is 350 years old.[1] Audacious claimants of change commemorate this birthday as a funeral rite. They speak grandly, of our own times as interesting times, of sovereignty's erosion, of moving beyond Westphalia, of a new medievalism, all realized through the expansion of the European Union, the rise of internationally sanctioned intervention, and governments' loss of control over goods, money, migrants, investment, drugs, and terrorists – moving across borders, ever quickening.[2] Predictably, to others, this talk is fustian. None of the Westphalia settlement's words is lapidary: The rise of state sovereignty at Westphalia, the robustness of state sovereignty since Westphalia, and the fall of state sovereignty today are all overrated.[3]

If the seers are right, then Westphalia is properly commemorated, and our times interesting. Changes in international politics after the Cold War are more fundamental than the usual sorts of changes that follow the usual major wars: crownings of new hegemons, constructions of new schemes for maintaining peace and order, and ascents of new victors of the game with new styles of play. If the seers are right, we are seeing a new game, one with new players and new rules, indeed, as I shall argue, a revision in the constitutional authority underlying international relations. Our literature, though, lacks a concept that would tell us whether this sort of change is taking place, and if so, how it compares in quality and scale with previous changes in international authority.

[1] I presented an earlier version of this paper at the 'Sovereignty at the Millennium: getting beyond Westphalia?' Panel at the Annual Convention of the International Studies Association, Minneapolis, Minnesota, March 17–21, 1998. For comments on previous drafts of this paper, I thank Martha Finnemore, Chris Hardy, Bryan Hehir, Stanley Hoffman, Robert Keohane, Andrew Moravcsik, and William Wohlforth. For institutional support, I also thank the Research Program on International Security, Center of International Studies, Princeton University, and Olin Institute for Strategic Studies, Harvard University.
[2] See essays in G. Lyons and M. Mastanduno, (eds), *Beyond Westphalia? State Sovereignty and International Intervention* (Baltimore, Johns Hopkins University Press, 1995); essays in T. Bierksteker and C. Weber, *State Sovereignty as Social Construct* (Cambridge, Cambridge University Press, 1996); J. Ruggie, 'Territoriality and beyond: problematizing modernity in international relations', *International Organization*, 47 (1993), 139–74. For the concept of the 'new medievalism', see H. Bull, *The Anarchical Society: A Study of Order in World Politics*, (New York, Columbia University Press, 1997), pp. 254–55, 264–76.
[3] See S. Krasner, 'Westphalia and All That', in J. Goldstein and R. Keohane, (eds), *Ideas and Foreign Policy: Beliefs, Institutions and Political Change* (Ithaca, Cornell University Press, 1993), pp. 253–64; and S. Krasner, 'Compromising Westphalia', *International Security*, 20 (1995/96), 115–151; H. Gelber, *Sovereignty Through Interdependence* (London, Kluwer Law, 1997).

So that is what I propose: To develop the concept of the constitution of international relations. In the first half of the paper, I explicate the concept. In the second half, I use it to characterize international history as one of successive constitutional changes, and finally to judge the allegations of contemporary revolution.

The Constitution of International Society

Behind wars and economic competition, prior to concerts, alliances, and balances of power, beneath agreements governing trade, armaments, and the environment, is the constitution of international society. This defining authority is what I want to identify and describe. Here is what I mean by it: *A constitution of international society is a set of norms, mutually agreed upon by polities who are members of the society, that define the holders of authority and their prerogatives, specifically in answer to three questions: Who are the legitimate polities? What are the rules for becoming one of these polities? And, what are the basic prerogatives of these polities? Constitutions of international society are both legitimate – that is, sanctioned by authoritative agreements – and practiced, generally respected by all polities which are powerful enough regularly to violate it.* Each part of this definition I will probe more deeply. What I now want to stress is the foundational nature of these constitutions. They are authors of orders, denoting the polities who carry on war and business, and the contours of their powers; they are etchers of blueprints, resembling the rules of baseball, which define the nine players, their strictures and allowances, the meaning and regulation of pitches, outs, strikes, steals, and balls.

Now in the international context, 'constitution' may seem strained. It is within borders that we are familiar with single documents which people call constitutions; there, constitutions are most developed, rich, complex, and respected. International constitutions are rarely called such, and are often strewn among separate treaties, conventions and customary law. But they are constitutional in this essential respect: they define internationally the traditional troika of executive, legislative, and judicial powers.

As international understandings, these constitutions refrain from defining *all* authority, at every level. Most international constitutions define polities with internal realms, where the inhabitants, or at least some of them, in turn define the character of their constitutional authority – e.g., monarchical, communist, social democratic, and so on. The modern state, as it emerged after Westphalia, is such a polity. But it is the international constitution which first defines this polity as an entity with the authority to determine further its own constitutional authority. It is the international constitution which defines the very meaning of internal and external realms. An international constitution, then, is more than simply a derivative of the collected constitutions of its individual polities. It is the framework that makes them individual polities. This is what emerged at Westphalia. In the negotiating halls of Münster and Osnabrück, Dutch and German rulers won a monopoly of constitutional powers, just as their counterparts elsewhere in Europe already enjoyed. But in order for these states to triumph, the rival authority of the Holy Roman Empire and the Catholic Church, who had once legislated, judged, and enforced laws and religious uniformity within these states' territories, had to be replaced. A sovereign state system required both state institutions within borders and the disappearance of authorities who would interfere from without. The international constitution defined both aspects.

But 'constitution' may still seem strained. We think of domestic constitutions, accurately or not, as creations of designers, but of international orders as foreign to idealistic fiat. But to articulate the international constitution is not to assert the cause of its genesis. Westphalia, for instance, arose in part from ideas of the Reformation, but also from centuries of economic, technological, and institutional evolution. On a utilitarian reading, a constitution is a set of functional rules which states adopt as they begin to communicate, trade, and carry on commerce. Neither is a constitution contrary to the Realist tradition: Constitutions create the very anarchic states system that makes war, balancing, and alliances possible.[4] Indeed, constitutions are part of normal international politics. When a Secretary of State visits a foreign minister or when a papal nuncio visits an Islamic Caliph, a recognition of constitutional authority – the authority for which the diplomat speaks – is implied. Elsewhere in this collection, in the context of the system of sovereign states, Alan James writes that sovereignty (a form of constitutional authority) gives states 'the capacity to "talk" to other states'.[5] To assert the constitution of international society is not to insist upon a fantastic construction but to exhume and reveal something we take for granted.

Exposing constitutions begins with finding them. As an agreement upon shared rules, an international constitution exists within an international society – 'a group of states (or, more generally, a group of independent political communities) which ... have established by dialogue and consent common rules and institutions for the conduct of their relations, and recognize their common interest in maintaining these arrangements'.[6] Of these rules and institutions, the constitution is that portion which defines the basic, constitutional authority of the member polities.

Because the society is international, the polities will be separate, but they might range in their separateness from the complete independence of sovereign states, to the distinct but overlapping authority of kings, nobles, pope, and emperor in medieval Europe, to the partially autonomous regions of a loosely centralized empire. A constitution of international society is often geographically bounded and might exist within a single civilization, as was the case with classical Greece, China, Sumeria, medieval Europe, and Renaissance Italy, but

---

[4] For Realists who acknowledge the importance of sovereignty as an institution, see H. Morgenthau, *Politics Among Nations: The Struggle for Power and Peace*, revised by K. Thompson (New York, Alfred A. Knopf, 6th ed., 1985); and K. Walz, *Theory of International Politics* (Reading MA, Addison-Wesley, 1979), p. 96.

[5] A. James, 'The practice of sovereign statehood in contemporary international society', *Political Studies*, 47 (1999), 457–73, p.466 (this issue).

[6] H. Bull and A. Watson, 'Introduction', in H. Bull and A. Watson, *The Expansion of International Society* (Oxford, Oxford University Press, 1984), p. 1. For other key works in the English School, see Bull, *The Anarchical Society*; M. Wight, *Systems of States* (London, Leicester University Press, 1977); M. Wight, *Power Politics* (Harmondsworth, Penguin, 1979); H. Butterfield and M. Wight, (eds), *Diplomatic Investigations* (London, Allen and Unwin, 1966); A. Watson, *The Evolution of International Society: A Comparative Historical Analysis* (London, Routledge, 1992); B. Buzan, 'From international system to international society: structural realism and regime theory meet the English school', *International Organization*, 47 (1993), 327–52; M. Shaw, 'There is no such thing as society: beyond individualism and statism in international security studies', *Review of International Studies*, 19 (1993), 159–75; and C. Brown, 'International theory and international society: the viability of the middle way?', *Review of International Studies*, 21 (1995), 183–96.

could also be global, as the current society of sovereign states has been since the fall of the European colonial empires. Or, a geographical constitution might coexist with a global one – the member states of the European Union, for instance, are also members of global international society. Finally, one geographically separate international society might carry on business with another, or with an empire. Medieval Europe, China, India, and the Ottoman Empire, Greece, Persia, and Rome – they fought, they traded, they exchanged diplomats, they developed rules to govern this interaction, but never united themselves under a common constitution. Much more common in ages before technology and communication became strong and dense ligatures, they were what Martin Wight called 'secondary systems of states'.[7]

The Three Faces of Authority

Constitutions of international society, then, define authority. I want to propose that this authority appears in three faces. All constitutions contain all three faces; every constitution's determination of them is its unique signature. Each face answers a different question about authority. The first face answers: Who are the polities in a given international society? The second face answers: Who may belong to the society? And, who may become one of these legitimate polities? The third face answers: What are the essential prerogatives of these polities? Together, these faces define constitutional authority for any international society.

The First Face of Authority

Most fundamentally, international constitutions prescribe the legitimate polities of an international society. A legitimate polity is simply one that the members of a society recognize as properly participating in the society. To ask who is a legitimate polity is analogous to asking who is a citizen in a domestic society. Since Westphalia, in the West, later throughout the globe, international constitutions have defined the legitimate polities mainly as states, possessing the quality of sovereignty. In this world, Burundi has a status that California does not, entitling it to diplomatic privileges and memberships in international organizations. The state is not the only form of legitimate polity, for other constitutions have prescribed other sorts of polities. Medieval Islam apportioned authority among a Caliph and scores of geographically far flung lesser figures, while high medieval Christendom admitted hundreds of diverse authorities, few of them sovereign, all linked together by unique privileges and prerogatives.[8] But I want to focus on the sovereign state, for it is the basis of our own constitution.

Sovereignty has suffered a troubled intellectual history. It has evolved over four centuries, making a single definition seem an immodest proposal.[9] Yet,

---

[7] Wight, *Systems of States*, pp. 24–25. I have relied heavily in this section on Watson, *The Evolution of International Society*.

[8] See Watson, *Evolution of International Society*, pp. 112–119.

[9] For skeptics of stable definitions of sovereignty, see L. Oppenheim, *International Law*, Vol. 1 (London, Longmans, Green, 1905), p. 103; R. Falk, 'Sovereignty', in *Oxford Companion to Politics of the World* (Oxford, Oxford University Press, 1993), p. 854; J. Bartelson, *A Genealogy of Sovereignty* (Cambridge, Cambridge University Press, 1995); S. Benn, 'Sovereignty', *Encyclopedia of Philosophy*, 7 (1955), 501–5; and E. H. Carr, *The Twenty Years' Crisis* (New York, Harper & Row, 1964).

there is, I believe, a formulation broad enough to encompass much of the diversity of definitions, but discrete enough to be useful: supreme authority within a territory.[10] Each element of the definition is crucial. Authority connotes legitimacy, the right to hold offices and powers. Sovereign authority is supreme authority; no human being is above it (even some philosophers of sovereignty such as Bodin still insisted upon the higher authority of God). Supremacy is what Bodin, Hobbes, and Grotius, sovereignty's first systematic articulators, had in mind, and it anchors most subsequent definitions.

Territoriality is also crucial: The collection of people over whom the holder of sovereignty rules is defined by virtue of its location within borders, not by some other principle such as family kinship or religious belief. The people within these borders may not necessarily conceive of themselves as a 'people' with a common identity; in the century of Westphalia, they rarely did. But their location within boundaries requires their allegiance to their sovereign. Today, virtually all political authority is territorial. Even institutions like the European Union or the United Nations are composed of territorial member states, rendering their authority territorially derived, too. By virtue of what quality are the citizens living under these institutions subject to their authority? By virtue of their religion? Tribe? Family? Nationality? No, by virtue of their residence in a state which has contracted into these institutions.[11]

These are the limits of specificity, for within the broad definition of supreme authority within a territory, all historical uses of the term have meant a particular form of sovereignty, reflecting one or another philosophy in one or another epoch: Sovereignty is never without an adjective. A compendium of these adjectives I cannot offer here. But three categories of adjectives capture sovereignty's variants. The first describes *holders* of sovereignty. Sovereignty need not lie in a single individual or legislature, as Bodin and Hobbes thought.[12] It could also reside in a triumvirate, a Committee of Public Safety, the people united in a General Will (as Rousseau thought), the people ruling through a constitution, or the law of the European Union.

Another relevant sort of adjective is the pair 'internal' and 'external', which are not distinct types of sovereignty, but complementary, always coexistent, aspects of sovereignty.[13] Every holder of sovereignty is Janus-faced. He is supremely authoritative within a territory; his community is free from outside authority. This feature of sovereignty echoes Alan James' notion of sovereignty

---

[10] There are many scholars who share roughly the definition of sovereignty that I develop herein. See J. Brierly, *The Law of Nations* (New York, Oxford University Press, 1963), p. 13; R. Keohane, 'Sovereignty, Interdependence, and International Institutions', in M. Smith and L. Miller, (eds), *Ideas and Ideals. Essays in Honor of Stanley Hoffmann* (Boulder CO, Westview, 1993), pp. 91–107; Waltz, *Theory of International Politics* p. 96; Morgenthau, *Politics among Nations*, p. 333; M. Fowler and J. Bunck, *Law, Power, and the Sovereign State* (University Park PA, Pennsylvania State University Press, 1995); Ruggie, 'Territoriality and beyond'; Kratochwil, 'Of Systems, Boundaries, and Territoriality: An Inquiry Into the Formation of the States-System'.

[11] On the importance of territoriality to sovereignty, see Ruggie, 'Territoriality and beyond', pp. 148–52; and H. Spruyt, *The Sovereign State and its Competitors* (Princeton, Princeton University press, 1994), pp. 34–36.

[12] See J. Bodin, *On Sovereignty* (Cambridge, Cambridge University Press, 1992); and T. Hobbes, *Leviathan* (Harmondsworth, Penguin, 1968).

[13] This is not to say that you cannot have one without the other. For instance, a state that is in the midst of civil war, but whose authority is unchallenged from the outside might have external sovereignty but not internal sovereignty. But when sovereignty is realized, both aspects are present.

as constitutional independence.[14] The key here is constitutional authority: A sovereign constitution is supreme within borders and independent of all other constitutional authorities. To James' notion, I add only that this independence depends on its recognition by outsiders, entailed in the international constitution. This recognition, to borrow an analogy used by other scholars, is to states what a no-trespassing law is to private property – the broad societal agreement that bequeaths property, or the state, its inviolability.[15]

The external sovereignty of the state is what international lawyers have in mind when they speak of sovereignty. It is what the United Nations Charter means by 'political independence and territorial integrity,' and the basis of its general prohibition of intervention. It is also what political scientists mean when they speak of international relations as anarchy, which means not necessarily chaos, violence, and riot, but simply the lack of a government, the absence of a higher authority which makes claims upon those who live under it. The external sovereignty of the state is compatible with a variety of holders of internal sovereignty. A monarch, the people, a constitution, a dictatorship, a theocracy, can each represent the state within borders and be immune from external intervention. Compared with internal sovereignty, external sovereignty has also remained relatively constant – not unrevised, but steady like a suit of armour whose plates and hinges are only occasionally updated, while the personality inside changes often, from revolution to revolution.

A final relevant pair of adjectives for describing kinds of sovereignty is 'absolute' and 'non-absolute'. At first, non-absoluteness might seem to contradict sovereignty's essential quality of supremacy. If sovereignty is supreme, how can it be anything but absolute? This is close to Alan James' argument: Sovereignty is either present or absent, never only partially realized.[16] I understand absoluteness, though, to refer not to the quality or magnitude of sovereignty, for if sovereignty were less than supreme in any particular matter, it would not indeed be sovereignty at all. But a holder of sovereignty need not be sovereign over all matters. For instance, a military junta might be sovereign in all matters except for its responsibility for upholding human rights, in which it is subject to the executive and judicial power of an outside body. Absoluteness refers to the scope of affairs over which a sovereign body governs within a particular territory: Is it supreme over all matters or merely some?

In those matters to which a sovereign state's authority does not extend, it is typically international law, or the law of an international institution that prescribes how authority is to be shared, that is sovereign. The government of France is supreme in defence policy but not in trade, which it governs jointly with the other EU members as prescribed by EU law, which is supreme in trade. The French constitution's sovereignty is non-absolute. Note that the supremacy of EU law in matters of trade does not mean that the EU monopolizes trade policy to the exclusivity of the member states. Rather, EU law defines the

---

[14] James, 'The practice of sovereign statehood in contemporary international society', p.466.

[15] See F. Kratochwil, 'Sovereignty as *Dominium*: Is There a Right of Humanitarian Intervention?', in Lyons and Mastanduno, *Beyond Westphalia?* (Baltimore, Johns Hopkins University Press, 1995), pp. 21–43; J. Ruggie, 'Continuity and Transformation in the World Polity: Toward a Neorealist Synthesis', in Robert O. Keohane, (ed.), *Neorealism and its Critics* (New York, Columbia University Press, 1986), pp. 131–157.

[16] James, 'The practice of sovereign statehood in contemporary international society', p. 463.

distribution of policy making prerogatives, as they are so complexly arrayed among members states and the component institutions of the Union.

Of course, sovereignty can also be absolute. For Bodin and Hobbes, sovereignty meant unconditional human authority, over all matters.[17] The absolute sovereignty of the state is archetypical modern sovereignty; it is the norm to which the EU and the emerging UN norm of humanitarian intervention are two exceptions. It renders international relations anarchical, for it makes states wholly autonomous; they are not required to yield or genuflect to any outside authority. It is the sort of sovereignty with which we are most familiar.

It was with the sovereign state that constitutions of international society coloured their first face, in Europe after Westphalia, and across the globe through colonial independence in the 1960s. Of course, the first face also tells us which polities are not legitimate. Westphalia, for instance, negated the Holy Roman Empire's substantive constitutional authority – the legislative and judicial authority of the Imperial Diet and other institutions, which had persisted well into the fifteenth century, and the executive authority to enforce religious uniformity within nascent states, which the Empire asserted through arms until Westphalia. What kinds of authorities can hold meaningful powers, what kinds cannot, is what the first face determines.

The Second Face of Authority

Every club has rules for membership, and these rules are tied closely to what it means to be a member. International societies, too, have rules that determine who enjoys, and can attain, the status of the legitimate polity, entitled to all of the privileges that legitimate polities enjoy – the second face of authority. The second face includes and excludes. According to its rules, societies grant their own members a thicker set of privileges – diplomatic immunities, commitments to consultation, restraint from intervention – than they grant to those they deem outsiders. Medieval Islamic legal theorists, for instance, divided the world into two realms, *dar al-Islam* (the realm of Islam) and *dar al-harb* (the realm of war).[18] Medieval Christendom practiced similar standards toward the rest of the world. Even Westphalia's signers still intended to create a constitution for Christian Europe, one whose provisions would apply only to Christian states, and not, for instance, to the Ottoman Empire. The Treaty of Münster begins, '[i]n the name of the most holy and individual Trinity'.[19] Today, the European Union, secular, defined by intricate modern law, purveys elaborate application procedures, that compose its standards of membership, its second face.

Along with distinguishing insiders and outsiders, international constitutions also propose the terms for dealing with outsiders. Many of the medieval

---

[17] In fact, this must be somewhat qualified even in the case of Bodin, for whom the sovereign is bound by natural law, is under a duty to respect the liberties and property of subjects as they are entitled to them, and is obligated to abide by his contracts with private citizens. There is no right to resistance, however, to correspond to these duties. See Bodin, *On Sovereignty*; and J. H. Franklin, *Jean Bodin and the Rise of Absolutist Theory* (Cambridge, Cambridge University Press, 1973).

[18] See S. Hashmi, 'International society and its Islamic malcontents', *The Fletcher Forum*, (1996), pp. 13–29.

[19] See F. Israel, (ed.), *Major Peace Treaties in Modern History, 1648–1967*, Vol. 1 (New York, McGraw-Hill Books, 1967).

Islamic theorists thought that members of the Islamic state were called to wage *jihad,* through both military and non-military means, against outsiders in order to expand the sphere of *dar al-Islam.* But they also forged a third realm, *dar al-sulh,* for states with which Muslims developed treaty obligations. With them, *jihad* was to be postponed. Societies almost always trade, ally, and negotiate with outsiders. But outsiders are still not legitimate polities, entitled to full privileges.

The Third Face of Authority

All legitimate polities, once they are members of a society, may perform some actions by virtue of their membership. Such standing prerogatives are constitutional; they define fundamental powers of states, of the European Union, of any legitimate polity; they compose the third face of authority. They differ from the rules of the first face in that they are not essential to the legitimate polity's definition. Just as a president could be a president without a line item veto power, a state could be a state even if non-intervention were not absolute. But if standing prerogatives are not essential, they are also steady, existing prior to the commitments that states contract into – alliances, trade agreements, sundry pacts governing sundry matters. In the eighteenth century, Vattel depicted the third face of authority when he defined international society as one of equal sovereign states, states whose prerogatives included the right to send diplomats and enter treaties, the duty not to invade, and, most of all, the obligation not to intervene. In a society of states, the third face tells us whether sovereignty is absolute or non-absolute, and if non-absolute, in which respects it is sovereign.[20] It completes the concept of the constitution of international society.

But What Exactly *are* Constitutions of International Society?

Constitutions of international society define constitutional authority, according to the three faces of authority. This is what they *do*. But it still may not be clear exactly what they *are*. Are they laws? Morals? Norms? The habitual behaviour of polities? How are they different from common agreements between polities which are not constitutional? Are constitutions still valid if violated? Do they amount to anything more than mere power? I stated above that international constitutions are sets of norms. By this hazardously contested, sometimes cryptic term, I mean rules which are viewed as obligatory by the broad majority of people living under them, and which are usually, customarily, practiced.[21] Norms here are quite similar to law, as legal positivists typically understand it. A constitutional norm is a unique kind of norm in that it constitutes polities and

[20] Similar to my argument about the third face of authority, Christian Reus-Smit argues that the 'constitutional structure of international society' defines 'pure procedural justice'. See C. Reus-Smit, 'The constitutional structure of international society', *International Organization*, 51 (1997), 568–570.

[21] Of course, norm has many meanings for social scientists, ranging from patterns of behaviour that result from the fear of sanctions, to customary behaviour, to moral beliefs, to standards that constitute the very identities of actors, whether they are tribes people or states. On the variety of definitions of norms in international relations, see J. Thompson, 'Norms in international relations: a conceptual analysis', *International Journal of Group Tensions*, 23 (1993), 67–83.

endows them with their basic prerogatives. There are two particular features of constitutions which further establish their distinctiveness, and which I want to describe further: their legitimacy and their practice.

By legitimate, I mean perceived to be obligatory, worthy of assent, by the polities living under the norm. Polities speak of constitutions as something they are mutually obligated to respect, and view the polity who violates them as one who breaches a promise – much like law. Constitutional provisions, then, are much more than behaviour, desirable or habitual. Britain's nineteenth century role as 'holder of the balance', applying military force on the European continent only to parry excessive great power expansion, was, no matter how consistent or wise, never seen as an obligation, either by Britain or by continental European powers. It was not a constitutional provision. Had Britain intervened in the Austrian Empire in order to overthrow a monarch or liberate a nation, by contrast, Britain would have violated the constitutional provision of non-intervention.

How do we identify legitimate constitutional provisions? How do we know when polities recognize obligation and which obligations they recognize? We simply look at the claims about obligation which the polities agree upon. In the modern west, provisions of international constitutions are usually codified; they can be discovered in founding charters and major treaties, and are regularly reaffirmed and reinforced in protocols, pacts, and pronouncements. Decolonization was legitimated in a 1960 UN Declaration; the laws of the European Community were approved in the 1957 Treaty of Rome and revised in the 1991 Maastricht Treaty; minority provisions were codified in nineteenth century treaties and the League of Nations Covenant. Sometimes, as with Westphalia's elevation of sovereign statehood, we must look beyond the mere text of a treaty to the signers' understandings of the treaty, just as judges in domestic society will look beyond the text of a law to the intentions of its signers. More rarely, constitutional provisions are matters of 'customary law', whose obligatory character is revealed in certain kinds of actions. For instance, the permissibility of intervention since the end of the Cold War has not been codified in a UN Declaration, but has achieved its legitimacy through several instances of the Security Council's approval of actual interventions.

That constitutional provisions are expressed as obligation in codification or custom distinguishes them not only from mere habitual behaviour but also from mere moral ideas, which need only exist in human minds, and which find their expression in books, speeches, or conversations. Constitutional provisions are not moral laws, natural laws or God's laws, nor are they the notions of Luther, Kant, Rousseau, or Madison, or even the ideas of philosophers of international relations like Grotius, Vattel, or Suarez, although they may be consistent with any of these ideas.

But constitutional provisions must not only be legitimate, but also generally adhered to, or their constitutional status, the distinction between mere moral ideas and constitutional provisions, would mean very little. *That is, the authority which the norms prescribe must correspond to actual practice.* Attendant upon the UN Declaration on colonies was the actual freeing of colonies. Following Westphalia, only states exercised significant power, and they rarely forcibly interfered in one another's religious affairs. The Holy Roman Empire, by contrast, still enjoyed codified constitutional powers after 1648, but states contemptuously ignored these powers: the Empire did not practice sovereignty

TABLE 1. Characteristics of International Behaviour

Characteristics of rules	Legitimate	Not legitimate
Practiced	Constitutional norms	Patterned behaviour (*Britain's role as holder of the balance*)
Not practiced	Merely formal constitutional provisions (*The Holy Roman Empire after Westphalia*)	Normatively unpatterned behaviour (*Any number of events in international relations – e.g. wars*)

in any meaningful way. With the criterion of practice, we can eliminate rules which are bare paper provisions. Table 1 shows international behaviours which share various combinations of legitimacy and practice, and identifies constitutions as possessing both features.

That international constitutions are both legitimate and practiced echoes what many scholars claim about sovereignty, that it has both *de jure* and *de facto* aspects. Some dissenters, though, want to define constitutions, sovereignty, as matters of mere coercive power. The state's loss of control over trade, communication, multinational corporations, the defence of its borders, and cross-border flows of people, money, and drugs, to them, is the decline, the twilight, the downfall of sovereignty.[22] For several reasons, I think this approach is mistaken. First, it elides the insight of constructivist scholars that authority is constituted at least in part by mutual recognition: A state does not practice sovereign powers, for instance, unless it is surrounded by a community of states that recognizes these powers.[23] Second, we lose the ability to describe situations where constitutional authority is constant, yet power varies. During three centuries of a European sovereign state system, the holder of hegemony, the polar distribution of power, metamorphosed several times with only occasional changes in the faces of authority. Today, even if state power is challenged by corporations, immigrants, and money flows, these trends have brought little change in constitutional authority. Or, we can imagine Burundi and Japan, two equally sovereign states, who enjoy similar diplomatic privileges, but differ wildly in their economic and military size. Such distinctions would hardly be intelligible if power were inseparable from sovereignty. Finally, an equation of constitutions with power would rob the constitution of its very distinctiveness. If sovereign statehood, for instance, is only a matter of power, then its existence and extent is nothing more than the sum total of all those forces, internal and external, military, economic, social, psychological, that

---

[22] See W. Wriston, *The Twilight of Sovereignty*, (New York, Scribners, 1992); K. Ohmae, *The End of the Nation State*, (New York, Harper Collins, 1995); R. Vernon, *Sovereignty at Bay*; R. Cooper, *The Economics of Interdependence: Economic Policy in the Atlantic Community*, (New York, McGraw-Hill, 1968).

[23] See A. Wendt, 'Collective identity formation and the international state', *American Political Science Review*, 88 (1994), 384–96; and Reus-Smit, 'The constitutional structure'.

compose this power, making sovereign statehood redundant. The same goes for other constitutions of international society as well.[24]

Besides matters of mere power, there are other entities which constitutions are not, and whose identification throws into sharper relief what international constitutions are. They are not agreements between already constituted polities, regulating their arms, trade, religion, environment, treatment of criminals, or thousand of other matters, agreements obligating them to perform certain actions under certain conditions, but which do not cede any standing constitutional authority.[25] Most international laws committing states to arbitration of disputes, and most multilateral organizations, although important to the character of international relations, acquire no constitutional authority from states. The collective security function of the United Nations, for instance, allows states to determine for themselves when they will participate in a war of enforcement, leaving their executive authority completely intact.

We also distinguish constitutions from their exceptions, aberrations, and violations. Some agreements do cede constitutional authority, but are signed between only two or a few polities, not the collectivity of polities in an international society, and thus fall short of revising an international constitution. Panama leases its canal zone to the US government; nineteenth century Britain maintains a sphere of influence in China, subject to only limited Chinese governance; the USA maintained the right to intervene in Cuba; the Soviet Union treated eastern European states as semi-sovereign satellites according to its Brezhnev Doctrine.[26] All of these are aberrations, not revisions.

Polities also violate international constitutions. States intervene; medieval barons violate the terms of dukes' authority; perhaps states continue to hold colonies after colonies have become illegitimate. When a polity violates a constitutional norm occasionally, in isolable instances, then the violation is just that, a violation, and not an annulment of the norm. But if there exist revisionist states which reject a norm and constantly violate it, then the norm effectively does not exist – it is not practiced. Revisionist states are powerful states, ones who can prevent the norm's practice or force other states to fight to preserve it. Eras of their reign are one of 'contested constitutions', meaning not that the old constitutional norm has been supplanted by a new one, but that no norm elicits general support at all. Although the 1555 Treaty of Augsburg prescribed sovereignty over religious matters within the Holy Roman Empire, neither Catholic nor Protestant powers accepted its terms, and in fact continued literally to invade one another's religious privacy. Only after 1648 was princes' sovereignty over religious practice accepted and respected and practiced. During revolutionary France and the expansion of Nazi Germany, the prohibition of intervention was constantly violated, while an aspiring empire

---

[24] Generally agreeing that sovereignty should be separated from power are theorists as diverse as Brierly, *The Law of Nations*, p. 13; Keohane, 'Sovereignty, Interdependence, and International Institutions'; Waltz, *Theory of International Politics*, p. 96; Morgenthau, *Politics among Nations*, p. 333.

[25] Keohane develops a separate term for the set of obligations that states occur through their treaty commitments – 'operational sovereignty'. See Keohane, 'Sovereignty, Interdependence, and International Institutions'.

[26] I draw these examples from Fowler and Bunck, *Law, Power, and the Sovereign State*, pp. 83–125.

challenged the state as the legitimate polity. These were times of contested constitutions.

Even when constitutions are respected, though, we should not make the mistake of thinking that they will necessarily be tranquil. Stable, uncontested constitutions are perfectly compatible with conflict, competition, even the worst sort of death and disaster, cruelty and holocaust, which all occur within agreed upon, legitimate, norms of authority. Constitutions are often less like the script of a choreographed dance, a routine that performers follow cooperatively, than they are like the rules of a jousting match or bull-fight, regulators of deathly competition. They do not eliminate conflict, but structure who fights it, and on what terms.

A Brief History of Constitutions of International Society in the West

With the concept of the constitution of international society, we can identify the authority structure of an international society in any time and place. How does an international society characterize the three faces of authority? This is our central question. Two other questions help us to establish a constitution's significance. First, what are its geographic boundaries? Is it global or regional? Harder to answer precisely but also quite important is a question which the three faces themselves do not answer: What is the intrinsic significance of the constitution? For instance, the founding of the European Coal and Steel Community in 1950, was, as I will argue, the most sweeping constitutional revision since Westphalia in that it revised all three faces of sovereignty. But in creating supranational authority over only two industries, it was arguably much less significant than rise of colonial independence, a revision of only the second face of sovereignty, but one which gave complete legal independence to scores of states and millions of people. Of course, the ECSC was significant for its future possibilities, but such significance, again, is hard to be exact about, and is only captured in description.

The constitution of international society also offers us a new way of recounting the history of international relations, one whose junctures and monuments will be very different from those stressed by the more traditional histories of rising and falling hegemons. It is rather a history of successive constitutions, told according to what I propose to call 'constitutional revolutions', which I define as a major redrawing of at least one of the three faces of authority. Each revolution, we can describe by the manner and thoroughness by which it fashions the three faces.

Below, I briefly tell such a history for the western international society of states as it has evolved since the Middle Ages. Although it is only one such history – we could tell similar histories of Islam, India, ancient Greece, ancient China[27] – it is the one with which we are most familiar, which reveals the origins of our contemporary society, which places present changes in comparative historical context, and which will, then, nicely illustrate the concept of international constitutions and their revolutions. I tell the history as a double movement: First, one of how the sovereign state system took over Europe, then the world; second, one of how sovereignty has begun to be circumscribed, largely during the twentieth century. Towards sovereignty, away from sovereignty – each

---

[27] For these histories, see A. Watson, *The Evolution of International Society.*

TABLE 2. Major Constitutional Revolutions Since the Middle Ages

Revolution in sovereignty	Revision of first face	Revision of second face	Revision of third face	Geographical boundaries
Westphalia (1648)	Sovereign states replace Holy Roman Empire	Polity must have basic characteristics of a state and be Christian	Government within state enjoys absolute sovereignty; non-intervention	Europe
Colonial independence (early 1960s)	None	Colonies entitled to statehood	None	Global
Minority treaties (19th century, post First World War)	League of Nations judicial and oversight functions	Minority agreements criterion for recognition as states	States subject to oversight of minority treatment	Eastern Europe
European Union	EU institutions 'pool' the sovereignty of states	Membership criteria specified by EU law	States no longer sovereign in areas specified by EU law	Europe, member states
Intervention	UN attains executive authority to enforce human rights and justice	None	States subject to outside enforcement of human rights practices	Potentially global

movement involves a few major revolutions. It was Westphalia, then colonial independence around 1960 whose constitutions brought us the system of sovereign states.

It was the rise of minority treaties in the late nineteenth and early twentieth centuries, the founding of the European Community, and the rise of internationally sanctioned intervention that have come to challenge it. How each revolution revised sovereignty's three faces and each constitution's geographic boundaries I summarize in Table 2. These features, as well as each constitution's intrinsic significance, I describe below.

Toward a System of Sovereign States

A constitution which prescribes a system of sovereign states in its purest form is one that holds that the sovereign state is the sole legitimate form of polity within a society, prescribes basic criteria for a polity to be recognized as a sovereign state – usually, that it possess a government that is in control of a people within a territory, and be capable of entering into international agreements – and posits non-intervention as the basic prerogative of sovereign states. This is how it renders the three faces. I doubt that such a pure system has ever existed. But something like it emerged at the Peace of Westphalia, then gradually spread around the world, finally becoming globally legitimized and practiced through the revolution of colonial independence around 1960.   .

The Revolution at Westphalia

In his classic 1948 article on Westphalia, international legal scholar Leo Gross called the settlement 'the majestic portal which leads from the old world into the new world'. Hans Morgenthau and other top political scientists have repeated the judgment; Westphalia is now metonymy for the modern international system.[28] The case for Westphalia is that before 1648, as long as the Thirty Years' War was still flickering, Europe's legitimate polities, the membership criteria, and the rules – the three faces of sovereignty – were not compatible with a constitution of sovereign statehood; afterwards, they were. This is not to assert Westphalia as instant metamorphosis, for elements of sovereign statehood had been accumulating for three centuries. Westphalia consolidated the modern system; it did not create it *ex nihilo*.[29] Nor was modernity perfectly achieved after the peace, when a few medieval anomalies persisted. But if Westphalia was not a consummate fissure, and needs more qualification than the conventional wisdom suggests, it was still, I want to argue, as clean as historical faults come.[30]

We can see the international constitution that emerged at Westphalia most sharply in relief against the previous season at its peak – High Medieval Europe. The *Respublica Christiana* prescribed the three faces of authority only very loosely. There was no supreme authority within a territory, manifestly no sovereignty. Some publicists and theologians claimed sovereignty for the Pope and Emperor, but neither figure approached the territorial supremacy that other historical emperors, Chinese and ancient Roman for instance, achieved. Both the Pope and the Emperor held authority over thousands of kings, nobles, knights, and of course, bishops and other ecclesiastics, but these same authorities held prerogatives – each, a unique set of prerogatives – against the Pope, the Emperor, and one another.

Neither was any body of law sovereign. While natural law was a universal standard of morality, it did not prescribe offices or powers in the way that the United States Constitution, for instance, does. Nor was the requirement of territoriality met. The *Respublica Christiana* comprised all Christians, living in Europe or abroad in the Holy Land. Can we even speak of a constitution for this international society? While no single treaty or body of law prescribed prerogatives, there did exist common standards of legitimacy which, by their

---

[28] Gross, 'The Peace of Westphalia', p. 28; Morgenthau, *Politics among Nations*, pp. 328–30.

[29] For a similar view, see Wight, *Systems of States*; and Tilly, *Coercion, Capital, and European States*.

[30] For a dissenting view, see S. Krasner, 'Westphalia and All That', and S. Krasner, 'Compromising Westphalia'.

very silence on the exact forms of authority, themselves permitted thousands of eclectic authorities: the ideals of Christendom, canon law, and feudal law.[31]

Following its apogee in the twelfth century or so, the Middle Ages began to shed its diversity as sovereign states arose in England, France, and Sweden. But by the eve of the Thirty Years War, a strong obstacle to modernity persisted in the heart of Europe: the Holy Roman Empire. Drawing upon extant powers from the medieval imperial constitution, closely allied with the King of Spain, the Holy Roman Emperor exercised authority, although not sovereign authority, throughout German and Dutch territories. Most importantly, he enforced religious uniformity and the powers of the Church.[32] In 1555, princes within the empire appeared to have taken this authority over religion for themselves in the Peace of Augsburg, whose principle *cuius regio, euis religio* ('whose the region, his the religion') allowed them to enforce their own faith within their own territory.[33] But Augsburg did not last. It remained continually contested, exploding eventually into the holy cataclysm of the Thirty Years' War. Not until the close of this war did a proscription of intervention for religion become accepted and respected and practiced; not, indeed, until 1648.

What, then, was this Peace of Westphalia of 1648? At first, the settlement's two component treaties, Münster and Osnabrück, may not seem like the constitution that established a system of sovereign states. Nowhere do the treaties explicitly declare such a principle.[34] The Holy Roman Empire signed both treaties – it was not abolished until 1806. But Westphalia was not without plan or principle, a design which we can only understand by looking beyond the literal text of the treaties to the understandings of its signers, its historical context, and the subsequent practice of states. Here we find the three faces of authority configured as a system of sovereign states.

[31] On medieval authority, see J. Strayer, *On the Medieval Origins of the Modern State* (Princeton, Princeton University Press, 1970); B. Tieney, *Crisis of Church and State* (Englewood Cliffs, NJ, Prentice-Hall, 1964); E. Kantorowicz, *The King's Two Bodies* (Princeton, Princeton University Press, 1957); M. Wilks, *The Problem of Sovereignty in the Middle Ages* (Cambridge, Cambridge University Press, 1964). Ruggie, 'Continuity and Transformation', p. 142; Spruyt, *The Sovereign State*, pp. 34–36; and Wilks, *The Problem of Sovereignty*. For a challenge to medieval historians' consensus that the Middle Ages generally lacked sovereignty, see M. Fischer, 'Feudal Europe, 800–1300: communal discourse and conflictual practices', *International Organization*, 46 (1992), 427–66. For responses to Fischer, see R. Hall and F. Kratochwil, 'Medieval tales: neorealist "science" and the abuse of history', *International Organization*, 47 (1993); and R. Hall, 'Moral authority as a power resource', *International Organization*, 51 (1997), 591–622.

[32] R. Kann, *A History of the Habsburg Empire* (Berkeley, The University of California Press, 1974), pp. 1–24; H. Koenigsberger, *The Habsburgs and Europe, 1516–1560* (Ithica, Cornell University Press, 1971); J. Berenger, *History of the Habsburg Empire* (London, 1994).

[33] H. Holborn, *A History of Modern Germany*, p. 243–46; G. Barraclough, *The Origins of Modern Germany*, pp. 371.

[34] For the texts of the treaties, see Israel, *Major Peace Treaties* (Münster); and C. Parry, *Consolidated Treaty Series* (Dobbs Ferry, NY, Oceana Publications, 1981), (Osnabrück). For a good interpretation of the settlement's meaning for international relations, see A. Osiander, *The States System of Europe* (Oxford, Clarendon, 1994), p. 72. On the settlement in general, see F. Dickmann, K. Goronzy, E. Schieche, H. Wagner, and E. Wermter, (eds), *Acta Pacis Westphalicae* (Münster, Aschendorff Verlagsbuchhandlung, 1962); F. Dickmann, *Der Westphaelische Frieden* (Münster, Aschendorff, 1965); F. Dickmann, 'Rechtsgedanke und Machtpolitik bei Richelieu. Studienen neu endeckten Quellen', *Historische Zeitschrift*, 196 (1963); G. Pages, *The Thirty Years War*, D. Maland (trans.) (New York, Harper & Row Publishers, 1970); G. Parker, *The Dutch Revolt* (Ithaca, Cornell University Press, 1977); J. Polisensky, *The Thirty Years' War*, R. Evans (trans.) (Berkeley, University of California Press, 1971); and T. Rabb (ed.), *The Thirty Year's War: Problems of Motive, Extent, and Effect* (Boston, Heath, 1964).

In several respects, Westphalia defined the state as the legitimate European polity – the first face of sovereignty. A leitmotiv in the settlement was the principle of autonomy, realized, for instance, in the 'liberties' that largely freed German states from imperial interference in their affairs. Equality – the equality of European states, the rejection of universal papal and imperial authority, the logical complement to autonomy – also appeared frequently. Many negotiators, especially the French, under the influence of Cardinal Richelieu's ideas, but also the Swedes, also envisioned a European equilibrium, a balance of power, that implied independent action among independent European states.[35]

State sovereignty was also evinced in the settlement's separate provisions, and in the practice of these provisions following Westphalia. The Holy Roman Empire continued to exist, but it became largely a deliberative body, little different from a contemporary alliance among sovereign states. One of the settlement's most important provisions decriminalized the right of German princes to ally outside the Empire. Virtually immediately after Westphalia, German princes would come to exercise independent power, just like states in an international system. The authority of the Emperor himself was effectively reduced to another sovereign, supreme within his central European Habsburg lands. The pope, too, saw his political power eviscerated. Elsewhere, statehood was simply recognized. The settlement effectively made the Swiss Confederation independent; a separate treaty recognized the sovereign independence of the Netherlands. Medieval anomalies persisted, to be sure. A few German bishoprics remained partially autonomous; and during short periods over the coming centuries, small German states would combine their armed forces through imperial institutions. But these were scattered exceptions. States were now the legitimate polity, prevailing as the new template for political authority in Europe.[36]

Westphalia's prescription for politics and religion also helped establish state sovereignty. This, too, we must discern beneath the text, which did not re-establish Augsburg's *cuius regio, euis religio*, but which committed princes to tolerating the religious freedom of enumerated proportions of Catholic, Lutherans, and Calvinists in their territories. But with respect to sovereignty, to constitutional authority, these agreements were little different from agreements between modern sovereign states to regulate prices or pollution within their borders. After Westphalia, unlike after Augsburg, neither princes nor the Emperor would intervene to contest religion within another prince's territory. It is this vital matter of authority that distinguishes the two settlements.[37]

What about the second face of authority? The practice of granting new states membership in the states system would become a precedent. By the eighteenth century, the criteria for membership were that new states should have the

---

[35] On the views of the French and the Swedes, see the careful study of A. Osiander, *The States System of Europe*, pp. 27, 41, 77–8, 80–89; Church, *Richelieu*, pp. 283–349; M. Roberts, *Gustavus Adolphus* (London, Longmans, Green, 1958); M. Roberts, *Essays in Swedish History* (London, Weidenfeld & Nicolson, 1967), pp. 82–110.

[36] Osiander, *The States System of Europe*, pp. 32, 38–39; P. Schroeder, *The Transformation of European Politics, 1763–1848* (Oxford, Clarendon, 1994). R. Kann, *A History of the Habsburg Empire*, p. 52, 54; Osiander, *The States System of Europe*, p. 46; G. Barraclough, *The Origins of Modern Germany*, pp. 381–87; Mattingly, *Renaissance Diplomacy* (Boston, Houghton Mifflin Company, 1955).

[37] Osiander, *The States System of Europe*, pp. 40, 49; Holborn, *A History of Modern Germany*, pp. 368–69; Barraclough, *The Origins of Modern Germany*, pp. 381–87.

fundamental attributes of statehood – a viable government, control within their territory, the ability to make and carry out treaties. At the time of Westphalia, a Christian culture was required, too: Russia and Poland, but not the Ottoman Empire, were admitted, and given full diplomatic privileges.[38] This requirement was gradually dropped over the following couple of centuries, as the second face of authority took on its modern form.

By contrast, the third face of authority, like the first face, took its modern form almost immediately after Westphalia. Non-intervention, the key prerogative of sovereign states, was not explicitly stated in the settlement, and would not be until the eighteenth century, when philosophers and lawyers openly espoused it.[39] But non-intervention became standard and expected state practice – religious war and Habsburg intervention exited European history. Over the following three centuries, non-intervention persisted, not unchallenged, not always respected – both Hitler and Napoleon attempted to overthrow these practices, many states would intervene – but perduring as normal, expected behaviour. It perdures today, even if it is beginning to crack.[40]

Westphalia remains the most significant revolution in sovereignty to date. It revised all three faces of authority, and established constitutional authority in the form of the sovereign states system. Subsequent constitutional revolutions have revised, not replaced the state – geographically extending it, revising the criteria for being recognized as one, amending its authority. Even the European Union, a new form of institution, involves states as states, rather than replacing or subsuming them. Geographically, though, the Westphalian settlement was quite bounded – confined to the European continent.

Westphalian Europe and the Rest of the World

Over the ensuing three hundred years, the history of sovereignty is largely the history of Westphalia's geographic extension. Until this extension was completed through the revolution of colonial independence in the 1960's, polities outside the European international society generally held one of three kinds of status in relation to Europe. Some were rivals and trading partners with Europe, but not ruled or monopolized by Europe: the East Indies and China in the seventeenth and eighteenth centuries, the Ottoman Empire up through the nineteenth century. Although Europe shared with these polities at least certain principles like *pact sunt servanda*, it did not recognize them as states or accord them the privileges of statehood, and neither did these polities, for that matter, grant Europeans equal status: To Ottoman Muslims or the Chinese, Europeans were infidels or vassals.[41] No constitution of international society was mutually, explicitly, agreed upon.

---

[38] Bull and Watson, *The Expansion*; G. Gong, *The Standard of 'Civilization' in International Society* (Oxford, Clarendon, 1984).

[39] See F. Hinsley, *Sovereignty* (Cambridge, Cambridge University Press, 1986); and Bartleson, *A Genealogy of Sovereignty*.

[40] G. Parker, *The Thirty Years' War* (London, Routledge, Kegan, and Paul, 1997), p. 217; R. Vincent, *Nonintervention and International Order* (Princeton, Princeton University Press, 1974).

[41] On the Ottomans, see T. Naff, 'The Ottoman Empire and the European States System', in Bull and Watson, *The Expansion*, pp. 143–170; and H. Bull, 'The Emergence of a Universal International Society', in Bull and Watson, *The Expansion*.

A second category of non-European, non-sovereign polities included those whom Europe treated as less than equal, but not as wholly subordinate, like a colony. In both China and the Ottoman empire during the last half of the nineteenth century and the first part of the twentieth, in areas of Africa, Asia, and the Middle East such as post-independence Egypt and Iran, in portions of Latin America, in the eastern European states which became independent in the nineteenth century – in all these polities, European powers exercised authority over assorted affairs which Westphalian states normally govern themselves. Europeans partitioned these lands into spheres of influence for trade; they maintained rights to military bases; they governed strategic plots of territory such as the Suez Canal zone; they took over the collection of debts and customs or even intervened to collect debts; and they exercised other sorts of authority. The rulers of such territories were autonomous in many other matters, but these significant exceptions to their absolute sovereignty, combined with the lack of international assent to their sovereign status, made them less than Westphalian sovereign states.[42]

Wholly ruled, completely subordinated, entirely under the sovereign rule of European states was a third category – colonies, which the British, the French, the Dutch, the Portuguese, the Belgians, the Americans, and the Germans held in the Americas, Asia, the Middle East, and Africa. In effect, colonies were extensions of Westphalian sovereign states: Their rulers were ultimately accountable to European rulers; other European powers could not legitimately intervene in their affairs; and their European rulers could bargain their fate with other European powers.

These three categories of polities existed in different proportions at different moments in the three centuries after Westphalia. Over time, the virtual partners declined, while the subordinated and colonized polities of the globe multiplied, culminating in the nineteenth century with the colonization of much of Africa, Asia, Central America, and the Middle East. During these centuries, a few polities also moved up the ladder, some from colonies to subordinate states, some to full membership in the Westphalian system. Many Latin American states became independent in the 1820s, although they were still subject to regular intervention when they defaulted on their loans, and were not included in conferences on peace and international law until the early twentieth century.[43] Others advanced to full Westphalia status – the USA in 1783 and Canada in 1867, for instance.[44]

For a polity to advance out of colonial status or become Westphalian, there needed to be no change in membership criteria, no change in the Westphalia constitution; the polity merely acceded according to the set criteria. But did the standards themselves ever change? In one sense the rules for membership, the second face, evolved. European states no longer demanded Christianity, but instead a secularized 'standard of civilization' for aspiring states. The standard meant that a polity would not be treated as a full member of the Westphalian system – entitled to non-intervention, allowed fully to govern its own affairs –

---

[42] See A. Watson, 'European International Society and its Expansion', in Bull and Watson, *The Expansion*; H. Bull, 'The Emergence of an International Society'.
[43] See R. Klein, *Sovereign Equality among States: The History of an Idea* (Toronto ON, University of Toronto Press, 1974).
[44] On Japan, see Gong, *The Standard*, pp. 28–29.

until it met certain criteria. It had to guarantee basic rights – of life, property, travel, commerce – to both its own people and foreign nations; it had to have an organized government and capacity for self-defence; it had to adhere generally to international law as well as provide a domestic system of justice; it had to maintain diplomatic representation; and, more vaguely, it had to conform to the norms and practices of civilized international society.[45] In practice, such a requirement was little different from the earlier Christian standard. It was at most an evolution, not a revolution, in the international constitution.

The Rise of Colonial Independence

The radical revolution in the second face which permitted all colonies to become full sovereign states did not arrive until around 1960. A widening and weakening of the previous criteria for being recognized as a state, the new norm of colonial independence held that colonies were entitled to statehood however weak their government, however scant their control over their territory, however inchoate their people.[46] This was the first victory of the principle of self-determination in an international constitution following Westphalia. General colonial independence attained legitimacy through a 1960 UN declaration: 'all peoples have the right to self-determination', and 'inadequacy of political, economic, and social and educational preparedness should never serve as a pretext for delaying independence'. The resolution condemned colonialism as 'alien subjugation, domination, and exploitation ... a denial of fundamental human rights'.[47] In the surrounding decade, it was practiced as Britain, France, and Belgium granted independence to the preponderance of their remaining colonies, just as the United States and the Netherlands had freed their colonies during the previous two decades, and as Germany and Spain had lost their empires well earlier.

Like Westphalia, the transition was not divinely neat: Some colonies had already been freed; others would trickle into independence during the next two decades; most egregiously, Portugal clung to Angola and Mozambique. But in the thought, word, and deed of the UN and the vast majority of states, including the colonial powers, it was now illegitimate for a state to govern a colony. Self-determination, though, had its limits. Only colonies were entitled to statehood, not nations or tribes either within colonies or within other states.

Colonial independence revised only the second face of authority. The sovereign state remained the legitimate form of polity; and the new states attained all of the privileges of sovereignty. But the significance of this revolution emerges in its magnitude: between 1955 and 1970, 78 colonies were released from political dependency, as sovereign statehood expanded to virtually the entire globe.

[45] Gong, *The Standard*, pp. 14–15.

[46] On weak sovereign states, see R. Jackson, *Quasi-states: Sovereignty, International Relations, and the Third World* (Cambridge, Cambridge University Press, 1990).

[47] General Assembly Resolution 1514, United Nations Declaration on the Granting of Independence to Colonial Peoples and Countries.

Away from a System of Sovereign States

The second movement in this history of post-medieval constitutions is the circumscription of sovereign statehood. It is a twentieth century movement, and the work of ideas which grew popular in the twentieth century – human rights and European federalism. We find it in three major revolutions, and in some more minor phenomena, too. Minority treaties, European integration, and internationally sanctioned intervention are the major ones. I will not describe them in detail here, for they are treated well by other papers in this collection (Wallace, Mayall, and Taylor). Rather, I describe briefly how they revised the three faces of authority.

Minority Treaties

The minority treaties of the nineteenth and early twentieth centuries, I almost hesitate to call a revolution, for they appeared over a century. But since they are all instances of a single innovation, I will treat them as a common phenomenon. Simply, they require that a new state, in order to be recognized by other states, sign treaties guaranteeing the protection of its minorities, religious, racial, and ethnic. Britain, France, and Russia imposed such treaties on eastern European states in 1830 and 1856, but it was not until the 1878 Treaty of Berlin that minority protection came to be a normal condition placed on new European states. The trend culminated in the settlement of World War One, when the victorious allies signed minority treaties with both the defeated states and new or enlarged states, and included in the League of Nations Covenant a provision to enforce the treaties through a regular monitoring function and a judicial arbitration system. The minority treaties, then, revised both the second and third faces of authority. They provided criteria for membership and subjected some of states' internal policies to oversight. During the 1920s, several cases of minority disputes were successfully resolved through the League's arbitration system. This norm, however, was deeply bounded, both geographically – it was confined to eastern Europe – and temporally: Hitler doomed its prospects and the arrangement has never since reappeared.[48]

The Return of European Unity

The first transition since Westphalia to change sweepingly all three faces of authority, the most thorough revolution in sovereignty since Westphalia, has been the 1950 creation of the European Coal and Steel Community, and its expansion into the European Community, and eventually the European Union. The EU, whose powers are explicitly and clearly legitimated through the Maastricht Treaty, signed in 1991, amounts to a separate constitution of international society, one that coexists with the larger international society of sovereign states of which its members are still a part.

For the first time since the demise of the Holy Roman Empire, a significant political authority other than the state, one with formal sovereign prerogatives,

---

[48] On minority treaties, see I. Claude, *National Minorities: An International Problem* (Cambridge, Harvard University Press, 1955); R. Pearson, *National Minorities in Eastern Europe 1848–1945*, (London, Macmillan Press, 1983); C. Macartney, *National States and National Minorities* (New York, Russell and Russell, 1968).

has become legitimate within the boundaries of the Westphalia system – a revision of the first face of authority. The EU is not a 'wholly other' institution, though, for it comprises states themselves, who have 'pooled' their sovereignty into a common 'supranational' institution.[49] But this institution exercises constitutional powers that are not reducible to the state's powers. Through the European Commission, which proposes legislation and administers the day-to-day affairs of the Union through a large bureaucracy, the union exercises executive powers. Through the Council of Ministers, particularly as it now votes on many matters through a qualified majority, as well as the European Parliament, the Union exercises legislative powers. Finally, through the European Court of Justice, whose rulings stand authoritative within member states, the Union asserts judicial authority.

As for the second face of authority, the EU constitution prescribes definite criteria for membership, including a well-defined regimen for application. Defining the third face of authority, the constitution also carefully apportions prerogatives over decision-making in matters of trade, monetary policy, market regulation, and other matters among the member states, the Council of Ministers, which is made up of the member states, and the EU bureaucracy itself. EU law is sovereign in only a limited number of areas, but member states are no longer sovereign in all areas; neither enjoys absolute sovereignty. The significance of the European integration revolution depends on the areas of governance which continue to come under the pooled authority of the Union institutions. The recent decision to create a common currency and monetary policy among eleven countries is a strong step beyond the institution's confinement to matters of trade and commerce, and a pooling of quite an important part of states' sovereignty.

Internationally Sanctioned Intervention

Since the end of the Cold War, a new revolution has begun to take place, one significant for its revision of a crucial norm established in the Westphalia revolution: non-intervention. It encompasses several cases in which the UN or another organization has sanctioned military force to remedy an injustice within the boundaries of a state, or has taken on the administration of typically domestic matters. In using military force, the UN has acted often without the consent of the target state's government or of one of the parties in a civil war, thus departing from previous UN peacekeeping operations, where the consent of all warring parties was a prerequisite. The purposes of these interventions have included the delivery of humanitarian supplies, the ending of civil war, the enforcement of democratic elections, the rebuilding of failed state institutions, and the arrest of war criminals. The venues have included Iraq, the former Yugoslavia, Somalia, and Rwanda, Haiti, Cambodia, Liberia, the Sudan, and elsewhere. Some have been failures; some have been mixed successes.[50]

---

[49] See R. Keohane and S. Hoffmann, 'Institutional Change in Europe in the 1980s', in R. Keohane and S. Hoffman (eds), *The New European Community: Decisionmaking and Institutional Change* (Boulder CO, Westview, 1991), pp. 1–39.

[50] For a helpful account of contemporary intervention, see O. Ramsbotham and T. Woodhouse, *Humanitarian Intervention in International Conflict* (Cambridge, Cambridge University Press, 1996).

In exactly what sense do these interventions revise the constitution of international relations? Paul Taylor argues that they represent new conditions which the UN system places on states' sovereignty, such that they are now accountable to a higher authority for upholding certain standards of civilized behaviour.[51] Through the three faces of authority, we can see how this trend translates into an amended international constitution. It gives the United Nations and other international organizations – NATO, the EU, others – the executive power to intervene in states' internal affairs under certain conditions. This is the first face revised. But these institutions are only weak alternative polities to the state, for their use of force requires the unanimous permission of the Security Council in the case of the UN, and of all states who would contribute their troops in the case of every organization.

Much stronger is what intervention implies for the third face of authority. Under some conditions, when they fail to uphold some standards of justice – usually, peace, order, basic human rights – some states will be subject to the intervention of outside states acting in cooperation with an international authority. The target states are no longer absolute in their sovereignty. In the history of international constitutions, this trend is quite significant, for it departs from non-intervention, perhaps the most enduring and prominent tenet of the Westphalia settlement. Non-intervention's most recent historical articulation occurs in the UN Charter, which states the principle more than once, and in subsequent UN resolutions and declarations. Throughout the Cold War, it remained robust, as the UN consistently refrained from endorsing actual interventions, including unilateral humanitarian interventions in Uganda, Cambodia, and Bangladesh.[52]

But this conceptual significance must be balanced by a recognition of the limits of the practice. First, the intervention has been limited and selective. Depending on exactly how one interprets intervention, it has been practiced upon somewhere between five and fifteen states since the end of the Cold War – out of a total of over 190 states in the world. Intervention has failed to occur, too, in many states with injustices quite similar to those where it has occurred. Second, intervention is legitimate only when authorized by the UN Security Council, whose right to authorize force Chapter VII of the Charter prescribes. Intervention is far from a unilateral right. Third, the legitimacy of the intervention is not universal. Countries like China often dissent, although China has notably refrained from vetoing any of the above interventions in the Security Council. Fourth, in most cases of intervention, the Security Council has claimed a 'threat to international peace and security', signaling its refusal openly to label its actions intervention or depart radically from its traditional interpretation of the Charter. Although the construal is implausible, for the conflicts and

---

[51] See P. Taylor, 'The United Nations in the 1990s: proactive cosmopolitanism and the issue of sovereignty', *Political Studies,* 47 (1999), 538-65. pp. 548–50.

[52] Article 2(4) prohibits unilateral intervention in the form of 'the threat or use of force against territorial integrity or political independence of any state, or in any other manner consistent with the Purposes of the United Nations', whereas Article 2(7) is directed against the intervention of the United Nations in matters which are in states' domestic jurisdictions. Subsequent UN Documents even more directly condemn intervention, especially unilateral intervention. For arguments that UN law forbids intervention, see L. Damrosch, 'Commentary on Collective Military Intervention to Enforce Human Rights', in L. Damrosch and D. Scheffer (eds), *Law and Force in the New International Order* (Boulder CO, Westview, 1991), pp. 215–23; and K. Pease and D. Forsythe, 'Human rights, humanitarian intervention, and world politics', *Human Rights Quarterly*, 15 (1993), 290–314.

injustices eliciting intervention were all primarily internal, it does reveal the UN's reluctance to endorse a general doctrine of intervention.[53] Finally, it is not clear how robustly the post-Cold War precedent of intervention will continue. The interventions thus far have enjoyed mixed success; the practice is far from a durable fixture in a new world order. Despite these caveats, however, intervention – widely endorsed and significantly practiced – now seems well within the Security Council's legitimate authority.

Other Circumscriptions of Sovereignty

These major revolutions do not recount an exhaustive history of international constitutions. But they are the key landmarks. Other constitutional revisions, while significant in their normative importance, have proven only minor in their transference of authority. In this category is the European Convention on Human Rights, whose judicial powers originated in 1953 and expanded through subsequent protocols, but whose accomplishments extend little further than changing a few legal procedures in a handful of its member states.[54] Still others have proved more constitutionally significant, but were short-lived. The Holy Alliance of conservative great powers following the Napoleonic wars, for instance, agreed to intervene jointly against domestic liberal revolutions, but did not practice this executive power beyond about seven years after they agreed to exercise it. Other constitutional revisions have achieved strong political support, but never the broad agreement among states to become constitutional provisions. Self-determination outside the colonial context is an example of this – a revolution that minorities around the globe have hoped for, but which has never been realized. All such stories – of smaller revisions, of revisions that were not – would be included in a comprehensive history of international constitutions.

Conclusions

The concept of the constitution of international society offers us a way of characterizing international relations, not by its distribution of power, not by its economic openness, not by its mechanisms for resolving conflict or maintaining peace, but by its very configuration of constitutional authority. The three faces of authority describe these constitutions, help us to compare them with each other, and enable us to see when and how they change. Constitutions and revolutions differ in their sweep: Some revise one face of authority, some, two, some, all three. We can compare, too, their geographical extent and the intrinsic significance of the matters over which they have authority. We can also distinguish intact constitutions, practiced and legitimated, from contested constitutions, from violations of constitutions, from agreed upon exceptions to constitutions, and from revolutions in constitutions.

---

[53] On the interpretations of Security Council resolutions on intervention, see D. Scheffer, 'Toward a modern doctrine of humanitarian intervention', *The University of Toledo Law Review*, 23 (1992), 253–294; J. Chopra and T. Weiss, 'Sovereignty is no longer sacrosanct: codifying humanitarian intervention', *Ethics and International Affairs*, 6 (1992), 95.

[54] See S. Krasner, 'Compromising Westphalia', *International Security*, 20 (1995/96), 125; J. Donnelly, *International Human Rights* (Boulder CO, Westview, 1992); and D. Forsythe, *Human Rights and World Politics* (Lincoln, University of Nebraska Press, 1989), p. 19.

What then, is the significance of today's trends in constitutional authority? Both the expansion of the EU and the rise of intervention are conceptually historic, for they revise long-standing features of the Westphalian revolution. The EU transforms all three faces of the Westphalia constitution; intervention revises the old principle of non-intervention. But tempering reserve is warranted, too. The geographic significance criterion reminds us that the EU is bounded to a continent, and that intervention is confined to scattered islands of egregious calamity. Other substantive attributes qualify these revolutions, too. The EU notably extends its reach to monetary affairs, but leaves state authority entirely intact over defence, education, health care, and scores of other matters. Intervention is mitigated by the restraint and discord of the members of the UN Security Council. So we see also the enduring strength of Westphalia's signature achievement: an international society where the sovereign state is the key legitimate polity. States remain key actors in the EU; and of all the world's states, only a few have been subjected to intervention. We see how distant we are, too, from the institutional world of the High Middle Ages, where the state was only the dimly discernible power of a king, an authority who was still linked to a nerve network of outside authorities to whom he was obligated, who was tied to authorities within his realm who swore allegiances to other authorities outside his realm, and who shared Christendom with thousands of other authorities, overlapping, vying, complex in their privileges. Where the state's authority is challenged, it is challenged significantly, but the challenge extends only to certain matters in certain places.

Sovereignty: Change and Continuity in a Fundamental Institution

Georg Sørensen

Only a few years ago, sovereignty used to be taken for granted in the study of world politics. J. D. B. Miller expressed the prevailing opinion in simple, but clear terms: 'Just as we know a camel or a chair when we see one, so we know a sovereign state. It is a political entity which is treated as a sovereign state by other sovereign states'.[1] Today, few would be satisfied with Miller's summation. Sovereignty is being intensely debated among scholars and practitioners of world politics. For example, the most recent International Studies Association meeting had 'The Westphalian System' as its overarching theme; the programme chair explicitly emphasized that 'traditional touchstones' such as sovereignty must now be 'open to question'.[2] In July 1998, a large conference took place in Munster in celebration of the 350 years birthday of the Westphalian treaties and discussing current interpretations of sovereignty.

There are several reasons for the renewed interest in sovereignty. Processes of globalization making the world hang closer together; humanitarian intervention in weak states and attempts to promote democracy and human rights on a global scale; new forms of intense cooperation in Europe and fresh attempts at regional integration elsewhere; the emergence of a large number of newly independent states; all these developments have helped spark new considerations about the possible implications for sovereignty. At the same time, both the end of the Cold War and the approach of a new millennium have boosted interest in the long lines of world politics. Real or perceived, such moments of transitions are watersheds which invite stocktaking. To know where we are going from here, we need to know where we came from.

The intense scholarly interest in sovereignty is most clearly evidenced in the spate of recent books and articles on the subject.[3] A central issue in most of

---

[1] J. D. B. Miller, *The World of States: Connected Essays* (London, 1981), p. 16.

[2] R. Denemark, 'A Note From the Program Chair', ISA Conference Program, Minneapolis 1998, p. 5.

[3] Only a selection of contributions can be mentioned here: F. H. Hinsley, *Sovereignty* (Cambridge, Cambridge University Press, 2nd edn, 1986); A. James, *Sovereign Statehood: the Basis of International Society* (London, Allen and Unwin, 1986); R. Lapidoth, 'Sovereignty in transition', *Journal of International Affairs*, 45 (1992), 50–74; S. D. Krasner, 'Sovereignty: an institutional perspective', *Comparative Political Studies*, 21 (1988), 66–94; N. Onuf, 'Sovereignty: outline of a conceptual history', *Alternatives*, 16 (1991), 425–46; R. H. Jackson, *Quasi-states: Sovereignty, International Relations and the Third World* (Cambridge, Cambridge University Press, 1990); R. O. Keohane, 'Hobbes's Dilemma and Institutional Change in World Politics: Sovereignty in International Society', in H. H. Holm and G. Sørensen (eds), *Whose World Order? Uneven Globalization and the End of the Cold War* (Boulder CO, Westview, 1995); G. Lyons and M. Mastanduno (eds), *Beyond Westphalia? Sovereignty and International Intervention* (Baltimore, Johns Hopkins Press, 1995); J. Bartelson, *A Genealogy of Sovereignty* (Cambridge, Cambridge University Press, 1995); S. Barkin and B. Cronin, 'The state and the nation: changing norms and the rules of sovereignty in international relations', *International Organization*, 49 (1995), 479–510.

these contributions concerns the question of change. Is sovereignty a stable and unchanging institution or has it undergone dramatic change, both in present times and in earlier periods? If there is dramatic change, is the institution in the process of disappearing or at least losing much of its significance? Should we consequently talk about 'the end of sovereignty' or 'the illusion of sovereignty' as many analysts indeed propose to do? The debate about change and continuity is also apparent in the contributions to the present issue of *Political Studies* with some arguing in favour of continuity (e.g. Alan James) and others (e.g. Paul Taylor) arguing in favour of change.

This article makes an attempt at resolving the continuity versus change debate by arguing in favour of both positions; there are core aspects of the institution of sovereignty which remain unchanged and there are other aspects of the institution which have changed dramatically over time. In making that argument, I employ a distinction between constitutive rules of sovereignty (which remain unchanged) and regulatory rules of sovereignty (which have changed in several ways), and I introduce the notion of different sovereignty games played by different types of sovereign states.

Sovereignty: Continuity of Constitutive Rules

If institutions are defined as 'persistent and connected sets of rules, formal and informal, that prescribe behavioural roles, constrain activity, and shape expectations'[4] then sovereignty is an institution. It is common to tie the emergence of that institution in with the peace of Westphalia in 1648 which undermined the power of the church and strengthened secular power. The choice between Catholicism and Protestantism became the privilege of local rulers; that is the principle of *cujus regio ejus religio*. The corresponding secular principle gives the King authority over his own realm: *Rex in regno suo est Imperator regni sui*. Dispersed medieval authority was replaced by centralized modern authority, the King and his government. The world did not change overnight at a specific point in time; elements of the old system remained in place for a long period. There was no momentous change from one day to the next in 1648. Still it is justified to look at 1648 as a crucial point in the transition from feudal to modern authority. The old system was decaying; a new system, with sovereign statehood as its basic principle of political organization was growing ever stronger. In 1648 we could, to borrow a phrase from Sir Ernest Barker, 'hear the cracking of the Middle Ages'.

In order to find out whether the institution of sovereignty is changing dramatically, we have to know what it was and is. It is helpful to look at the rules of sovereignty as making up a special kind of game played by a special type of player, the sovereign state.[5] We may distinguish between two qualitatively different kinds of rules in the sovereignty game: constitutive rules and regulative rules.[6]

---

[4] R. O. Keohane, 'Multilateralism: an agenda for research', *International Journal*, 45 (1990), 732.

[5] The game metaphor is also employed in Jackson, *Quasi-states*, p. 34. My reflections on sovereignty games in this paper is greatly indebted to intense discussions with Robert Jackson.

[6] A distinction introduced by J. Rawls, 'Two concepts of justice', *Philosophical Review*, 64 (1955), 1–33; the use of it here is based on J. R. Searle, *The Construction of Social Reality* (London, Penguin, 1995).

Constitutive rules are foundational,[7] they define the core features of what sovereignty is. Constitutive rules 'do not merely regulate, they also create the very possibility of certain activities'.[8] This type of foundational rules, says Searle, comes in systems which characteristically have the form: 'X counts as Y in context C'.

Let us try to apply this reasoning to sovereignty. First, what are the features of the entities which satisfy the X term in the game of sovereignty? Not any association can become sovereign; transnational corporations, churches, or football clubs do not satisfy the X term. Only a certain type of player does, the one we label 'state'. Which features must the state have to satisfy the X term? It is commonly agreed that three elements are necessary: territory, people, and government.[9] Georg Schwarzenberger and E. D. Brown put it in the following way:

> The State in quest of recognition must have a stable government ... it must rule supreme within a territory – with more or less settled frontiers – and it must exercise control over a certain number of people. These features have come to be taken as the essential characteristics of independent states.[10]

That is to say, the emergence of the constitutive rules of sovereignty (the Y term) is predicated upon the previous existence of states with a delimited territory, a stable population, and a government. A well-known study of international law published in 1968 makes the point in the following way: 'The international legal order does not provide foundation for the State; it presupposes the State's existence. Recognizing the appearance on a territory of a political entity showing the characteristics generally attributed to the State, it merely invests it with personality in the law of nations'.[11] Robert Jackson concludes: 'Classical international law is therefore the child and not the parent of states'.[12]

Once we have the X term we can proceed to the constitutive rule of sovereignty (the Y term). What is the definitorial content of sovereignty that is bestowed on some (but not all) states? It is recognition of the fact that the state entity possesses constitutional independence. As emphasized by Alan James, sovereignty 'in this fundamental sense, amounts to constitutional independence'. Constitutional independence, according to James, is 'a legal, an absolute, and a unitary condition'. That it is a legal condition means that sovereignty is a juridical arrangement under international law. The sovereign state stands apart from other all other sovereign entities, it is 'constitutionally apart'.[13] That means the sovereign state is legally equal to all other sovereign states. Irrespective of the substantial differences between sovereign states in economic, political, social, and other respects, sovereignty entails equal membership of the international society of states, with similar rights and

---

[7] For a similar point, see D. Philpott, 'Westphalia, authority, and international society', *Political Studies*, 47 (1999), 566–89, p.567 (this issue).

[8] Searle, *The Construction of Social Reality*, p. 27.

[9] See A. James, 'The practice of sovereign statehood in contemporary international society', *Political Studies*, 47 (1999), 457–73 (this issue).

[10] Quoted from Jackson, *Quasi-states*, p. 53.

[11] C. de Visscher, *Theory and Reality in Public International Law* (Princeton, Princeton University Press, 1968), p. 174–5.

[12] Jackson, *Quasi-states*, p. 53.

[13] A. James, 'The practice of sovereign statehood in contemporary international society', p. 462.

obligations. The fact that every sovereign member state, irrespective of differences in substantial powers, has one vote in the UN general assembly is a concrete expression of this legal equality.

Constitutional independence is also an absolute condition; it is either present or absent. Other juridical categories share that quality; a person is either married or not, there is no legal status of being 75% married. A person is either a citizen of a particular country or not, there is no legal status of being 75% Dane. The same goes for sovereignty; a state does either have sovereignty in the sense of constitutional independence or it does not have it. There is no half-way house, no legal in-between. (Some will object that the EU is exactly such an in-between condition, but that is misleading as will be argued below).

Finally, sovereignty as constitutional independence is a unitary condition. That means that the sovereign state is of one piece; there is one supreme authority deciding over internal as well as external affairs. Such is the case even in federal states or states with a high degree of political decentralization; powers may have been delegated, but there is one supreme authority.

To sum up so far: the constitutive content of sovereignty can be seen as a foundational rule in the form of 'X counts as Y in context C'. The X term are states with territory, people, and government. The Y term is constitutional independence which is a legal, absolute, and unitary condition. Context C is of course the international society of states. It has been customary in the neorealist tradition to talk of an international system, invoking the image of states as billiard balls. The above discussion of sovereignty immediately reveals why this image is misleading. Relations between sovereign states involve social acts of recognition and of mutual obligations between states. Hedley Bull and Adam Watson made the distinction between system and society clear in their definition of international society: 'a group of states (or more generally, a group of independent political communities) which not merely form a system, in the sense that the behaviour of each is a necessary factor in the calculation of others, but also have established by dialogue and consent common rules and institutions for the conduct of their relations, and recognize their common interest in maintaining these arrangements'.[14] Note that the act of recognition confers a special status on states. The sheer physical features of the X term (territory, people, government) are not in themselves sufficient to guarantee the status and function specified by the Y term; as emphasized by Searle, 'collective agreement about the possession of the status is constitutive of having the status, and having the status is essential to the performance of the function assigned to that status'.[15]

It is necessary to emphasize, even if the formulation is awkward, that the constitutive rule content of sovereignty is constitutional independence in the sense discussed above. It is this constitutive content which has remained fundamentally unchanged since it became the dominant principle of political organization in the seventeenth century. In that sense there is continuity, not change, in the institution of sovereignty. The history of sovereignty from then to now is a history of the victorious expansion of the principle of political organization embodied in sovereignty: constitutional independence. Several authors have recorded the history of that expansion; Hendrik Spruyt has

---

[14] H. Bull, *The Anarchical Society* (London, Macmillan, 1977), p. 13.
[15] Searle, *The Construction of Social Reality*, p. 51.

recently argued that there was nothing inevitable about the process and traces the complex interplay between actors and structures in the triumph of sovereign statehood.[16] Charles Tilly also notes how the sovereign state has outcompeted a large number of rival forms of political organization since its first establishment in Europe.[17] None of this can be covered here. I follow Ruggie (quoting Tilly) in emphasizing that 'once the system of modern states was consolidated, however, the process of fundamental transformation ceased: "[states] have all remained recognizably of the same species up to our own time" '.[18] The sovereign state remains the preferred form of political organization; no serious competitor has emerged.[19] One simple way of gauging the popularity of sovereign statehood is the threefold increase in the number of sovereign states since 1945.

Another way of bringing home the point that constitutional independence is a permanent feature of sovereignty is to visit authors who want to discuss changes in sovereignty. Even if that is their main aim, they note the continuity in the aspect of sovereignty which is constitutional independence. Joseph Camilleri and Jim Falk, for example, discuss at great length the contemporary challenges and changes in sovereignty, but they also note how the world came to be organized in states who did not 'acknowledge an external authority higher than their own', and that 'the trappings of legal sovereignty remain intact'.[20] Robert Keohane analyses the changes in sovereignty in the context of EU, but also notes the stable, unchanging element in sovereignty, namely that a state has 'independence from the authority of any other nation and equality with it under international law'.[21] Robert Jackson identifies the changes in sovereignty driven by the emergence of quasi-states, but he also stresses the stable core of sovereignty: 'constitutional independence of other states'.[22] Samuel Barkin and Bruce Cronin analyse how 'the rules of sovereignty vary', yet they employ a fixed notion of state sovereignty: 'institutional authority within a set of clearly demarcated boundaries'.[23] Finally Cynthia Weber studies 'various meanings of sovereignty' but she still holds on to a constant core of that concept, namely sovereignty as the legitimate foundation of state authority.[24]

In sum, there is a stable element in sovereignty which marks the continuity of that institution. That stable element is the constitutive core of sovereignty: constitutional independence possessed by states which have territory, people, and government. The comprehensive talk about changes in sovereignty should not ignore this vital element of continuity. This does not mean that there have been no changes in the institution of sovereignty. There have been very

---

[16] H. Spruyt, *The Sovereign State and its Competitors* (Princeton, Princeton University Press, 1994).

[17] C. Tilly, *Coercion, Capital, and European States AD 990–1990* (Cambridge MA, Basil Blackwell, 1990).

[18] J. G. Ruggie, *Constructing the World Polity* (London, Routledge, 1998), p. 191.

[19] R. H. Jackson, 'Continuity and Change in the States System', in R. H. Jackson and A. James (eds), *States in a Changing World* (Oxford, Clarendon, 1993), pp. 346–69.

[20] J. A. Camilleri and J. Falk, *The End of Sovereignty* (Aldershot, Edward Elgar, 1992), pp. 28, 99.

[21] Keohane, 'Hobbes's Dilemma and Institutional Change', p. 172 (Keohane quotes H. Morgenthau).

[22] Jackson, *Quasi-states*, p. 32.

[23] Barkin and Cronin, 'The state and the nation', pp. 128, 111.

[24] C. Weber, *Simulating Sovereignty: Intervention, the State and Symbolic Exchange* (Cambridge, Cambridge University Press, 1995), pp. 29–30.

substantial changes in sovereignty's regulative rules, the rules that the sovereignty game is played by.

Sovereignty: Change in Regulative Rules

Before embarking on a discussion of the changes in sovereignty having to do with regulative rules it is helpful to introduce an important distinction. It has been emphasized several times above that sovereignty is an institution, that is, a set of rules. Those rules should not be conflated with the positive, substantial content of sovereign statehood. The fact that small or weak states were always less powerful actors does not make Denmark or Ghana less sovereign; irrespective of their substantial weakness these countries do have sovereignty in the form of constitutional independence. The fact that there is mutual dependence between countries does not annul the existence of sovereignty as constitutional independence. The substantial, positive content of sovereignty has always been contested,[25] the rules of sovereignty exist irrespective of the fact that many sovereign states have not always actually enjoyed the autonomy implied in the notion of constitutional independence. In that sense it is misleading to talk about the 'end of sovereignty' with reference to such substantial features as economic globalization or the like. The institution of sovereignty and the actual degree of state autonomy are two different things. This should not be taken to mean that there is no relationship at all between the rules of the sovereignty institution and these substantial developments. To the contrary, substantial developments often trigger changes in the rules of sovereignty, as will be discussed below.

Changes in sovereignty pertain to changes in sovereignty's regulative rules. Regulative rules 'regulate antecedently existing activities'.[26] The freeway speed limit is an example of a regulative rule, regulating the antecedently existing activity of driving. The regulative rules of sovereignty regulate interaction between the antecedently existing entities that are sovereign states. How do states go about dealing with each other in war and peace, who gets to be a member of the society of states on what qualifications, are examples of areas of regulative rule. Such regulative rules would not be meaningful or necessary without the prior of existence of the special type of player which is subject to regulation: the sovereign state. In other words, the constitutive rules come first, the regulative rules second; without the former there would be no object of the latter.

The regulative rules of the sovereignty game have changed in several ways over time. One important area of change concerns the rules of admission. For a very long time, the sovereignty game was a European game, played by a European society of sovereign states. Other would-be members were held out because the Europeans found they did not satisfy the basic criteria for statehood: a delimited territory, a stable population, and a dependable government with the will and capacity to carry out international obligations. When non-European states eventually became members, they did so by meeting the membership criteria set up by the Europeans. Consequently, the international

---

[25] See S. D. Krasner, 'Westphalia and All That', in J. Goldstein and R. O. Keohane (eds), *Ideas and Foreign Policy* (Ithaca, Cornell University Press, 1993), pp. 235–64.
[26] Searle, *The Construction of Social Reality*, p. 27.

society of states was 'based on a selective membership principle which discriminated between a superior class of sovereign states and an inferior class of various dependencies'.[27]

The precise criteria for recognition have always been a subject of debate in the society of states and for a very long period there were no clear rules supported by all sovereign states.[28] This reflects a situation where countries could be players in the sovereignty game without actually having the formal recognition by all other members. Britain attempted to block the entry of the United States into the society of states by reference to the norm of mother state acceptance – i.e. the USA's recognition by other states depended on prior acceptance of such sovereignty by Britain. France did not accept this claim and recognized the United States already in 1778; British recognition did not follow until 1783.

After the Congress of Vienna in 1815 rules of recognition became clearer, but were still subject to exemptions which reflected the specific interests of the European great powers. The emergence of nationalism and ideas about the nation were also reflected in recognition practices, but it was not until 1919 that the principle of popular sovereignty – i.e. the idea that nations have a right to self determination – became the official basis for recognition. Yet as John Mayall emphasizes, clear guidelines for implementation of this principle were never formulated. It proved extremely difficult to answer the innocent question: Which are 'the appropriate collective selves whose right to self-determination must be recognized as the basis of the new political order?'.[29]

With the adoption of the Universal Declaration of Human Rights in 1948, the issue of human rights obtained a more prominent position on the international agenda. Yet human rights did not emerge in the principles of recognition until after the end of the Cold War and even in this recent period demands for certain human rights standards have not been consistently applied to the recognition of the new states emerging from the Soviet Union and Yugoslavia.

I cannot further pursue the discussion of recognition rules here. Even from these few remarks it ought to be clear that the rules of admission to the society of states have changed in several ways over time. Let me turn to the rule of the sovereignty game itself. Once the membership issue is decided, by what rules is the game played? Robert Jackson identifies a number of playing rules, among them 'non-intervention, making and honouring of treaties, diplomacy conducted in accordance with accepted practices, and in the broadest sense a framework of international law ... In short, the rules include every convention and practice of international life which moderate and indeed civilize the relations of states.'[30]

It is immediately clear that these regulative rules of the sovereignty game have changed substantially over time. The geographical expansion of the international society of states has combined with a trend towards a more dense

---

[27] Jackson, *Quasi-states*, p. 61.

[28] Some even argue that the situation of 'historically diffuse' principles of recognition continue right up to the present day; see Ø. Österud, 'The narrow gate: entry to the club of sovereign states', *Review of International Studies*, 23 (1997), 167–84. For the view that there is a detectable pattern in recognition practices, see K. Hyldelund, Anerkendelsesprincipper, MA thesis (Aarhus, Dept. of Political Science, 1997).

[29] J. Mayall, 'Sovereignty, nationalism and self-determination', *Political Studies*, 47 (1999), 474–502, p.476 (this issue).

[30] Jackson, *Quasi-states*, p. 35.

regulation of the relations between states. International regimes have been set up in a large number of areas; the size and number of international organizations has grown dramatically; after the end of the Cold War new practices of humanitarian intervention in weak or failed states have developed. In order to record such changes of regulative rules in detail, we would have to consult diplomatic history, the development of international law, the evolution of intervention practices, and so on. This is not necessary for the present argument. What must be emphasized here is the dynamic and changing content of the sovereignty institution's regulative rules. They have developed and adapted over time in the context of a society of states which has itself undergone dramatic development and change in substantial terms: the modern state of the late twentieth century is a species quite far apart from the absolutist state of the seventeenth century. Given this high degree of dynamic development, is there any way of finding systematic patterns in the way which the institution of sovereignty confronts us today? The following section makes an attempt to do this by employing the notion of different sovereignty games.

Games of Sovereignty in Present-day International Society

The above discussion makes clear that the debate about whether sovereignty has changed in every respect or remains wholly unchanged is really not helpful. There is a stable element of continuity in sovereignty, embodied in the constitutive rule of constitutional independence. And there is a dynamic element of change in sovereignty, embodied in the institution's regulative rules. And there is a third element of dynamic change which is often mixed up with the two others mentioned here, namely the development of substantial, empirical statehood, that is, the concrete features of statehood as they have developed from the absolutist state of the seventeenth century to the modern welfare states of this century. If we consider these three elements to be different aspects of sovereign statehood, then it is very often the case that those talking about continuity of sovereignty and those talking about change of sovereignty are really not addressing the same aspect; the 'change people' talk about the development and change of substantial statehood, or development and change of sovereignty's regulative rules, or some mix of the two.[31] The 'continuity people' most often talk about the stable rule of constitutional independence.[32] Both are right, but the discussion is not very productive, because they address different aspects of the complex phenomenon that is sovereign statehood.

Is it possible to find ways of synthesizing that complex entity which is sovereign statehood in a way which respects both change and continuity and which also encompasses the three aspects of sovereign statehood discussed here? It should be clear by now that any detailed historical picture will always be flimsy instead of neat and clean, with one clear-cut sovereignty game for all states; for example, the Holy Roman Empire did not officially end until 1806, long after the Westphalian Peace; the present international system has states which have substantial statehood but no formal recognition of constitutional independence (e.g. Taiwan); the regulative rules of sovereignty, perhaps

---

[31] See for example Camilleri and Falk, *The End of Sovereignty?*, and Weber, *Simulating Sovereignty*.

[32] See for example James, 'The Practice of Sovereign Statehood'.

especially those concerning principles for recognition, have always been a matter of contention and debate among powerful states in the international society.

Instead of looking in vain for one synthesis which will never be empirically accurate, I suggest the use of Weberian ideal types. The ideal type is not an accurate description of historical reality; it is a construct which elucidates typical features of that reality so as to bring out their essential elements. What I propose in other words, is to construct three ideal types which bring out the different, typical ways in which the sovereignty game is played out in present-day international society. The raw material for these ideal types will be drawn from the three aspects of sovereign statehood identified above: (a) constitutive rules; (b) regulative rules; and (c) substantial, empirical statehood. I am going to identify three different ideal type sovereignty games: The Westphalian game; the Post-Colonial game; and the Postmodern game.

The first level, that of constitutive rules, is the stable element which is unvarying across the games: all three games are played by states which have constitutional independence as members of the society of states. In terms of differentiating between types of games, therefore, this first level drops out. The second level, that of regulative rules, is more difficult to handle because there are several such rules, as was demonstrated earlier. I have chosen to focus on two regulative rules which have always been considered vitally important, even 'grundnorms' or 'golden rules'[33] of the sovereignty game: non-intervention and reciprocity. Non-intervention is the prohibition against foreign interference in the domestic affairs of other states; reciprocity is the principle of *quid pro quo*, the 'exchange of roughly equivalent values'[34] between the legally equal partners of the sovereignty game. The point is that these two 'grundnorms' are played out in different ways in the sovereignty games discussed below and these differences help us capture the distinct features of each game.

The third level concerns substantial statehood. All participants in the three games satisfy the X-term of sovereign statehood discussed earlier, even if one category of players does it only just barely: there is a territory, a population and some form of government. But beyond these basic aspects, the players of the three games differ substantially in their empirical statehood, on the following dimensions: structure and content of the economy, structure and content of the polity, and the relationship between nation and state, that is, the issue of nationhood.

We now have the necessary tools for identifying the different ideal types of sovereignty games.

The Westphalian Sovereignty Game

This first ideal type is a stylized version of the sovereignty game that developed after the peace of Westphalia. Let me begin with the substantial statehood profile in the Westphalian game. Between the seventeenth and the twentieth

---

[33] See Jackson, *Quasi-states*.

[34] R. O. Keohane, 'Reciprocity in international relations', *International Organization*, 40 (1986), 1–27; the full definition offered by Keohane runs: 'Reciprocity refers to exchanges of roughly equivalent values in which the actions of each party are contingent on the prior actions of the others in such a way that good is returned for good, and bad for bad', p. 8.

century, states became modern, that is, they developed their substantial state-hood in a variety of ways. In ideal type terms, the Westphalian game is played by a modern state. As regards the economy, the modern state is based on a self-sustaining national economy which is the result of the interplay between industrial and technological modernization and state regulation and interven-tion. The national economy is not self-sustaining in the sense that it is autarchic; it is rather what some development theorists call auto-centric, meaning that the decisive intra- and inter-sectoral links in the economy are domestic.[35] It could be labelled a mercantilist national economy, containing sectors for means of production as well as consumption. It is a homogenous economy with sectors at similar, high levels of development. There can be a high level of foreign trade, but the external linkages are less important than the internal; the economic structure is introvert rather than extrovert.

At the political level, the modern state is governed by an effective institutional machinery based on the rule of law and on popular legitimacy. Compared to earlier types of state in history, the modern state has vastly expanded its regulative powers and its capacity for control and surveillance of the popula-tion. Yet even if the modern state controls the means of violence, its rule is based less on coercion than on consent and legitimacy. In other words, the modern state possesses what Michael Mann calls infrastructural as opposed to despotic power.[36] The power of the state is matched by the civil and political rights of citizens. In that sense, the modern state is both strong and weak: strong in regulative, control, and surveillance capacities; weak in that it depends on the legitimacy stemming from popular support.[37]

The modern state is a nation-state. Political community was created in modern states over an extended period of time. Territory came first; the state building elites first consolidated control over a territory and only in a later phase came the construction of a nation. This building of a national community was helped by two factors, one material, the other non-material. The material factor was the welfare, security, and order provided by the state; the non-material factor was the idea of a national community provided by mythology, inter-pretations of history, and ideology. Put differently, political community is based on two types of legitimacy: vertical legitimacy (the connection between state and society, the notion that the state elite and its institutions have a right to rule); and horizontal legitimacy, defining the membership and the boundaries of the political community of people.[38] The nationalism of the nation-state thus contains two different elements which exist in harmony: a territorially based idea of *Gesellschaft*, the community of citizens within defined borders; and the ethnic idea of *Gemeinschaft*, the community of people defined by the nation.

[35] See for example D. Senghaas, *The European Experience: a Historical Critique of Development Theory* (Leamington Spa, Berg, 1985).

[36] 'Infrastructural Power is the institutional capacity of a central state ... to penetrate its territories and logically implement decisions. This is collective power, "power through" society ... Infrastructural power is a two-way street: It also enables civil society parties to control the state ...', M. Mann, *The Sources of Social Power, Vol. II* (Cambridge, Cambridge University Press, 1993), p. 59.

[37] The historical development of this whole interplay between state and society is analysed in A. Giddens, *The Nation-State and Violence* (Cambridge, Polity, 1985), especially p. 205–6.

[38] K. J. Holsti, *The State, War and the State of War* (Cambridge, Cambridge University Press, 1996).

It should be clear that modern Westphalian states embody a well-developed substantial statehood in both economic, political, and socio-cultural terms. Let me turn to the sovereignty-game that they play, based on non-intervention and reciprocity. For modern, Westphalian states, non-intervention is the right of state-leaders to conduct their affairs without outside interference. The reverse side of that right is the duty to refrain from interfering in the domestic affairs of other countries. The modern, Westphalian sovereignty-game is one of self-help; states are individually responsible for looking after their own security and welfare: the state decides for itself 'how it will cope with its internal and external problems, including whether or not to seek assistance from others ... States develop their own strategies, chart their own courses, make their own decisions about how to meet whatever needs they experience and whatever desires they develop'.[39] That situation is of course not only one of opportunity, but also of constraint: 'Statesmen are free within the situation they find themselves which consists externally of other states and internally of their subjects. This is obviously a circumstance of constrained choice ...'.[40]

The dealings with other states are based on reciprocity, that is, they involve a notion of symmetry, of giving and taking for mutual benefit. In the present context, reciprocity should be seen less as a bargaining strategy employed by single actors and more as a systemic norm according to which bargains between parties are made. A game based on reciprocity is a symmetric game where the players enjoy equal opportunity to benefit from bi- and multilateral trans-actions. Reciprocity in this sense is expressed, for example, in the 1947 adoption of the General Agreement of Tariffs and Trade (the GATT). That organization is based on rules which are basically liberal in character. The basic norm is the 'most-favoured-nation' rule which stipulates equal treatment in commercial relations between states, regardless of size, power, location, and any further particulars about them.

In sum, the Westphalian sovereignty game features substantial, capable states in a self-help game based on non-intervention and reciprocity. Many IR-theorists, perhaps especially neorealists, have thought of the Westphalian sovereignty game as the standard game played by all independent states. But this view is misleading. There are two other distinct types of sovereignty game in the present international system.

The Post-colonial Sovereignty Game

This sovereignty game emerged when decolonization extended constitutional independence to the former Western colonies in the Third World. A new type of player then joined the society of states, a weak player with severe deficiencies in substantial terms.[41] Even the basic possession of territory, people, and govern-ment was frequently more formal than real. Ex-colonies took over the borders established by the colonial powers; rarely did the newly independent states exercise effective control over their nominally allotted territories.

---

[39] K. N. Waltz, *Theory of International Politics* (Reading, Addison-Wesley, 1979), p. 96.

[40] Jackson, *Quasi-states*, p. 6.

[41] For an in-depth analysis, see Jackson, *Quasi-states*, and C. Clapham, *Africa and the International System* (Cambridge, Cambridge University Press, 1996).

Populations were divided along ethnic, linguistic, socio-cultural, and other lines. Governments became based on weak and underdeveloped institutions most often in the hands of tiny elites that sought to exploit their positions to their own advantage.

Post-colonial states do not have national economies in the sense of coherent main sectors within a unified economic space. They are dependent mono-economies based on the export of one or a few primary goods and the import of sophisticated, technology-intensive products. Large parts of the populations are outside of the formal sectors, living in localized subsistence-economies at very low standards.

The weak, post-colonial states are not nation-states. The people inside former colonial borders were communities only in the sense that they shared a border drawn by others. Their idea of nationalism was a negative one: get rid of the colonizers. When that project succeeded, there was no positive notion of community left over. Political elites made some attempts to construct such a notion, but they quickly gave up trying and in general that project was a huge failure. Therefore, political community was not created, neither in the *Gesell-schaft*, nor in the *Gemeinschaft* sense. The communities that prevailed were the different ethnic sub-groups which competed for access to state power and resources, sometimes building frail alliances amongst each other.

It is clear that the legal equality between modern and post-colonial states is not matched by substantial equality; post-colonial states are much weaker players. As a consequence, post-colonial states display a distinctly different game of sovereignty. Contrary to what neorealists claim, the international system is not one of self-help for post-colonial states. Exactly the opposite: it is non-self help. Weak, post-colonial states are unable to put up a defence against threats from the outside; instead, they rely on the international community to provide the absolute security guarantee of non-intervention. In more general terms, the main security problem in post-colonial states is domestic rather than international. The traditional security dilemma is turned on its head.

Post-colonial states cannot systematically base their relations with developed countries on reciprocity. They need special, preferential treatment from the developed world. That is the basis for the emergence of development assistance regimes where economic aid flows from rich, developed countries to poor, underdeveloped countries. This is a replacement of the liberal, equal opportunity principle in relations between states with a principle of special, preferential treatment of the weak party. In a similar vein, the GATT regime has special provisions for weak, post-colonial states which amounts to a change from reciprocity between equals to a situation of non-reciprocity between unequals.

Economic and other aid gives the donors an amount of influence over the domestic affairs of recipients. That puts pressure on the principle of non-intervention. Economic conditionalities and, of late, political conditionalities have been tied to development assistance. Even if such conditionalities do not represent a sharp deviation from non-intervention (because they are based on negotiated agreements between the parties), they do demonstrate how non-intervention is under pressure in the case of weak, post-colonial states. The decisive shift from non-intervention to intervention comes in the case of state failure. Since the end of the Cold War, the international community has in several instances undertaken intervention in failed states in order to provide security for innocent civilians. Such intervention is always fraught with problems because they are never undertaken solely with humanitarian objectives in mind.[42] These issues cannot be taken up here. What must be stressed is that the international society has yet to come up with an effective formula for dealing with the special security and welfare problems in weak, post-colonial states. The peculiar sovereignty game played by post-colonial states is a reflection of that situation.

The Postmodern Sovereignty Game

This is a sovereignty game based on intense cooperation between sovereign states. The European Union currently represents the case where such supra-national cooperation has gone farthest. West European cooperation was pushed by the lessons of World War Two; getting Germany and France to work together was a way a avoiding new disasters in Europe. But what began as inter-state cooperation between what was basically Westphalian ideal type states in the 1950s has developed in qualitative new ways since then. The members of the EU are no longer 'Westphalian' in terms of their substantial statehood. They exemplify a new type of statehood which is not modern in the ways described earlier. For lack of a better term, this new form of statehood can be labelled 'postmodern'; my intention in employing this term is merely to stress that the states in question have developed beyond 'modern' in important respects; 'late modern' is another possible label for these states. Postmodern states are characterized by transnationally integrated, globalized economies; by multi-level governance; and by identities that are no longer exclusively tied to that nation-state.

The process of economic globalization contains two main elements; one is the increase of all kinds of economic relations between countries, that is, intensified economic interdependence. The other is the gradual replacement of national economies by a global economic system based on a consolidated global marketplace for production, distribution and consumption.[43] Post-modern states are characterized by globalized economies. Compared to 'Westphalian' economies, in globalized economies external linkages are as important or even more important than internal linkages; the economic structure is extrovert rather than introvert. The 'national' economy is no longer self-sustaining; it is part of a larger, globalized economic space.

Economic globalization provides a decisive incentive for more intense supra-national political cooperation, because such cooperation is a way of recapturing some of those powers of political regulation which have been lost at the national level due to the process of globalization. States bargain with their sovereignty, their territorial authority, in the sense that they allow other states to influence the regulation of their domestic affairs in return for influence over the domestic affairs of these other countries.[44] It is such processes which lead to the creation of multi-level governance. Instead of purely or mainly national political

---

[42] See foe example A. Roberts, *Humanitarian Action in War*, Adelphi Paper 305 (Oxford, Oxford university Press, 1996).

[43] See P. Hirst and G. Thompson, 'The problem of "globalization": international economic relations, national economic management and the formation of trading blocs', *Economy and Society*, 21 (1992), 341–72.

[44] See Keohane, 'Hobbes's Dilemma and Institutional Change'.

regulation, there develops a complex network of supra-national, national, and sub-national regulation.

Multi-level governance in a globalized economic space changes the foundations for national identities. Recall that the political community of 'Westphalian' states is based on *Gesellschaft* and *Gemeinschaft*. The *Gesellschaft* component changes because borders are increasingly perforated in a context of supra-national governance. In the EU, for example, there is an integrated labour market and citizens can freely pick up jobs in other member countries. The *Gemeinschaft* component changes because the community of people defined by the nation now has other concepts of community emerging stronger next to it, in particular local identities and supra-national identities. This need not lead to transfer of loyalties from one level to another; in Europe, it appears to lead to more complex sets of identities and loyalties. Political community, then, is no longer exclusively defined by the state, but by a new context of multi-level governance.

The sovereignty game played by postmodern states differs in basic respects from the 'Westphalian' sovereignty game. The rule of non-intervention is seriously modified in the sense that an opening has been created for legitimate outside intervention by member states in national affairs. This is most clearly evident in the Single Market Treaty where a majority of member states may define rules applicable to all members. And this 'First Pillar' cooperation is set to expand to cover additional areas in coming years.

As regards reciprocity, postmodern cooperation involves some redistribution of economic resources across national boundaries which is not based strictly on member countries, but also on regions within member countries. Whereas in the Westphalian game, the rule of reciprocity is basically that of equal or fair competition, in post-modern game it is cooperation rather than competition. For example, poor regions get special, preferential treatment. This resembles the aid regime described in the post-colonial game, but there is a decisive difference. In the EU context, there is an institutional network with overseeing powers. That is, EU-institutions have the possibility of controlling whether aid for poor regions is actually used according to intentions and take corrective measures if this is not the case. A similar combination of cooperation and control is absent from the post-colonial sovereignty game.

There is an intense discussion in Europe concerning the relationship between the regulative rules of sovereignty and constitutional independence. In particular, those that are sceptical towards EU-cooperation find that the modifications of regulative rules described here are in the process of going so far (or have indeed already done so) that they have consequences for the constitutive rule of sovereignty: constitutional independence. The argument is that integration via modification of regulative rules can proceed so far that constitutional independence ceases to exist in more than purely nominal terms: there is no way out anymore. The counterargument is that constitutional independence remains intact; countries dissatisfied with EU-developments can, should they so wish, discontinue their membership. I support this counterargument,[45] but the discussion indicates how far-reaching modifications of sovereignty's regulative

---

[45] G. Sørensen, *Suverænitet: Formel og faktisk* (Copenhagen, Danish Institute for International Affairs, 1997).

rules raises new debates about the institution. Sovereignty becomes a contested concept.

Conclusion

The institution of sovereignty is changing, but there are also core elements of continuity. The debate about what happens with sovereignty is plagued by the confusion of three distinct aspects of sovereign statehood: (a) the constitutive rules of sovereignty; (b) the regulative rules of sovereignty; and (c) substantial, empirical statehood. I have combined these three elements in the above presentation of three distinct sovereignty games in present-day international society: The Westphalian game; the post-colonial game, and the postmodern game. In ideal typical terms, these three games describe and explain how sovereignty is played out in today's world.

  What about the future of sovereignty? The implication of the argument in the present paper is that any argument about 'end of sovereignty' is profoundly misleading. What happens is that the institution changes in order to adapt to new challenges mainly stimulated by changes in substantial statehood. The three games identified above will probably stay with us for the foreseeable future. Changes in the post-colonial game will demand either a change of the legal context so as to introduce forms of sovereignty which fall short of constitutional independence, or change in the empirical statehood of weak states towards far more substantial statehood. Neither prospect is likely. Changes in the post-modern game is predicated upon either a set-back toward more conventional forms of inter-state cooperation, or progress towards more genuine federal structures. None of those prospects are likely either. Most probably, change in sovereignty will emerge from the development of the classical, modern Westphalian sovereignty game in yet new directions not covered by the two other ideal types discussed here.

Contributors

CHRISTOPHER CLAPHAM is Professor of Politics and International Relations at Lancaster University. Recent publications include *Africa and the International System: the Politics of State Survival*, and an edited collection, *African Guerillas*. He is the editor of *The Journal of Modern African Studies*.

ROBERT JACKSON is Professor of Political Science at the University of British Columbia. He is the author/editor of eight books, including: *The Global Covenant: Human Conduct in World of States* (forthcoming), *Introduction to International Relations* (co-author Georg Sørensen, 1999), *Quasi-States: Sovereignty, International Relations and the Third World* (1990). He is currently writing a book entitled *Sovereignty: History of an idea*.

ALAN JAMES spent his career at the London School of Economics and Keele University. He is former Chairman of the British International Studies Association and has held visiting appointments in the US, India, Nigeria and Japan. His works include, *Sovereign Statehood: the Basis of International Order* (1986); *Peacekeeping in International Politics* (1990); and *Britain and the Congo Crisis, 1960-63* (1996). Currently he is working on the Cyprus Crisis of 1963-64 and, with G. R. Berridge, on a dictionary of diplomacy.

JAMES MAYALL is Sir Patrick Sheehy Professor of International Relations and Director of the Centre of International Studies at the University of Cambridge. Previous publications include *Nationalism and International Society* (1990). He is also editor/contributor of *The New Interventionism: UN Experience in Cambodia, Former Yugoslavia and Somalia* (1996).

DANIEL PHILPOTT is an Assistant Professor of Political Science at the University of California, Santa Barbara. He has written on self-determination, sovereignty, and ethics and international relations. He is currently completing a book on the origins and development of the sovereign states system.

GEORG SØRENSEN is Professor of Political Science at the University of Aarhus, Denmark. Recent books include: *Democracy and Democratization: Processes and Prospects in a Changing World* (2nd ed., 1998); *Introduction to International Relations* (with Robert Jackson, 1999). His current project is *Forms of Anarchy and Types of State: the International Domestic Connection*.

PAUL TAYLOR is Professor of International Relations and Chair of the Department, at the London School of Economics, where he specialises in international organization within the European Union and the United Nations system. Most recently he has published *International Organization in the Modern World* (1993) and *The European Union in the 1990s* (1996). He has edited and contributed to a number of books on international organization, with A. J. R. Groom, and most recently with Daws and Adamczick-Gerteis, *Documents on the Reform of the United Nations* (1997). He was editor of the *Review of International Studies* between 1994 and 1997.

WILLIAM WALLACE is Professor of International Relations at the London School of Economics. He was previously Director of Studies at the Royal Institute of International Affairs, and Walter F. Hallstein Fellow at St Antony's College, Oxford. His most recent books include: *Regional Integration: the West European Experience* (1994) and *Policy-Making in the European Union* (with Helen Wallace and others, 1996).

Index